Caroline Rose

# Dear Riley Rose,

The story of a woman and her dog..
and how they saved each other

**Dear Riley Rose,**
**The story of a woman and her dog.. and how they saved each other**
Copyright © 2024 by **Caroline Rose**. All rights reserved.

No part of this book may be used or reproduced in any manner whatsoever without written permission, except in the case of brief quotations embodied in critical articles and reviews. For more information, e-mail all inquiries to info@manhattanbookgroup.com.

Published by Manhattan Book Group, LLC
447 Broadway | 2nd Floor #354 | New York, NY 10013 | USA
1.800.767.0531 | (212) 634-7677 | www.manhattanbookgroup.com

Printed in the United States of America.

ISBN-13:   978-1-963844-10-8 (paperback)
           978-1-963844-11-5 (hardback)

*To my brother, for without you, this life would not be possible.*

*Love you endlessly.*

*Miss you every day.*

## Dear Riley Rose,

I'd like to tell you a story.
It's a love story—a fairy tale of sorts.
It's the story of us—Caroline and Riley, Riley and Caroline—and our journey toward finding each other.
It's a story of healing, love, and acceptance.
I'm going to tell you our story because it's something special, something magical, something big.
You were there, by my side.
You were there for the ride.
It's not that you need to know; it's that I need to tell it.
And I need to tell it from my perspective.
So that's what I'm going to do so that you can feel the hope of it all, the hope of us.
You and I together were bigger than our struggles.
And our story is one worth honoring.

## Contents

Prologue / ix

1 The Diagnosis / 1
2 MD Anderson / 11
3 Finding Riley / 17
4 Jacob / 29
5 The Rock / 35
6 Round 2 / 45
7 Anchor of Guilt / 53
8 The Story of My Closet / 63
9 Tommy Rose / 71
10 The Lump / 75
11 Finding Francis / 85
12 Motherhood Swirled with Chemo / 91
13 My Lifeline / 97
14 Nurse Jan / 113
15 Mommy's Tennis Ball / 123

16 Deepest Level of Right / 135
17 Bravo and Babas / 143
18 God, Please / 151
19 Hopeful Success / 161
20 Rose-Colored Glasses / 175
21 Christmas Cards / 191
22 The Nod / 205
23 Soulmate / 211
24 Fucking Awesome / 219
25 A Boy, a Ball, and a Boat / 229
26 The Waiting Game / 239
27 The Dash / 251

Acknowledgements / 259

# PROLOGUE

## Dear Riley Rose,

Clarity and Courage. Two words. One plan.

For so many years, I never asked. I only told. With clenched fists, I directed my life to follow my meticulously written script. I had to achieve the plan. There were no other options. Head down. Work hard. Zero distractions.

Organic chemistry and biology of the human body consumed my world. 4:40 a.m., my days began. I arrived at the gym by 5. My treadmill of choice was second from the left, first row by the windows. This jog took exactly fifty-two minutes, the first five miles holding steady at a pace of 6.0 mph. The speed of the last mile was meticulously increased to ensure a few seconds would be shaved off the previous run time. A two-and-a-half-minute cool-down followed the run, leaving just enough time to claim my favorite bike in the spinning studio.

After five minutes of in-the-saddle arm weights while waiting for the class to begin, I pushed through my high-intensity fifty-five-minute spin class, always getting a well-deserved and life-affirming shout-out from the instructor. This schedule allowed exactly twenty minutes to shower and dress in the gym locker room so I could beat the traffic from Santa Monica to downtown.

If all went according to schedule, which, barring a natural disaster or major traffic accident on the 10 Freeway, it did, I'd arrive at Starbucks at exactly 7:05. This gave me an hour and forty minutes to have my venti black coffee and raisin-topped oatmeal before packing up my school books and walking to the science building on the University of Southern California campus. By 9 a.m., I was seated in the front row of either my organic chemistry or molecular biology class. By 10:30, I was walking to the library to study for my upcoming medical school exams. By 2:30, I was back home reviewing my upcoming marathon route.

One marathon completed when I was twenty-two years old was not enough. Instead of finish line celebrations, with fists still clenched, I consumed myself with new goals, faster goals, "better" goals. As my number of marathons run grew larger, my finishing times grew smaller. And when that was no longer enough, I added triathlons into the mix. And then mountain climbing.

And then…the truth of what I had been running from, hiding from, caught up to me. Instead of directing and controlling, I was yielding and submitting. The quiet was deafening. The stillness, excruciating. The reality, terrifying.

The life I had curated, perfected, mastered, was slipping away through my tightly clenched fist. And no matter how hard I squeezed, I couldn't hold on to the perfection.

And then…I found you.

I wasn't even sure I wanted you, but then I saw my fists soften. I noticed my gaze lift. I felt my shoulders loosen. And, for the first time maybe ever, I was quiet. Truly quiet. And I asked. And I listened. And I heard.

Clarity and Courage.

These two simple words started our life together. Caroline and Riley, Riley and Caroline, one name rarely said without the other. You and I entered into our special dance, me leading at first, you carrying at the end. I didn't change you. We changed each other. We healed each other. We saved each other.

Over the years, the noise quieted. My speed slowed. My palms opened. 26.2 miles became 26.2 steps around the nurse's station. A 4:40 a.m. wake-up meant another blood-draw. Molecular biology became the study of my own ailing body.

That became tolerable. It became doable. It became normal.

Because I had you.

Riley Rose, you were my cure. Your love was my medicine. Your acceptance, my prognosis.

Because of you, I was able to live. Because of you, I was able to love. Because of you, I was able to receive.

Clarity and Courage. Asking and accepting. Listening and learning.

Palms open.

Heart full.

Inner truth heard.

Clarity and Courage.

Two words.

One prayer.

CHAPTER 1

# The Diagnosis

**Dear Riley Rose,**

I'd been willing to take my chances. It's scary to think now what would've happened if I'd had. And yet it's scary to think about what did happen because I didn't.

It was one of those gorgeous Texas fall mornings. The sky was a deep, crystal-clear shade of blue. The leaves were starting to change, and the air was crisp and cool. A cold front had blown in the night before, bringing the energetic air with it. Growing up, I lived for those freshly cool mornings. Fall always felt like a new beginning. The school year was still unfamiliar. Football was underway, bringing the Friday night social scene with it. Snakes were going into hibernation, and the dreaded mosquitoes were on their final countdown before the first freeze.

I was back in San Antonio for the Thanksgiving holiday, which meant fun nights with my high school friends before leaving to spend the big family holiday at my aunt and uncle's ranch. I'd flown in from my temporary home in Los Angeles the night before. I'd known in advance that my first morning home would start with an unpleasant trip to the blood lab, but I never could have predicted how my day would end.

Unfortunately for me, the ordered blood work I'd needed to have drawn required fasting, and fasting meant no coffee or pre-jog snack, so unfortunately my ritualistic early morning run was not going to be possible. My daily pre-dawn jogs gave me my routine adrenaline fix, and as I quickly learned regular adrenaline rushes became addictive.

That day, I'd especially needed that fix or else I knew I'd have no chance of functioning as my most fun and energetic self that evening. At that time, missing a run for me was like being a battery that hadn't been plugged into the socket, and a night out with old friends whom I hadn't seen in a while would require a full charge.

Thankfully, needles had never bothered me. However, my dad's overabundance of caution tendencies sometimes did. I guess being a neurosurgeon will do that to you. After twenty-seven years of being Dad's daughter, I'd learned that Dad didn't believe in taking chances. In his line of work, there was zero room for risk because one tiny error could quite literally lead to death. My brother and I used to joke and say, "What, Dad, like it's hard? It's not like it's brain surgery!" Dad always smiled at our veiled respect.

Although we joked about it, Chad and I were in constant awe of our dad and what he did daily. Dad's profession and the skill with which he performed his surgeries will always be one of the things in my life for which I am the proudest.

Respect and humor aside, despite our assurances, Dad was concerned about both of his kids traveling to Africa with the goal of climbing Mount Kilimanjaro. However, Dad also knew he couldn't change our minds about going. Therefore, with our upcoming trip to Africa just one short month away, Dad had scheduled extensive blood work with the unstated messages, "Let's just be extra sure y'all are healthy before traveling to a very far away country where I will not be there to help if you need me."

I arrived five minutes early. Being on time would be, in my mind, late. Nurse Betty was waiting for me. I'd only been to the blood-draw lab once before, but one of the unavoidable benefits that came with being the child of a well-loved and highly respected surgeon was having every nurse and technician know all about me and my brother. After all, our pictures covered the south wall of operating room 7. I wasn't surprised when Nurse Betty smothered me with a massive bear hug before sitting me down and slapping my arm to find a vein.

Nurse Betty had worked as a phlebotomist for over twenty years.

"Sweetheart, your veins are tiny! You have the veins of a sixty-year-old!" Nurse Betty remarked.

"Thank you?" I half asked, half stated.

"Now I rarely leave a mark, but I see a bruise starting to form, so you might need to keep some pressure on your arm for a few minutes. It will help minimize the bruising."

Bruising? Oh dear. That would not look cute with the top I planned to wear out that night. I noticed Nurse Betty's gaze. Her hazel eyes reflected a swirl of remorse and confusion. After so many years, Nurse Betty had perfected the art of "sticking without bruising" and was clearly confounded.

I tried to assure Nurse Betty that I really didn't mind, and in that moment that was the truth. Thankfully for Nurse Betty, my hunger pains trumped my vanity.

I was halfway home when my car phone rang.

"Caroline, it's Dad."

"Hey, Dad. I saw Nurse Betty. She's the best."

"Um-hum. Yeah, she's great. Listen. I just saw your lab results. There's been a mistake on your platelets. I need you to come back and have your blood redrawn."

Ugh. And I'd been so close to finally getting food.

"Dad, seriously? I feel like I'm about to pass out. I haven't eaten in fourteen hours. Can't we let this one slide?" Silly me. I knew as well as anyone that Dad didn't let things slide.

Every time Chad and I left the house, Dad asked if our cars had gas in the tanks and if we'd checked the air in the tires. At night, Dad triple-checked the house locks, and when we traveled we arrived to the airport three hours in advance for any family trip—even pre-9/11 domestic flights. You know, just in case.

Knowing my African fate hung in the balance, I begrudgingly turned the car around. Nurse Betty was once again waiting for me. This time, her eyes seemed a bit darker. Her hug wasn't as eager, and our conversation did not flow as effortlessly. As Nurse Betty worked to find a new vein, she again commented on my unusualness.

"Has anyone ever told you how small your veins are? I've never seen veins quite this small on someone so young before," Nurse Betty remarked.

"Humm," I distractedly replied.

"Honey," Nurse Betty started, "don't you think it's odd that your platelets came back so low? I mean, they were red flag low. But I guess that would explain that nasty bruise I gave you."

My interest was piqued. I'd learned in medical school that platelets clotted our blood, so maybe that was why I now had a bruise the size of a naval orange on my right forearm. Maybe that was also why the tiny cut on my finger from the gym the week before bled for two days before I was finally able to take off the Band-Aid. But none of that would make sense, because there was no way my platelets were as low as my labs had said they were. After all, I'd just run my fastest marathon time in San Diego. I ran this seventh marathon three minutes faster than Boston and thirteen minutes faster than New York. I'd also just completed the LA triathlon and had been training to climb Mount Kilimanjaro. None of this would have been possible if my platelets were truly red flag low. A mistake, just like Dad had said. Just a mistake.

Until it wasn't.

Forty-five minutes later, my car phone rang again. In a very different voice, Dad asked, "Where are you?"

"Hey, Dad, I'm pulling up to lunch with Mom. I'm absolutely famished."

"Caroline, I canceled your two o'clock appointment for your vaccinations." I was stunned. And not happy.

"Wait, Dad. What? WHY? I must get those shots today. Why would you cancel that appointment without talking to me first?" I was waiting for his answer, but no words followed. Dad paused for one second too long.

"Listen. The results from your second round of blood work were the same as your first. There's no mistake. Your platelets are at a critically low level, and we need to know why. I've called Dr. Mions."

"Who?"

"Dr. Mions. He's a hematologist and a friend, and he's agreed to see you in an hour. I've canceled my afternoon surgery, and I'll meet you at his office." Now it was my turn to take a beat-too-long pause.

"Dad, why'd you cancel your surgery? In the twenty-seven years I've known you, you've never, ever canceled a surgery."

"Have Mom drive you. Meet me in an hour. Y'all can park in my office parking lot. Dr. Mions's office is across the street. See you soon."

My blood was drawn for the third time that day. Only that third time, one vial turned into sixteen. I wondered if I'd get drunker faster that night with the decreased blood volume.

Dad introduced me to Dr. Mions. No pleasantries were exchanged. There was no time. Instead, the older doctor in the white coat greeted me with the question that would thrust me out of the only life I'd ever known and into a foreign existence.

"Hello, I'm Dr. Mions. Caroline, how long have those lumps been in your neck?"

Nice to meet you too.

"What lumps?"

Dr. Mions looked at my parents.

"Kim, Warren, why don't y'all wait in my office? I'm going to take Caroline into the exam room."

In shocking silence, Dr. Mions spent exactly two minutes checking my body for lumps. I didn't move a muscle. I wondered what thoughts were forming behind his tired eyes. Was that a faint smile or a deep frown? Was his soft breath sound a sigh of relief or a repressed gasp of knowing? I didn't want to find out.

"Caroline, why don't you wait for me in my office?" Dr. Mions asked through his furrowed brow.

So it was a frown. Damn it.

Mom and Dad were already sitting in chairs that were positioned in front of Dr. Mions's desk. I cautiously sat down in the empty chair in between my parents and tightly gripped the seat. Dr. Mions wasted no time.

"Kim, Warren, Caroline, I'm not going to lie to you. I think this is lymphoma."

"Lym—what?" I asked.

"Lymphoma. It's a type of blood cancer," Dr. Mions explained in a deadpan voice.

"Cancer? You're kidding me, right?" Mom rhetorically asked. She and I were sharing the same level of misunderstanding.

She wasn't finished. "My daughter does *not* have cancer. I mean, look at her. She doesn't look sick to me!" Everyone turned to look at me as if hoping to find some outward indication that I did not in fact have an invisible disease growing inside of my body that was currently in the process of trying to take me down.

Dr. Mions spoke more monotone words. His voice began to mix in with the soft rock station playing over the medical office speakers. Bryan

Adams singing "Summer of '69." I'd always liked that song. I haven't listened to it since.

A muffled sob interrupted the catchy chorus. I turned to looked at Dad. He looked up at me with teary eyes.

Up until that day in Dr. Mions's office, the only time I'd seen my dad cry had been the day we took his mother's clothing to Goodwill. She had passed away suddenly from a brain tumor when I was in sixth grade. I had loved my grandmother deeply but was still taken aback when I saw my larger-than-life father pull the car over a block away from the Bellville, Texas, Goodwill donation location and hug the steering wheel until he was able to resume our drive. The memory of that day stuck with me and, even though it had been many years in the past, so did the sob.

Dad pulled himself together and stepped into neurosurgeon crisis mode. He worked quickly and efficiently with Dr. Mions to get a plan put into motion. It was decided that one of my lymph nodes would need to be removed. This unlucky lymph node would be biopsied and studied, and the information yielded from this sliced and diced node would give us a definitive diagnosis.

Unfortunately, this happened to be the Tuesday afternoon before Thanksgiving. Medical offices were closing early, and people were starting to leave town. In an effort to expedite this cancer hunt, Dad masterfully played his "doctor-to-doctor favor" card and had me scheduled for surgery at 7 a.m. the following morning.

As mom pulled her car onto Medical Drive, I caught a glimpse of myself in the rearview mirror. That California winter tan was still aglow. My long golden-brown hair hung loosely around my face. I could still see a trace of a tan line on my chest from the special swimsuit sports bra I had worn recently in the LA triathlon. I couldn't understand. Was this what a cancer patient looked like?

The surgery the following morning and corresponding biopsy confirmed the lymphoma. Dad found me in his bed, on Mom's side. I don't remember why I was in their bed instead of mine, but I do remember being violently ill from the anesthesia. Dad delivered the words that should have created a "moment that changed my life forever," but all I felt was nausea and…nothing.

Maybe my body had already known what my mind had not. And maybe that knowledge had prepared me for what I'd deep down already known.

Two days later, we were gathered at my aunt and uncle's ranch with my mom's side of the family. Mom had already called Aunt Karol, Uncle Paul, Gigi, Granddad, Chad, Cousin Kelly, Cousin Paul, and Cousin Paul's soon-to-be wife, Katie, and told them the news. Since Mom and her sister talked on the phone multiple times a day, I knew Aunt Karol had been kept in the loop each step of the way.

It was Thursday, November 25th, 2024. Not only was it the day after my cancer diagnosis, but it was also the national day of giving thanks. While Aunt Karol busied herself in the kitchen with the Thanksgiving turkey, I sat on a kitchen barstool and looked around the room. I felt like both the center of attention and invisible at the same time. My diagnosis was the unseen puppet master that was controlling all my family's reactions in their own unique ways.

Aunt Karol busied herself with constant temperature checks on the turkey and sweet potatoes. Mom focused her efforts on creating the world's most elaborate floral centerpiece. Chad immersed himself in yelling at the television during the college football games, and Dad kept pacing around the room checking his watch. Granddad retreated a little bit more into his worn leather armchair and covered himself with a thick wool blanket. Uncle Paul was on the ranch landline calling in favors and using his connections at MD Anderson Cancer Center to get me an appointment with the best possible doctor.

Cousin Kelly tasted different dinner wines, and Grandmother Gigi just kept trying to feed me. Cousin Paul and his fiancée, Katie, consumed themselves with picking out the perfect music to fit the mood, but what music represented denial and gratitude wrapped together in a pretty little bow? All the while, I resisted the urge to pull out my medical school books and study for my upcoming finals. Studying always made me feel more in control of my destiny.

Thankfully, Uncle Paul had been involved with MD Anderson. His phone calls resulted in me having an appointment at nine o'clock the following Monday morning. Now that we had a starting point, we could try to enjoy our meal together as a family.

Gigi always began our Thanksgiving meal with a blessing before going around the table and everyone saying the one thing for which they were the most grateful. However, that year, after Gigi's blessing, instead of leading us off with a quote on the importance of giving thanks, which was our sign to begin the circle of gratitude affirmations, Aunt Karol silently and mercifully picked up her fork, signaling us to all dig in.

That night, I decided to sleep in the same room with Cousin Kelly. We used to share a room back when the most pressing problems we faced were trying to sleep through the pain of the fiberglass splinters that covered our backsides from the old ranch swimming pool slide.

As Kelly and I were about to recap the latest celebrity gossip, Cousin Paul came in and sat down beside me. As he put his arm around me, I had a moment of believing it really was just like old times. Being in that room together felt so comforting and so safe. For that brief moment in time, I forgot about the invisible new invader that now also occupied our intimate and familiar space.

That night at the ranch, in our childhood bedroom, with Paul and Kelly sitting close to me on the bed, I'd only been a cancer patient for twenty-four hours. It still seemed too surreal to be true. I was convinced there must be some mistake. How could I possibly call my closest friends when I got home and tell them that I had cancer?

No one who had been told about my diagnosis had really known what to say to me, and I in turn didn't know what to say to them. False assurances felt painfully insincere. I was savoring the isolation of being on the ranch with my family and not having to talk about "it" almost more than the perfectly cooked turkey we'd enjoyed hours before.

Paul, Kelly, and I stared at the wall, silent. It felt sacrilegious to say anything other than the truth. I searched for unfamiliar words. After a few minutes, Paul turned to me and said,

"Well, Caroline, fuck this."

Unexpected relief slowly spread across my body.

Yes. Fuck this.

Fuck all of this.

And fuck pretending like anything about this was okay.

For the first time since my hug with Nurse Betty, I felt a connection. Since the moment the diagnosis had been confirmed, I'd been walking around with a fake smile and reassuring hugs for everyone in my family. They never asked for it, but I never wanted them to worry. But in that moment, Paul gave me permission to acknowledge my feelings, the deep, dark, scary, ugly, uncensored feelings. As the grazing cows outside our window had been permanently scarred with the brand of the ranch, I knew I too had been forever marked as a cancer patient.

The three of us went back to staring at the wall. Neither Kelly nor Paul interrupted the silence, and I was grateful. In the stillness, I began to carefully try on the cancer patient label.

I tried to imagine what my life would look like now that I was "sick." I tried to force my fingers to feel my freshly, invisibly branded skin. I willed my mind to process this new diagnosis. I asked my body to rise to the challenge. And I begged my heart not to feel.

## CHAPTER 2

# MD Anderson

**Dear Riley,**

Nothing can ever prepare you for your first day at a cancer center. Walking into the clinic building at MD Anderson for the first time was equal parts terrifying and comforting, new and familiar, nerve-wracking and calming. I first noticed the gorgeous flowers planted in the meditative garden with the tastefully designed sign pointing to the complementary yoga classes. The grand carport stood tall and proud and welcomed visitors with rays of sunshine peering through the glass roof. The valets smiled with a cheerful, "Good morning!" Volunteers in blue vests welcomed us as we walked through the sliding glass doors. They were ready with hot cups of tea and peppermints for anyone who needed a treat. In the lobby, exotic fish seemed to smile at us from their large, colorful aquarium.

Our first stop was the information desk. An older man sat behind the desk and asked Mom, Dad, and me if we needed help. I looked this man in his kind eyes and said, "Yes, sir. I'd love some help. I'm a new patient here and don't know where to go."

"Well, young lady, I'd be happy to. What's your medical record number?"

"Oh, I don't have one yet. I'm not actually a cancer patient—just a patient. So I don't have a medical record number."

"I see. So you don't have cancer—that's a relief! I thought you looked too young to be a patient here. This place is reserved for us old folk," the nice man replied with a wink.

"Yeah, well, I guess I technically do have cancer," I reluctantly and begrudgingly responded.

"I see. What kind of cancer do you have?"

"Lymphoma."

"The leukemia/lymphoma department is on the eighth floor, but if your doctor wants you to get labs first, you'll need to make a stop at the main lab on the second floor."

"Thank you, sir. I appreciate your help. Oh, and do you know where I could get some of those peppermints they were passing out by the front doors?"

"I actually have a handful right here." He reached into his vest pocket. "All the volunteers keep peppermints on hand because the patients undergoing chemotherapy say they're the only thing that helps to get the metallic taste of the medicine out of their mouths."

The peppermints no longer sounded appealing.

After thanking the volunteer for his help, Mom, Dad, and I headed for the B elevator bank and proceeded to the second floor. The blood draw was uneventful. Ms. Belinda found my vein on the first try. She filled the purple, red, black-spotted, turquoise, lavender, yellow, and blue tubes up to the top with my blood before asking me to verify the patient labels. I laughed along with the phlebotomists as they joked around with each other. They seemed like one big happy, joy-filled, blood-drawing family.

After Ms. Belinda secured the cotton pad and wrap around my still bleeding IV needle site, our next stop was the eighth floor. The lymphoma waiting room looked a bit different than our previous stops thus far. I saw more people with bald heads and scarves. Many people were in wheelchairs as they were too weak to walk. One woman was hooked up to oxygen.

I took a moment as I knew I needed to gear up for this next appointment. I was approaching it like I approached everything in my life, with total focus and domination. I liked to set a goal and do whatever I had to do to achieve it. Goals made sense to me. I liked that they could be measured and that I had total control over whether or not I achieved them.

Mom, Dad, and I sat down in the last few empty chairs in the waiting room. Fox News was playing on the TVs. I wasn't sure what to do next. I saw some people walking up to a desk with a check-in sign hanging above. I told Mom and Dad I'd be right back. I stood and walked to the rounded black desk.

The lady sitting behind the desk had the name "Florence" stitched into her MD Anderson logo shirt. Florence greeted me, "Hey there, honey. Sign in on this form and then take a seat. We'll call you back in a few."

It took me a few minutes to sign in. A form so seemingly simple, yet I didn't know the answers to any of the questions. Even through her smiling eyes and welcoming words, Florence intimidated me a little with her seat in the gatekeeper's chair. No one went through the brown double doors without getting through Florence first.

Mom, Dad, and I waited for about twenty minutes in the crowded waiting room. As we sat next to each other watching the news, I started to sink into my green-checked chair a bit. For the first time all morning, I took a breath—a real breath—and relaxed my neck against the wall. I looked to my right and saw a middle-aged woman with no hair, wearing a mask. She was holding the hand of the man next to her, presumably her husband. She was calmly reading *Southern Accents* while her husband enjoyed the *Houston Chronicle*. I looked to my left. Several patients sat with unknown companions next to them. All wore masks, and no one had hair. Some ladies covered their heads with delicate scarves. Others chose warm caps. The men preferred to expose their bald heads. I saw no tears. I saw no fear. I saw no anger. I saw people surrounded by other people doing what they needed to do to live another day.

"Caroline?" Florence announced to the room.

"Yes! That's me!" I eagerly shouted as if I were hailing my medical school professor with the correct answer.

"Come on back. The doctor will see you now."

After thanking Florence, Mom, Dad, and I proceeded to walk through the brown double doors away from the waiting room and into my future.

Dr. Barbara Frank and I hit it off right away. She was from Italy, and I had lived in Italy during my semester abroad. Granted, our experiences in her homeland were probably quite different, but I still felt an instant kinship. I later read in one of Dr. Frank's dictation notes from our initial meeting that she had described me as an "intelligent, cheerful, and otherwise healthy twenty-seven-year-old female." It was true. Apart from this cancer that was supposedly growing somewhere in my body, I really was at the top of my game.

"The biopsy results tell us that you have a B-cell, follicular, fast-growing, and aggressive form of non-Hodgkin's lymphoma."

*Uh-huh.*

"We know you have this disease, but we won't know how widespread it is until we run all of the stage testing."

*Makes sense.*

"I'm going to go ahead and put in an order for the necessary tests. I'm hoping we can get started as early as today."

I liked that Dr. Frank was not one to waste time.

"The next week will be very difficult for you, both mentally and physically. I just want you to be prepared."

*Have you seen these biceps? Won't be a problem.*

"I'd like to meet you and your family back here in my office one week from today. By then we'll have all our test results and will be able to devise a game plan."

I always did love a good plan of action.

"If you don't mind waiting here for a few minutes, I'm going to see if I can get you in for your bone marrow biopsy this afternoon."

I noticed the wetness on Mom's cheek but chose to look away. I also noticed the worry lines on Dr. Frank's forehead but preferred to think of them as damage done from too many hours of drinking wine underneath the Tuscan sun. I noticed the twisting in my stomach and chose to label it as a hunger pain. My mind was working overtime to stop the flow of information from my heart to my head. All roadblocks were on high alert. No emotion was getting through without a full search.

However, deep down, I knew that the emotional tide had started to turn. I reminded myself that this was not a time for worry. MD Anderson was a happy place, full of smiling faces and kind people. I had learned in med school that laughter helped the immune system, and it seemed like now, more than ever, in this place where all patients were playing a literal game of Life and no one knew who'd be left standing, the need for increasing our chances of winning had become higher than ever.

CHAPTER 3

# Finding Riley

**Dear Riley,**

Living life in remission can be a real mind trick. When your cancer goes into hiding, it's as if you've won the race you fought so hard to win but then looked down and noticed you were no longer even on the track. You actually realize you were not on any track of any kind. Sure, you'd won the battle with The Cancer for the time being, but instead of celebrating in a winner's circle you find yourself tiptoeing through the dark, searching for a way forward.

I was twenty-seven. Tom and I had been married for three short months. I'd been in remission for six. I was trying to navigate married life and my hide-and-seek-playing cancer simultaneously. Nothing looked familiar. Little made sense. I was struggling and knew it. I needed comfort and knew how to find it.

For as long as I could remember, animals had always been my go-to source of solace. In childhood, my horse, Brimstone, filled any lonely voids. He and I were a formidable pair on the hunter-jumper circuit and shocked everyone, myself included, when we rose up the ranks to gain a national ranking. Brimstone knew we could do it. I didn't have the confidence in myself that he always had in me, but I did believe in us as a team. Brimstone took care of me, and when we finally retired from the sport together and turned Brimstone out for a life of retirement in a gorgeous Colorado pasture, I entered back into life without my teammate and source of support.

Teenage years are tricky. No one escapes unscathed. But thank God I listened to my gut and told my family that we needed a dog. In seventh grade, I used my dad's birthday as an excuse to go to the pound and rescue a scrappy, street-smart yellow Lab. Rudder was only about a year old at the time. Lord knows what his life was like before joining our family, but Rudder didn't seem to carry any emotional scars. He ended up being my dad's shadow and constant companion, but he reserved a bit of his love for me. Having Rudder in the house was comfort enough.

So maybe it was me honoring my need for canine companionship, veiled by my need to do something good and save an animal from certain death. Maybe it was another example of an impulsive, ill-thought-out decision that could end in heartbreak and disappointment. Or maybe, just maybe, doing the Google search of "rescue dogs Los Angeles" was an incredible, perfect example of allowing myself to sit in the moment and listen to my inner voice. I choose to believe the latter.

Being so newly out of my extensive and exhaustive series of chemo treatments, I knew I was in no condition to be able to take on the massive emotional baggage and physical injuries a rescue dog could bring to the table, and you, Riley Rose, were in no way able to take on the burden I was about to give back to you. Yet when I typed in my Google search and saw Ace of Hearts Dog Rescue pop up, I clicked.

Oh, but wait, I'd not thought of one major roadblock in my plan—Landlord Jerry. Tom and I had spent weeks looking for the perfect rental in which to begin married life and had just moved into our precious, tiny, and perfect Santa Monica cottage. Landlord Jerry was a tough older man from the East Coast (New Jersey to be precise) who had made it very clear that NO PETS were allowed. Bringing a dog home would result in our immediate eviction.

And yet I kept clicking.

Ace of Hearts Dog Rescue described itself as being an LA-based dog rescue organization that pulled dogs from local shelters on the day of euthanasia. Having just visited death's door myself, I was drawn to the promise of life. I saw the faces of those dogs whose lives had barely been saved and thought, *My picture could have been listed alongside those innocent creatures.*

We'd all knocked on Heaven's door but were turned away and given another chance, so maybe it was only fitting for us to find each other. Maybe Landlord Jerry would understand the emotional significance and make an exception to his pet policy. I kept clicking through the pages and staring at face after face of defenseless dogs and pleading eyes, but I never clicked on the "more info" tab.

And then I saw you. Riley, I remember that moment so clearly, almost as if it still exists. I was sitting in our back office with the midday sun beaming through the vine-covered trellis. There was already a chill in the early winter air. From my lovely viewpoint, I looked through the computer to see you lying on the cold, hard cement floor with your large, emaciated body curled up into a defensive ball and your face looking halfway up at the human who was taking the picture. I saw me in you.

I clicked.

No one knew for sure what your first year of life had been like, but they knew enough. You were around eleven months old. The rescue organization found you in a pet store in the Beverly Center. You had been born in a puppy mill in Missouri, separated from your mom days into your life and placed in a small cage. You traveled in your cage from Missouri to Los Angeles, where you were put on display in the pet store for all the puppy-loving families to see. One family took you home but returned you days later. They said you were "too much."

After spending a few months on the shelves of the pet store, you were deemed "unsellable," so you were moved to the back of the store. No one in the rescue group knew how long you'd spent in the back, but they did know that you were suffering. Being a Great Dane and Lab mix, you were, even as a puppy, large. You were very, very large. But your cage was small. Very, very small.

Yet no one let you out.

As your size grew, the space in your cage shrank. Your muscles were never able to form correctly, which resulted in the need for massive reconstructive surgery. As if that were not enough, the circular burn marks branded all over your body, paired with your lifelong intense fear of hairdryers, indicated abuse in the form of burning with the grooming dryer hose through the bars of your prison—I mean, cage. That was later confirmed by an ex-employee when the pet store was put on trial for animal abuse and subsequently shut down.

It's no wonder your ability to trust was damaged. It was clearly stated in the description under your photo that even though you'd endured serious abuse and neglect (every rib was visible through your malnourished white coat) you never were violent or aggressive.

You were a gentle giant and terrified all the time. The only other thing they knew about your personality was that you loved tennis balls. You were unable to chase them because your limp was too severe, but you seemed to keep the tennis balls with you, almost like a security blanket. Almost like a friend.

I called the number listed under your picture and said I'd like to come meet you. Your foster home was an apartment off of La Brea. I made an appointment for 6 p.m. that very evening. My next phone call was to Tom. He was in his first few months of his new financial job in Downtown Los Angeles. We'd loved every day of married life thus far, still very much in the honeymoon phase. Tom was incredibly grateful that I had agreed to move out to Los Angeles so he could pursue this job opportunity, so he was pretty open to most of my crazy ideas. This, however, could result in an eviction, which was not what we wanted.

When I called Tom and told him I needed him to meet me at this apartment behind Burger King on La Brea, he had to ask why. I finally told him about you, and his first comment was, "Well, I hope it's a small dog, because you know Landlord Jerry doesn't allow animals." I'd seen your weight listed at 111 pounds but decided to leave that detail out and instead asked for trust. And then I also decided to trust. Tom agreed to meet me.

As we approached the apartment, I looked up and saw that the front door was ajar, but the screen was closed. It was as if you knew we were coming. Even though standing was painful and difficult for you, there you were, waiting for us. You were tall and lanky behind the screen. It was dark outside, and only dim lights were on in the apartment.

You did not bark. You did not wag your tail. You just stood there, watching us. As we got closer, we noticed the slobbery, wet tennis ball safely held in your mouth.

Your foster mom gave us as much information as she could, which was not much. She said you were quiet and distrustful but kind as could be. She worried you might not be able to trust again. She described the reconstructive surgery that would need to be paid for by the family that agreed to adopt you. She knew you loved your tennis balls but said you were unable to chase them due to your malformations. You seemed calm and broken.

You seemed…lost. Or was that me?

Tom asked the questions. I listened and never took my eyes off you. Your eyes darted all around me, never daring direct contact. Your foster mom said several other families had come to meet you, but no one wanted to take on the financial cost of the surgery. Understandable. I didn't think Tom did either. We walked over to pet you. You stiffened as we reached down to stroke your back. You bit down on your tennis ball harder. We said goodbye.

The decision was up to me. Tom wanted me to find out the exact cost of the surgery and also asked that I call Landlord Jerry to clear this with him. I assured Tom I'd do both of those very necessary and responsible things before we made our decision. I did neither. I knew that if I called Landlord Jerry that he'd say no. And I knew if I found out the exact cost of the surgery that Tom would think I'd lost my damn mind. And who could've blamed him?

Tom was counting on his Type-A wife whom he'd married only three months earlier to make the responsible decision. This patient and level-headed man knew my practical side would prevail, as it always had before. So you can imagine his surprise when I called him on our car ride home the following afternoon to tell him that we were now a family of three.

Oh, Riley Rose. That car ride home. You, in the backseat, not moving a muscle. Me, with both hands on the wheel in the ten and two position. My first thought upon pulling into my parking place in front of our garage was a loud and clear, *What the hell do I do now?*

You cowered when I reached my hand out to you and violently shook when I managed to break through the force field and actually touch your body. After slow, calming, and gentle movements, I was able to get the leash clipped onto your collar. I decided to take you for a short walk down the street. That would be a nice first step.

Ahh—our first walk. You using all the strength you had to pull away from me and me using all the strength I had to bring you back. Do you remember me sitting on the curb two houses down from ours and bursting into tears? You were so damaged. I cried for your pain, and I cried for your fear, and I cried for my own broken self. I cried because I was scared and thought by bringing you home to live with us that you could alleviate some of my fear.

But I realized on that walk that I was going to need to help you before you could help me. I just wasn't sure if I was capable of giving any more of myself to anyone else.

For two days, you stayed in your corner, and I stayed in mine. Tom tried to bond with you. I knew he didn't agree with my decision, but he was giving me space to realize my own mistake. He also knew me well enough to know that if he told me to return you to the rescue group that I'd fight him tooth and nail. The realization would have to come from me. It wasn't hard to keep you hidden from Landlord Jerry, as you never left your corner except to step outside to our courtyard to do your business before retreating back into your safe place.

The breakthrough happened on day three while I was cooking dinner. The smell of steaks filled the air. Out of the corner of my eye, I saw you slowly limp into the kitchen. You sat down and looked halfway up at me, the drool coming down like rivers from the sides of your mouth. I knew what you wanted. And I was more than happy to give it to you.

I gave you my entire steak. I'd never seen you smile before. But that night, standing there in our tiny kitchen, you did. The corners of your mouth stretched backwards as your large, floppy ears relaxed onto your soft head. With each chew of your mouth, your eyes narrowed more and more as joy and newfound euphoria seeped through your steak-loving, mouth-salivating, food-obsessed gaze. I was so encouraged by this breakthrough that without thinking twice I gave you Tom's steak as well. Food was clearly the way to your heart. Watching you experience your first steak was like watching a child see the ocean for the first time. That night, in our kitchen, the world righted itself. I found my balance and you, in turn, found yours. We were no longer strangers. You were Riley and I was Caroline. Very nice to meet you.

Instead of staying the night in your corner of the living room, that night, you decided to sleep on your new dog bed on the floor of our bedroom. A week later, you found your way into our queen bed. Tom and I were both pushed to the outer edges as you relaxed and sprawled out between the two of us. You were slowly starting to put on some weight. Tom and I used to laugh in the middle of the night when your snoring would wake us up. We'd look up and, in the glow of the bedside clock, we could just make out the relaxed smile draped across your handsome face as you slept between your new family.

Before agreeing to surgery, I decided to try building up your strength through swimming. I knew you'd never seen the ocean, let alone any body of water, so I assumed you might be reluctant to jump into the vast open sea. But I also knew I had a secret weapon: your tennis ball. You would follow that ball anywhere, and I planned on using that to my advantage.

I started slow, tossing your ball a few feet into the waves. Your sweet soul was torn between energetic puppy enthusiasm and a malformed and abused body. I watched as you forgot about your physical limitations and tried to bound through the water and "run" along the sand after your ball.

Each morning, I'd throw your ball farther and farther out into the waves. Over time, your swimming gradually improved, as did your muscle strength. Your severe limp turned into more of a slight limp, which in time turned into an almost undetectable limp. No limp meant no surgery, and no surgery meant no large medical bill. Up to that point, we'd managed to keep you hidden from Landlord Jerry. Our two big potential roadblocks were starting to seem like non-issues. My decision to bring you home to live with us started to seem, well, brilliant.

Until…we got caught.

It was an ordinary Tuesday afternoon. You and I were driving home from our early afternoon trip to the dog park. We had just turned onto our street when I saw the police lights. My pulse quickened as I sped up. Three cop cars were parked directly in front of our house. Our neighbors stood in our shared driveway talking to—Landlord Jerry. Crap.

After telling you to "get down and hide," I slowly parked and stepped out of the car. I felt like I was under arrest. I had broken the rules and had finally been caught.

Slowly, tentatively, I approached Landlord Jerry.

"Hey, Jerry. How are you?"

"Well, as you can probably see, I've been better."

"Yeah, so, uhh, what happened?" I asked while holding my breath and bracing for impact.

"Some fucker broke into my properties!" Oh no. This was not good. Or was it? Maybe in this commotion, Landlord Jerry wouldn't notice you hanging your large head out the passenger side window.

Landlord Jerry owned several units that shared the same driveway. Our rental cottage was positioned in the front along the street. His other apartments were lined up in a row behind our home. From the looks of it, all his properties had been hit.

"Sir, you got lucky on this one," Mr. Policeman said as he walked to our position on the driveway.

"Lucky? What the fuck is lucky about this?" Jerry yelled in response.

"Well, sir, if that large dog wasn't living in the front house, you'd have a much more serious situation on your hands."

Tick, tick, boom.

"Dog? I don't allow fucking dogs in my properties! Who has a fucking dog?" he howled.

Mr. Policeman took this as an actual question instead of a rhetorical one, like I was hoping, and was pleased to answer. "The tenant of the front cottage owns a dog. Apparently, a very large dog."

I felt Landlord Jerry's gaze come over me like solid ice.

But Mr. Policeman wasn't done. "And it's because of that very large dog that we only have cop cars and no ambulances. You may want to thank that dog for saving your foul-mouthed ass."

Silence. Utter and total silence. Landlord Jerry's gaze was still bearing down on me. I didn't know what to do. I didn't know where to look. I couldn't imagine what I should say. I just knew I was infinitely grateful to have law enforcement officials by my side to witness the impending explosion from Landlord Jerry.

"Caroline, where is your dog now?"

"Umm, he's…" I pointed in your direction.

"I want to meet him," Landlord Jerry responded.

"Okay. I'll go get him. Be right back."

I glanced up at Mr. Policeman and tried to gauge if his look meant, *run while you still can*, or *I can't wait to see what happens next*. I walked up to your side of the car and opened your door. You gingerly jumped out of the passenger seat and paused as you assessed the crime scene. I gave you a quick scratch behind your right ear as I reassured you the police would protect us. I urged you to follow me as I prayed that was the truth.

Landlord Jerry was still standing in the exact spot I'd left him. My neighbors were huddled together in front of the first apartment. Mr. Policeman was preparing to enjoy the show.

"Umm, Jerry. This is Riley. Riley Rose."

"Caroline, how long have you had Riley?"

"A few weeks." Months actually, but who was counting?

"And he lives with you?"

"Yes."

"Does he bite?" Landlord Jerry wanted to know.

"No."

"But he looks like he bites. You know, because he's fucking huge."

"Umm, I guess so," I answered, confused as to where the conversation was headed.

"Good. That's good. Okay, Riley can stay."

"Stay where?" I was not tracking.

"Stay where? Stay with you. What the fuck d'ya think I meant? He can stay in the house. Just make sure people know he's in the house. I don't want to get another call from a fucking cop telling me my properties have been broken into. Make sure this—what'd you say the dog's name was?"

"Riley. Riley Rose."

"Yeah, make sure people see Riley Rose and see how fucking big he is. And tell anyone who asks that he bites—that he's a fucking Rottweiler when you piss him off."

And, with that, Landlord Jerry turned on his heels, walked to his car, and drove away.

I found out later that the culprit had been watching the comings and goings of all of us who lived along the shared driveway. He knew when we were home and knew when we were gone. The thief had a terrible fear of dogs so specifically waited for "the big yellow dog" in the front house to leave before making his move. Even knowing you and I were away from home, the burglar didn't break into our house. Mr. Policeman thought he was too afraid to get too close—just in case.

Aside from defying Landlord Jerry's pet clause and working around the possible large medical bills, bringing you into my life seemed like such an obvious thing to do. True, I was scared and nervous and doubted my decision-making abilities but, beneath all of that, beneath all of the negative, I saw the possible good that could far outweigh the possible bad. And, because I was searching for post-cancer-remission-approved methods of self-soothing, I clicked.

Prior to us finding each other, I was a runner. A big runner. Running was the physical manifestation of my internal drive for perfection. Nashville was my first marathon. I was a junior in college and signed up on a whim. My finishing time was a respectable four and a half hours. I knew I could do better, so I spent the next year purposefully training with a goal of four hours. I finished in three hours and thirty-eight minutes. I had qualified for Boston. I was hooked.

The next few years found me living in New York City and working for NBC Sports. During my time in New York, I ran four more marathons: Dallas, Austin, New York, and Boston. Running was my thing. I'd lose myself in my training runs. It was a meditative time for me. The thinking I did while running was always my deepest, most honest thinking, and without that time to center myself I felt lost.

I deeply missed my long runs. It pained me not to have my next marathon on the calendar. My triathlon bike sat in the back corner of my garage, and my forty-pound weighted vest for training on the Santa Monica stairs sat in the back of my Yukon, both gathering dust. Running long distances was no longer an option for my forever-weakened body. I was furious and riddled with loss. So many miles in me lost—left un-run—simply because I had no gas in the tank. After cancer, I tried to get back into running. My mind was ready, but my body was not.

I was living a personal goal-less life with so many desires still to achieve.

With my mind restless and my body still weakened, I was lost. My chemo regimen required four weeks of maintenance treatments every six months, which made it virtually impossible to go back to school or get a job. Everyone kept telling me to rest, but I was tired of resting. I was sick of being sick. I was done being broken.

On that fateful December morning when I entered a Google search only to find your empty eyes staring back at me, I was, in my own way, acknowledging the void within me. Or maybe I was searching for another being more broken than me. Or possibly I wanted a project, something I could focus on other than recovery. Maybe I was yearning for companionship.

Whatever the reason, clicking on your picture three months into my first remission was my first act in the last of my listless ways. Finding you brought me back to life. By choosing you, I was honoring me. By rescuing you, I was finding me. We were becoming Caroline and Riley, Riley and Caroline, two souls in need of saving. One partnership in need of protecting. One bond in need of finding.

## CHAPTER 4

## Jacob

**Dear Ri Rose,**

Do you remember Jacob? He was the seven-year-old boy who lived in the apartment above the garage behind our rental cottage. Jacob lived with his mom, Marlaina, and attended the public school down the street. He never had friends over and rarely played outside. Before you came to live with us, we barely knew him.

One afternoon in early October, just two weeks after Tom and I had moved in and right in the middle of my IVF treatments, Jacob knocked on our door. He and his mom had made a batch of cookies and wanted to give them to us as a "welcome to the shared driveway" gesture.

Even though I was enduring hormone shots and raging mood swings to try to safeguard our option to have children in the future, I still didn't feel any sort of a tug on my heartstrings when I saw our neighbor's child standing at my front door holding warm homemade cookies.

Ri, when you first met Jacob, Tom and I had lived in the cottage for three months and you'd only lived with us a little over a week. You and I were still trying to find our stride. I was still holding my breath, not wanting to disappoint our new rescue dog. You were quiet and hard to read. I lived to hear your tail thump against the hardwood floor. That sound meant I'd done something right, that I'd pleased you in some way. A scratch behind the ear worked sometimes. Food worked—every time.

There we were, two flawed beings just trying to figure out how to live. The Cancer had thrown my life path down the garbage disposal and shredded my ambition into unrecognizable pieces. My "job" was still to rest, to take care of myself, to heal. What did that even mean? Doing "nothing" may have healed my broken-down physical body, but it was destroying my soul.

This was also the time you had been ordered to rest. Your muscles needed time to strengthen before we pushed you too hard. The vet had given me strict orders: no more than twenty minutes of exercise a day. So, instead of doing what we both really wanted to do, what our souls yearned to do, we sat. And we silently suffered.

From the moment I was diagnosed, the doctors were very clear that they could treat my lymphoma but couldn't cure it. There was not yet a cure for this intelligent disease. Of course, I had the thought, well then why would I even fight it in the first place? What was the point?

Until my uncle came into my room one night while I was in utter despair and told me that he'd just attended a meeting at MD Anderson and was amazed by how many new treatments were under development.

Uncle Paul looked at me, slumped on the floor in the corner of his guest bedroom and said, "Listen, your goal isn't to cure this cancer. Your goal needs to be remission. Do the best possible treatment option available to you right now, and use that to get into remission. That will buy you time for the new research that is currently in the pipeline to become a viable treatment option, and that new treatment could be the cure. Just take baby steps and buy time."

Buy time. Baby steps. One foot in front of the other. Get into remission. Get into that promised land of a reprieve. Fight like hell until I get a scan that shows no traces of my lymphoma. Have a bone marrow biopsy that doesn't detect The Cancer in my bone marrow. Keep moving forward, keep working hard, and get into remission. Buy time.

Ri, was that what you were doing? When I thought about your life before we found each other, I wondered sometimes how you'd survived. Did you have a wise old uncle in the cage above you in the pet store giving you words of doggie wisdom and encouraging you to hold on for one more day? Did you even know the joys life could bring? Had you ever even had a taste of the good life? That first night we spent together as a new family, I worried life had broken you, but every time I heard that thump of your tail on the floor, I smiled because it gave me hope that you were still you, whoever that was. You just needed time to let down your guard. I understood. You could take all the time you needed.

So, Ri, you and I both fought. We both won. We both got out of our bad situations. And there we were, both in "remission" from the horrors that life could bring. We were both in a temporary holding pattern of time, a waiting period. We were two planes circling the skies, waiting for air traffic control to tell us it was time to land, time to fight, time to face life and all the scary things that came with it. I knew I'd have to fight for my life once again, and you knew that you'd once again have to go out and face the world.

True, our days were long, uneventful, and honestly boring at times, but at least we knew that in those moments we were safe from the outside. And when we were eventually told to come in for a landing, we'd no longer be two separate planes but instead co-pilots navigating the common plane of our partnership and landing in our shared life—together.

Knowing The Cancer was going to eventually come back, Tom and I froze our embryos immediately after getting married. I knew that when it came back, the next step would be to have a bone marrow transplant, and fertility post-transplant was, I'd been told, not an option. So, by doing IVF, which meant harvesting and freezing embryos, we were covering our parenting bases. Neither Tom nor I was ready for parenthood. And then you arrived.

I'd received the call from our fertility doctor that seventeen and a half of our embryos had survived the three-day growing process and were ready to be frozen. I didn't know if that was good or bad and couldn't understand what the half meant, but I didn't really have an interest in knowing. Tom and I had done what we'd needed to do to plan for the future, but any joy the moment might have held ended when the nurse removed my IV after the egg retrieval procedure. The bruises on my legs from the shots were still sore and healing. I was told they were larger and deeper than normal. Must be from my lingering funky platelet count.

I thanked the doctor and hung up the phone. I looked at you on your bed and said, "Ri, they said it's good news. Maybe one day you'll have a brother or sister."

That look in your eye was so…indifferent.

Then we heard a knock on the door. You didn't bark. You gingerly stood up, found your balance, and limped over.

"Who is it?" I asked.

"It's Jacob."

I opened our front door and saw little Jacob standing on our doorstep.

"My mom said you got a dog, and I was wondering if I could meet him."

"Of course you can. Jacob, this is Riley. He's very sweet but also very scared and nervous, so it might take him some time to warm up to you."

The last word hadn't even left my mouth when you walked right up to Jacob and gently pawed his shin. Then you raised your head and looked at Jacob in the eye.

Jacob reached down and roughly patted you on top of your head. You didn't retreat.

"He looks pretty friendly to me. I got a skateboard for my birthday. Could your dog come watch me skateboard in the driveway?"

"Sure, I think that'd be OK. He can't really run, so be careful that he doesn't get too excited."

I closed the black wrought iron gate at the front of the driveway and took a seat on our front step. You followed Jacob to the bottom of the outdoor staircase that led up to his apartment. Jacob put on his helmet and knee pads. You sniffed around and found a sunny spot in the corner of the driveway.

Jacob talked to you the entire time he rode his skateboard. He was so excited to show you his new "moves." You sat and watched every one of them, never taking your eyes off him. Every once in a while, you'd glance back to be sure I was watching. If I'd stand up to go in and check on dinner, you'd rise from your spot on the cement to follow me inside. As long as I was sitting where you could see me, you were content to hang with your new buddy.

As the weeks passed by and your legs and trust grew stronger, so did your penchant for food-stealing mischief. You started small by sneaking pieces of scraps from the countertop and found that the "trouble" you got into was absolutely worth the tasty prize. Always better to ask for forgiveness than permission.

One afternoon in January, you, Jacob, and I were in the middle of our new after-school routine. Jacob was growing on me, and I found myself looking forward to his soft knocks on the door. I was sitting on the front step reading *Us Weekly* while Jacob was riding his skateboard up and down the driveway. You were, predictably, sitting in your corner spot, soaking up the Santa Monica afternoon sun. I was enthralled in an article about the Jen/Brad/Angelina love triangle, so I didn't see you get up from your spot and ascend the staircase to Jacob's apartment.

The murmur of the afternoon traffic creeping down nearby Wilshire Boulevard was interrupted by the loud chaos that ensued.

"RILEY! NOOOOOOOOO! BAD BOY!"

It was Jacob's mom, Marlaina.

Next thing I knew, you were running full speed out of Jacob's apartment and back down the stairs to the driveway. I noticed something bulging out of your mouth. What in the world?

"Ha ha! Caroline, look! Riley ate all the hamburger meat that Mom was going to cook for dinner!" exclaimed Jacob.

Oh no, Ri. Tell me you didn't.

I ran over as Jacob's mom was running down the stairs. Jacob had jumped off his skateboard and was standing beside you with tears of laughter running down his freckled cheeks. "Oh my gosh. Marlaina, I'm SO sorry. I can't believe Riley did this. How can I make this up to you?"

Marlaina was about to reassure me (I assume) when we heard a loud grunt and then a gurgle. Jacob, Marlaina, and I all looked down at you as your body seemed to lurch forward and backward while the grunts grew louder and louder. This ended with a spectacular vomit, all over Marlaina's shoes. As I silently died inside, Jacob fell to the ground, rolling with laughter. Marlaina smiled her kind smile and told me not to worry while you started licking her brown flats in an effort to once again eat what you had just thrown up.

There really was nothing left to do except put you in the car and drive to In-N-Out to buy dinner for our neighbors. After the old dinner had been cleaned up and the new dinner had been delivered, I did what I suspected every parent did after their child acted in a socially irresponsible manner. I contemplated my still-developing parenting style and wondered if there were any mommy and me groups for moms of emotionally damaged rescue dogs.

Was I being too lenient and letting you get away with too much? I didn't want to be one of those parents who was run by her children. This tail was not going to wag this dog. You and I were still new to each other. We were establishing our own unique ways.

Ri, I really didn't want to mess that up. The stakes were too high. I thought about it and and after much contemplation kept coming back to the same conclusion—your tail wasn't wagging the dog. No, Ri, that wasn't our style. Our truth was this—your tail was already wagging my heart.

# CHAPTER 5

# The Rock

**Dear Ri,**

It seems like yesterday that I brought you to my special place for the first time. Ri, you and I had just flown into Austin from LAX on Christmas Day with Tom and Chad. When I saw your eyes drooping down to the ground in the Austin baggage claim, I felt horrible for making the decision to give you that extra doggie Valium. I thought knocking you out would be the humane thing to do, but it looked more like you had just returned from a Grateful Dead concert.

Bringing you to the lake was the greatest Christmas present of all. I was so excited to show you where I grew up and was equally excited to introduce my family to you. Mom and Dad were waiting for us in the driveway. You sobered up a bit during the hour-and-fifteen-minute drive from the Austin airport to the lake house, so you were able to make a good first impression.

Dad came up to the car and eagerly opened the door to the backseat. He gave me a hug and then switched his gaze to you—you kept your droopy eyes downcast toward the rubber mat on the floor.

The Texas winter sun was shining brightly in the cloudless blue sky, and the smell of the wood-burning fireplace filled the air. All the leaves had fallen to the ground, exposing the bare tree branches until spring. As the fresh air filled the car, your nose started to twitch, indicating your piquing interest. I jumped out of the car and inhaled the familiar scent. Dad took my place in the backseat and stroked your head. You allowed that.

After the luggage had been brought in and all the hellos had been said, I looked for you and found you still safely in the backseat. Dad was still by your side. Your head had moved a little closer to his leg. Dad suggested we take you on a walk, to The Rock. I agreed. Upon hearing the word "walk," you lifted your head a bit. Dad slowly moved his hands around your back and slowly, gently pulled you toward the open car door. You didn't resist.

Dad was able to help you to the ground and held on to your still-protruding rib cage as you found your balance on the gravel driveway. Dad and I turned and started up the hill—you followed, like I knew you would.

Dad and I walked up the hill while you limped behind. I entertained Dad with the story of how our flight was almost delayed because there were too many large animals on the plane and how Chad had jokingly blamed me. Dad wanted to know how the first two weeks with you had been and if I thought you would need the reconstructive shoulder surgery. I told him I honestly didn't know but was hopeful that we could find a way to strengthen your muscles without putting you through another massive trauma.

As we ascended the hill, the gravel driveway beneath our feet turned into a roughly paved road. The surrounding land was filled with thick brush and oak trees. At the end of the road, instead of following the paved curve to the right, we took a left onto the almost hidden dirt trail.

The landscape opened and turned into a flat, open space, untouched by humanity. The granite that was then underneath our feet formed a massive peninsula that jetted out into the lake. The views, as well as the beauty, were infinite. I liked to call this private and spiritual place, my place, The Rock.

I found my flat stone, perfect for sitting, waiting for me in the same place I'd left it a few months prior. Dad walked you down to the edge of the water. The Rock offered you a gentle slope into the lake, in case you wanted to venture in. Dad pulled a tennis ball out of his jacket pocket. Of course, he'd planned ahead. Your ears perked up, and your tail stood at attention. Your eyes fixed on the ball. You didn't move a muscle.

Dad tossed the ball a foot into the water. You were able to easily retrieve the ball by wading a few steps down the gentle slope. You brought it back to Dad and dropped it at his feet. Dad smiled as he picked up the ball. It was then that I realized he had a plan. Dad threw the ball two feet into the water. You fetched your prized possession and brought it back. Dad then threw your ball three feet. And then four. After a few minutes of this confidence-building warm-up, Dad took the ball you'd dropped at his feet and threw it ten feet out into the water, well past the shallow slope of The Rock. In your excitement, you didn't realize that the ground would suddenly fall out from under you as you ran farther and farther into the water.

You began to panic, unable to swim or float. I jumped up from my seat, but Dad gave me the signal to wait. Dad had The Faith.

Your weak legs slapped at the water and your head wildly thrashed around, looking for any signs of help. Your body was straight up and down, perfectly positioned to sink like a torpedo to the bottom of the lake. With each thrash against the water, your ball floated farther and farther away from shore. I couldn't watch. I closed my eyes.

The jarring sound of splashing water began to subside and I instead began to hear soothing sounds of lapping waves. I opened my eyes and saw that your body had straightened on top of the water. You'd sighted your ball, and your focus had turned from the Heavens above to the fuzzy yellow ball on the horizon. Your four legs moved in effortless harmony. Your enormous paws acted as flippers, giving you speed uncommon in such a large animal. After finding your beloved ball and effortlessly swimming back to shore, you found your footing on the slippery slope of The Rock.

You walked out of the water with the ball proudly in your mouth, shook off the excess water, paused to look up at me, then walked to Dad and dropped the ball at his feet.

I think it was appropriate that your first trip to The Rock left you feeling like you were struggling to keep your head above water, just as mine was one of trying to find calm in the midst of my flailing about. The Rock was the first place I came after completing my first two weeks at MD Anderson. I'd been feeling like a dog trying to swim for the first time whose feet had unexpectedly fallen off the ledge. I had been in "go" mode since learning about The Cancer and desperately needed some time and space to take it all in. I needed a safe place away from everyone else's feelings to be able to say "I'm scared" out loud with no fear of an emotional response to that truth bomb. So I came to The Rock.

The lake was the perfect place to recover in between treatments. I'd been told to stay away from people and germs because the poison, I mean chemo, would pretty much decimate my germ-fighting defenses. All my test results had shown The Cancer to be basically everywhere: It was in my stomach, my spleen, all my lymph nodes, and even in my bone marrow, therefore classifying it as Stage IV (AKA scary as fuck). In the hours I spent lying in bed on the long chemo days in the infusion unit at MD Anderson watching the red poison creep into my veins through the clear tubing, I wondered where the medicine was going and tried to imagine what it would kill. I had so many questions that I'd not thought to ask at the beginning. There just hadn't been time. We'd met with Dr. Frank the Monday after my week of stage testing. She'd immediately scheduled my first round of chemo for the following day. That was how aggressive The Cancer was. That was what I was up against.

As I sat on my favorite flat stone on The Rock that morning after MD Anderson, no longer a chemo virgin, I closed my eyes and felt the gentle breeze on my cheeks. The long hair that I was about to lose was pulled up in my favorite high messy bun. The only sounds I could hear were distant hums of ski boat engines and the rhythmic clicking of the pump inside my black fanny pack, pumping the fifth and final medication that made up the R-CHOP chemo cocktail into my veins.

Ri, a short month prior to The Cancer, I ran the Santa Monica steps with a forty-pound weighted vest, preparing for my upcoming trip to climb Mount Kilimanjaro. Instead of staying away from life, I should've been boarding a plane to Africa with my brother for the ultimate adventure that life had to offer. When did my body turn against me? Didn't it know the consequence its rebellion would have on my life?

My previous chosen goal of acing my medical school finals had suddenly been replaced with the forced goal of remission. I would've said cure instead of remission, but Dr. Frank had made it very clear that The Cancer had no cure. She said that my specific type of lymphoma was very unusual, very specific, very aggressive, and very smart. They could treat it, but they couldn't cure it. The Cancer would come back. Remission would only be a temporary reprieve of an unknown length for me to regather my fighting strength.

During those eight rounds of chemo, I went to The Rock daily. It was my church, my hospital, my support group, and my recreational activity all in one. I spoke to The Rock, told him my fears. He was a wonderful listener. He heard my joys when Tom proposed after the fourth round of chemo and my fears when after the fifth round Dr. Frank didn't think The Cancer was going into remission. In that case, we would've had to move directly into a bone marrow transplant. A transplant was risky as hell with a 25 percent mortality rate.

The Rock heard my fears and caught the tears I cried as I pondered what to do if The Cancer didn't go into remission and I had to move immediately into a bone marrow transplant. I knew that even if I did survive I'd almost certainly not be able to have children. How could I marry this man whom I loved so deeply if I knew I wouldn't be able to give him a family?

The wedding was put on hold, and a back-up plan was put in place. If the scan after Round 6 of chemo had not shown a total remission, we would've canceled the wedding that Mom had been planning, and we would've moved to Plan B. There wouldn't have been much time between the scan and the transplant. We would've needed a new wedding that was simple, quick, and easy.

Tom and I could've only said these Plan B vows if we'd both been relentlessly honest. We would've needed more than just love. I would've needed Tom to think this through and understand what marrying The Cancer and me really meant. He would've needed to say, "I do" in a place of pure realism. The Plan B: "I'll marry you but may not live longer than the next three months, and if I do survive I'll be faced with a lifetime of side effects and, oh right, also won't be able to give you children." It would've been a wedding on The Rock.

I knew my only focus those three weeks before the crucial scan needed to be on healing my body, but instead I found myself focusing on everyone but myself. I worried about the effect that a failed treatment plan would have on Tom, on my parents, Chad, my doctors. They'd all invested so much into healing me. I didn't want to let them down. I didn't think I could stand to see them cry another tear. I didn't allow myself to sit in my suffering. I was too busy trying to reassure those around me that I'd be fine. But would I?

My scans came back clean. The celebrations began. As a friend who knew my mom back in my college days so lovingly liked to say, she imagined that upon hearing the news that my cancer was officially "in remission," my mom's first action was to reach for the red emergency phone and call the wedding planner to exclaim, "This is NOT a drill. I repeat, this is NOT a drill. The wedding is ON. Move, people, MOVE!" She knew my mom well.

We were all crowded together in the small sterile exam room in the lymphoma department at MD Anderson. My family and the doctors involved in my case had all wanted to be present for the big reveal. I was seated in the center of the cramped room, on top of the examination table covered with protective butcher paper. My doctors and loved ones formed a horseshoe of support around me. I felt so alone.

Dr. Frank had the honor of giving us the good news. As soon as she said the word "remission," my supporters erupted into their own individual version of pure joy. Tom enveloped me in a massive hug then looked to Dr. Frank for a high five. Kara, Dr. Frank's PA, started to cheer. Chad did a fist pump and slapped Dad on the back. Mom burst into happy tears and reached for Kleenex to blot the black mascara tear trails that had formed on her cheeks. Dr. Frank was humbly brushing off the thanks and praise as my family marveled at her brilliance. We'd done it.

I'd been in that exam room with everyone else and had heard the same words come out of Dr. Frank's mouth. My brain had processed the words the same as everyone else, but I was frozen. I had been able to clearly see the joy in that exam room floating all around us, thick as a dark cloud of soot. I had seen this joy from a distance and had desperately wanted to reach out and grab some. Something in me hadn't been able to allow myself to partake in the celebration.

For everyone else, remission had meant we'd won. Tom and I could get married, and life could resume. Everyone and everything could go back to normal. But, for me, remission meant something very different. It meant The Waiting had officially begun. The Cancer had officially set the countdown for our next matchup and had refused to give me any clue as to how much time was actually on the clock.

For the most part, I'd known what the next three months of my life had in store. I knew I'd finish out my last two rounds of chemo before spending the summer picking out wedding and bridesmaid dresses and the various wigs that I would wear to the wedding events. I'd help Mom in the planning, giving my opinion when needed. I'd try to get into yoga and would avoid tan lines at all costs. Tom and I would be married in early September and would then go on our honeymoon to Cabo. But then what? What would be the normal that I was expected to be thrilled to get back to?

The "then what" turned out to be you, Ri Rose. You became the color that softened the anxiety of not knowing. My waiting game and internal battle between putting my college degree to good use and doing something productive, versus resting, relaxing, and taking care of my body for God knows how long until we face The Cancer again—that battle led me to you.

The new path with The Cancer had led me to an animal that had only known how to sit with his suffering. My enemy had given me a being that only knew how to live in "remission," only knew how to live in between burns from the hairdryer, only knew how to be a master of his own moment. So, thanks to The Cancer, we found each other.

So, Riley, as I sat again on my favorite flat stone on The Rock a few months after your perilous swimming experience and one year after finding out about The Cancer, I thought about your ability to conquer your fears so openly and honestly. Granted, you didn't know you would lose your footing on that granite slope, and you probably wouldn't have chosen to go into the deep water without knowing how to swim if you'd been given a choice, but you found yourself in a position that was sink or swim. Ri, you swam. Then you swam again.

Watching you being thrust into an unexpected and terrifying situation and coming through it like you did, I wondered if I'd be able to do the same. When The Cancer came back, would I be able to level out and find my stride or would I sink straight to the bottom? Would I be able to cling to hope in the distance as you did to the tennis ball on the horizon? I knew The Cancer would come back. Our fight wasn't over. I was in The Waiting, a holding pattern. The Cancer was resting, regaining strength for Round 2. We'd left on good terms, so my resentment toward my opponent had lessened. It had even given me a wonderful parting gift in you.

Ever since our first meeting, The Cancer had given me a sense of purpose and a clear path forward. I'd been given a goal and had achieved it. We'd found a rhythm in our dance, and I was happy to let The Cancer lead the way. I appreciated a strong leader and for the time being was content to follow, but just when I felt we were hitting our stride, The Cancer left without warning with only a promise to return.

Thankfully, I didn't have to wait long. Five months after the Google search that brought you and me together and only ten months since The Cancer had said goodbye, my faithful adversary came out of hiding, rested and ready to go on the attack again. What a beautifully odd mercy. Welcome back, amigo. Game on.

CHAPTER 6

# Round 2

**Dear Riley,**

There I was—back in the ring. Just me against my opponent. This was Muhammad Ali vs. Sugar Ray Leonard, the Hatfields vs. the McCoys, Taylor Swift vs. Kanye West. The Cancer had dictated the terms, picked the time and place, and I'd shown up. Bets were being placed within the medical community. Statistics and mortality rates were being thrown around, but I didn't let my unfavorable position weaken my resolve to win. I always did like to bet on the underdog.

I found the lump on Easter weekend, 2006. The acorn-sized lymph node under my skin had popped up on my underwear line, same spot as before. My first phone call was to Dr. Frank. She agreed with me that it was most likely a "recurrence," doctor speak for, "I did the best I could, but your disease is too powerful for me to stop."

She was transferring me out of the lymphoma department and into the stem cell transplant center. I'd officially become somebody else's problem.

You knew I couldn't fly to Houston and face the music without you, Ri, so back to the airport we went and into the dark and scary world of the under-the-plane blackness you rode.

Aunt Karol and Uncle Paul were sort of happy to see you. Their gorgeous home, filled with antiques and delicate fabrics and breakable decorative pieces never stood a chance against your big paws and wild tail.

My new doctor was an older man from Sweden named Dr. Andersson. I longed for the familiar faces of Kara and Dr. Frank but understood that The Cancer was bringing its A game, and in order to stand a chance of winning I needed to bring in the big guns: the doctors in the stem cell transplant division. Dr. Andersson repeated the week of stage testing then met with us to go over the results and treatment options.

Because I was so young, with a potentially long life ahead of me, I was presenting Dr. Andersson with a unique challenge in comparison to the rest of his patients, who were, on average, over the age of sixty. Dr. Andersson was tasked with trying to balance our goal of crushing my cancer while still preserving my post-transplant quality of life, assuming I still had one.

I was only twenty-eight years old. In any other world, I would have a long and healthy life ahead of me, but in my world with The Cancer, my future would only exist if I agreed to an extremely aggressive treatment plan that would most certainly include long-term side effects.

Dr. Andersson and the team of stem cell transplant doctors had discussed the particulars of my case and had agreed on the protocol.

During my first eight rounds of chemo, Chad had been tested and identified as a perfect bone marrow match, which was surprising to me, as we had different blood types and siblings were rarely matches. I remember him calling to tell me the good news.

"Well, I guess you're not adopted after all. I just got the test results and turns out I'm a perfect match." He then proceeded to tell me how incredibly lucky I was to be receiving such superb donor cells.

Knowing that my brother was a perfect match made the prospect of getting back in the ring with The Cancer a lot less scary. My older brother's cells were now my snug lace-up boxing gloves, fitting my body to perfection and designed solely to protect me. Chad had always been my protector. His love had shielded me from any harm that was under his control, and now that his cells were increasing my ability to hit back with a stronger punch, he was back in a position of power over an uncontrollable disease.

When I asked Chad to donate his stem cells, he said yes before I could even finish the question. Now that I think about it, I may have never even asked. He knew I needed his cells, and asking would have implied there had been a question as to whether or not he would give them to me.

My transplant protocol specified that I'd need to do a combo of radiation injected into my body with crazy-aggressive chemo. This plan would require me to be admitted to the hospital for about a month while the chemo killed off my broken immune system so that the new stem cells from my brother could find their way into my bone marrow and regrow into a new, healthy, functioning immune system. My faulty immune system wasn't able to red flag the normally occurring cancer cells that grew in everyone's bodies, therefore it allowed The Cancer to grow with no obstacles. A new immune system grown from healthy donor cells would, in theory, be able to red flag The Cancer and kill it off before it had a chance to grow back. If everything went according to plan, this new immune system would be The Cure.

There really was not much discussion because this was my only option. It was risky as hell, but what was the alternative? To give up before I'd even tried? Dr. Andersson was the first person to ever use words like: death, mortality, and advanced directive. Before being admitted, I'd need to decide if I wanted to be kept on life support if something were to happen and, if so, for how long. I needed to clearly state that all my money and belongings would go to Tom and told him that, if something were to happen, I wanted him to get remarried. Everything was excruciatingly straightforward because it was all very obvious and clear, until I thought about you.

By this time, you and I were one, Caroline and Riley, one name rarely said without the other. Since our meeting, you and I had never spent one day apart, and now here we were facing an uncertain amount of time away from each other with the distinct possibility of never being together again. I forced myself to push any and all thoughts of you out of my head. You brought too much realness to what I needed to be a businesslike, transactional situation.

I left for MD Anderson on a Sunday afternoon. My first chemo was scheduled for 4:30 Monday morning. You and I were lying on the sofa in Aunt Karol and Uncle Paul's TV room. You were tired from chasing tennis balls in the backyard, and I was trying to numb my mind with reality TV. Your jaw was clenched around your tennis ball, even as you slept. I knew what was about to happen, and I think you did too.

Tom came in and told me it was time. I felt the tears falling out of my eyes. I leaned over and folded my body over yours. You didn't move. I willed you to understand. I needed you to know that I was doing this for you. This was our only chance at a future together, so even though we would be apart in the short term, it would all be worth it when we saw each other again. *If* we saw each other again.

My first stem cell transplant was tough, very tough. I spent twenty-nine days as an inpatient on the eleventh floor of the MD Anderson Cancer Center Hospital. I endured five days of chemo that kicked my ass, along with numerous infusions of a terrifying radiation into my weary veins. My hair fell out again almost immediately, and my skin turned gray within days. My appetite, along with my personality, shriveled up and left the room. I began the process of retreating into myself. I wanted to keep the events that were happening to me at a distance. I refused to look at the bags of chemo. I barely made eye contact with the nurses. Maybe if I didn't participate, I wouldn't be scarred. Maybe.

During my long stay in the hospital, the news of your antics kept me entertained. One morning, I heard you ate Aunt Karol's bowl of chocolate-covered coffee beans. Mom called the vet and learned that the concern for dogs was the caffeine found in chocolate (she decided not to to tell them about the caffeine-filled beans inside the chocolate). They said you might just have a little more energy than normal. Mom sat outside in her bathrobe for twelve hours straight throwing tennis balls for your jacked-up caffeinated self and waited for your overstimulated system to return to normal.

Then there was the time Aunt Karol took you on a walk around her cul-de-sac. She never liked to use leashes and assumed you'd stay close. You did well, sweet boy, until you saw that cat. You ran down the neighbor's long driveway, hot on the cat's heels. Aunt Karol lost sight of you until she saw your body flash across the front windows of the gorgeous French chalet home you'd entered through the back door. Aunt Karol loves to retell the story and says that all she could see were images of the black cat darting across the front house windows and you running closely behind, wild with excitement.

Then there were the workmen who were doing repairs around Aunt Karol's home for a few weeks during your stay. You loved to find your way into their cars and pull out their brown-bag lunches for your own personal enjoyment. On more than one occasion, they found you in the corner of the living room licking the last of the Milky Way or Doritos wrappers.

Trusting other people to look after you while I was away was giving up control and leaning into blind faith. I started off wondering where you were and what you were doing. I was consumed with worry that you thought I'd abandoned you. Mom and Aunt Karol had the best of intentions in their promise to look after you like you were their own, but they weren't me.

They didn't know that showers sent you shaking into the corner of the garage because you knew a hairdryer would most likely follow. They wouldn't know to take several folded paper towels to the dinner table so they could wipe up your rivers of drool. How could they understand what you needed emotionally? Worry for you consumed me, until it didn't.

At some point, I stopped thinking of you. I never let my thoughts turn toward the world outside the four white walls of my room on the eleventh floor. My TV did a good enough job of keeping me connected to non-hospital life. The daytime talk show hosts became my friends.

The medicine had taken its toll, and I no longer had any energy left for anything other than taking a shower every morning and going on my walks around the nurses' station three times a day. As the days passed, my ability to shut off everyone and everything increased. I stopped caring, even about you.

Mail came daily. Tom opened cards from well-wishers and taped them up onto my walls. My gaze easily washed over the wall of support. Those cards were sent from people I knew in my past life. My gaze stayed fixed on my new friends on the TV directly in front of my bed.

One day, about halfway through my hospital stay, I opened my eyes to find a poster taped under the TV. Tom had decided to put it directly in my line of vision. The poster had been sent by our dog park friends and was decorated with pictures of you, me, and all our human and canine buddies. The smiles and paws blinded me. I was about to ask Tom to please move it to the invisible wall of support but paused.

I now locked eyes with these familiar faces on the poster board in my hospital room. These dog lovers were our people. This was our dog park posse, cheering us on from afar. These were the people who were the first to hear the news that, because of all the swimming and hiking and tennis ball chasing, you no longer needed reconstructive surgery.

We had initially bonded over our love for our dogs and ended up coming together on a level playing field where our titles and labels stayed outside the dog park gates. And the result was a collection of beautiful, long-lasting, authentic friendships. Ri, you gave that to me. So, then I needed to give you something in return—I needed to fight.

As scary as it would be to re-engage in a battle with an uncertain outcome, I knew I owed it to you to step into that vulnerability. Sometimes I felt guilty about bringing you into my life when I was dealing with a stage IV incurable cancer. I left that part out on my adoption application. I was worried I'd be denied because of my pre-existing condition.

I think I'd honestly tricked myself into believing I was normal. I was normal, right? I mean, I was married and had you and my dog park friends, all normal life stuff. My new LA dog park friends didn't even know about my health history until Chris overheard a comment made by a non-groupie wondering why anyone would choose to have hair as short as mine.

Chris defended my honor without even knowing that my short hair wasn't by choice. When I gave him a hug to thank him, I felt he was owed an explanation, so I introduced my new friends to my invisible sidekick, The Cancer.

As I held my gaze at eye level and really took in the details of the poster hanging directly in front of me, I felt my built-up force field of invisibility starting to crack. I focused my attention on those friends and slowly began to feel them staring back at me, their gazes seeming to say, "We see you, Caroline. Even without Riley, we see you and accept you and love you. Never forget the people and dogs who love you both and who can't wait to welcome you back, so please do what you have to do to come home."

I began to wonder where you were and what you were doing. My gaze shifted toward the light under the thick brown door leading to the hallway. Were other patients out walking? Were there children playing in the lobby? Was it sunny outside? Was it rush hour traffic? Were you able to go on a walk today? Where'd you choose to sleep at night?

Optimism came in and out of the room with each lab report that showed my blood counts wavering. Fear threatened to take over, but the dog park poster kept it at bay. The "We Miss You" written in dark-green block letters served as a portal to hope. The handwritten notes from various groupies brought a forgotten smile to my dry and cracked lips. The center of the poster was filled with a stunning picture of you looking incredibly handsome. You were standing at attention, eyes transfixed on the ball being held over the picture taker's head. Your body looked strong and relaxed. Your eyes held a glimmer of joy. I was so proud.

A few days after the poster was hung on the wall, I found myself less eager to turn on the television portal to emotional numbness and instead began to use some of the time in my long days to sit in silence. I turned off the sing-songy voices of my new daytime friends coming from the morning shows so I could quietly focus on my breathing. I began to reconnect with myself.

I checked in with my body and asked it how it was doing. I wanted to know if it thought we could win this fight. I turned my gaze to the dog park poster and began to talk to you. I told you that I was sorry, so very sorry. We had too many great things to live for, mainly for life together with Tom, for the three of us.

I may not have been the best candidate to bring home a dog who needed long-term love and care when I didn't even know how much longer I'd be alive, but there we were, Riley and Caroline, Caroline and Riley. The odds may have been stacked against us, but it wasn't the first time. We were renegades, doing things our own way. The Cancer had come between us, but only for a bit. I asked you to give me some time to get back in the ring. I knew you wanted to be with me, but this was something that, with Tom's unwavering support, I had to do on my own. I wanted to beat The Cancer once and for all so we could finally start living. I had made a promise to love and protect you, whatever that might look like—and right now it looked like the underdog opening her eyes, unblocking her heart, and fighting like hell.

So, bookies, who're you going to bet on now, The Cancer or the patient? As I was slowly learning, always put your money on the loyalty of a wingman.

CHAPTER 7

Anchor of Guilt

My sweet Riley Rose,

What a difference a year makes.

And that was the year our family of three became a family of four.

You and I were having the loveliest day together—Caroline, Riley, and our newest little addition. We'd just taken Ellie on our afternoon walk—me pushing the heavy jogging stroller and you sniffing the freshly blooming spring flowers. We were settling in to do tummy time on the jungle-themed play mat while our new favorite show, *Reba*, played in the background on our newly installed nursery TV. You found your favorite napping spot in between the play mat and the front of Ellie's crib on the woven, gender-neutral Pottery Barn Kids rug. Once you both were relaxed, I stretched out on the rug—you on my left, Ellie on my right.

I was comforted by the sounds of your rhythmic breathing. Ellie's squeals and gurgles reassured me that in that moment, I was doing something right. The sound of Reba's voice was like having an old friend in the room with us. My heart was light. My heart was...happy. And then, almost reflexively, my gaze turned upward to the shelf above the TV, and I felt the dark storm clouds move in as quickly as a Texas summer thunderstorm. My sunshine of happiness was again clouded by the incredible loss that had happened not so long before.

Ri, at the time, you and I were still fairly new to Pasadena. When we became responsible for a little human being, we abandoned our Caroline and Riley adventures and instead focused our extra energy on trying to make mom friends. But having a three-month-old with a severe case of acid reflux made things difficult.

I'd tried to take Ellie to a parent-ed class at a local church after I'd overheard a mom on the playground telling her friend that it was "the" parenting class, but we'd been asked to leave after the first hour because Ellie had screamed at the top of her lungs while the other babies were quietly nursing from their mothers' breasts.

Ellie didn't want to take her bottle of formula because I didn't have my large blow-up bouncy ball with me, and I had learned early on that the only way she could or would take a bottle of mom guilt over not being able to breastfeed was to be violently bounced up and down while she drank. The doctor said her screaming had something to do with her being premature and the muscle separating her throat and stomach not being properly formed. It would correct itself, in time. Nine months to be exact. So you and I did the only thing we could—we didn't leave the house until Ellie was able to drink a bottle without screaming like she was being tortured. In truth, I didn't mind so much. I enjoyed our days together in the nursery, you curled up on the woven rug and me in the white lounge rocker with Ellie in my lap and news of the 2008 Obama vs. Hillary race keeping me thoroughly entertained.

Ellie's nursery was the front room of our cottage in our new hometown of Pasadena, California. Toward the end of my bone marrow transplant, Tom and I had to decide where we would live after I was given the OK by my doctors to go back out and live my life. Tom's job was still in Los Angeles, but we both agreed that Santa Monica was too crowded for life post-transplant. I needed quiet and easy, and that led us to Pasadena.

From my hospital bed at MD Anderson, we found an 1,100-square-foot cottage for sale on the internet and bought it sight unseen. After Dr. Andersson gave me a hug and told me he'd see me back in three months, Tom and I loaded up the back of my gray Yukon with our clothes and belongings, folded down the middle seats to make room for your dog bed, and set out the three of us for the twenty-three-hour, 1,200-mile journey from Houston to Los Angeles.

You made it almost all the way to El Paso before you told us you'd had enough. You not so subtly stood up in the backseat, paced around in tiny circles and started pawing our seats from behind. We tried to tell you that we were already halfway, but you were having none of it. You started barking and used your mouth to toss your tennis ball onto our laps. Tom and I knew better than to try to reason with you, so from El Paso to Pasadena we stopped every two hours at rest stops to throw balls for you. And after twenty minutes of Riley time, we'd load you up into our backseat and resume the drive.

Our Pasadena cottage was different from what I'd expected, although I'm not sure what I thought would be waiting for us when we arrived. The first thing I noticed was the large wooden sign posted in the small grassy front yard with the real estate agency's name printed in large letters across the front and the bold SOLD sign attached to the top. That word seemed so absolute. This cottage was ours, for real. This was not a temporary rental that we could walk away from when we were ready to move along, this was OURS, this was permanent, this was grown-up, and this was scary.

As time passed, we settled in nicely to our new Pasadena routine. Tom enjoyed the shorter commute to his Downtown Los Angeles office, and you and I looked forward to exploring our new town together. Even though we lived in this new slower-paced community, we still had our sense of adventure. You and I had both fought too hard for life not to get out and live it.

We went to Hollywood to hike or drove down south to the dog beach. On occasion, we got up early and battled the morning traffic to the Brentwood dog park to visit our old friends or drove north to our favorite beach spots in Malibu. You and I were still us, the adventurous pair, wingmen to the end, always up for a new experience. And then I got pregnant.

Seeing as Tom and I decided to thaw two of our frozen embryos and transfer them via IVF, the pregnancy wasn't really a shock, but finding out both embryos had taken on our first try and that we were having twins—now THAT was a shock. We were having a boy and a girl, a dream come true, especially after being told fertility post-transplant wouldn't be an option. Here we were again—blazing our own trail and never accepting a fate that wasn't our own. I'd proven that fertility post-transplant was most definitely an option—twice over.

The first trimester passed with nausea and exhaustion. It was impossible to know if my symptoms were from the pregnancy or residual side effects from the transplant eight months prior. But even with my growing belly and challenging feelings of sickness, you and I were still determined to forge ahead and get involved in our new community. I didn't have a friend yet, so I decided to join a volunteer group for a local children's museum. I'd heard that the "who's who" of the young Pasadena moms all belonged to this organization, so I thought it was a good place to start.

With my excitement of finally belonging to a local social group, I quickly took on too much and learned my first lesson in volunteering: If you give an inch, they take a mile. You patiently waited in the car while I spent hours in meetings talking about raffle items and table arrangements. Other days, you came into Pottery Barn Kids with me and found your favorite spot on the blue and white boys' room rug display while I met with the design team for the millionth time, trying to decide how to decorate a nursery for both a boy and a girl. It was a happy time, an easy time, a hopeful time. And then…

The twins were twenty-four weeks along. I had my scheduled appointment with my OB that Wednesday afternoon. You were, per usual, waiting for me in the parking lot, lying on your dog bed in the back of my Yukon, the back window wide open. As I imagined you turning circles to find your napping position, I was lying back onto the exam table, feeling the cold gel on my tummy. The ultrasound wand applied light pressure on my skin and pressed down onto my growing babies and started to move around over the twin on the bottom, our girl.

Her heart rate was strong. She was growing as expected. All looked good. The wand moved higher. The doctor grew silent. The wand moved faster while the pressure grew harder. I raised my head slightly only to see wrinkles on my doctor's forehead. The world began to spin.

Tom arrived a half hour later. Dr. Macer told us that our son was no longer alive. His heart had stopped beating. No one knew why. Since he was positioned above his sister, he would need to stay in my body until she was born. Our goal now was to do everything we could to get our daughter to full term. Tom walked me to the car. I had my arms wrapped around my belly, my babies.

Your head popped out of the back window. It was all too much for me to understand. I could feel my babies. I'd seen his face. How could he be gone?

Just the day before we'd been picking out gender-neutral fabrics and matching cribs. Tom and I had discussed the best double strollers and had read countless books on raising twins. Our dual college funds had been set up, and names had been picked out. The baby shower invitation, given by Mom's friends in Texas, was proudly displayed on our refrigerator. "Twice the Blessings, Twice the Love, Two Little Miracles from Above."

Ri, how was I supposed to do this? What was I supposed to do with the extra love that was reserved for my extra miracle? How could I move through that incredible loss?

Eleanor Grace Rose was born exactly ten weeks later at exactly thirty-four weeks weighing exactly five pounds, nine ounces. Ever since we'd said good-bye to the son we'd never met, I had been counting down the days until I was able to hold my living child. I needed to be able to see her so that I could know that she was healthy. I'd needed to be able to hold her to understand that she was alive. I'd needed to be able to kiss her to accept that she was real.

Every day of my singular pregnancy with Ellie was spent in my double occupancy uterus was a day of terror. What if I lost her the same way we'd lost our son? How could I not have known that I'd lost him? How did I fail him before I'd ever known him? No, I needed to be sure. I needed her to live outside of my unreliable body.

I did not, however, need her to join me in the outside world quite as early as she actually arrived. Six weeks before her due date, my water broke. Or, at least, I thought it had. In fact, Ellie's brother's amniotic sac had begun to leak fluid. After realizing that this mystery liquid was indeed our son's amniotic fluid and not just my water breaking, the doctors were worried that our son's fluid would infect his sister's body, so the decision was made to deliver our babies early via C-section. We were warned that our daughter could be in the NICU for six to eight weeks because she may not be able to breathe or swallow on her own. I appreciated the warning. It helped me to manage my nonexistent expectations.

A few minutes after I arrived in the operating room, Ellie was born. She was a healthy size for a preemie born six weeks early. Immediately after she was born, the doctors held her up off to the side of my vision field so I could see her face before quickly whisking her away to the NICU. We were prepared for the worst. Tom and I were getting used to hearing the unthinkable news that only happened to other people, but our little Ellie was a glorious exception. Our baby girl was born with the strength of two babies. She shocked everyone by breathing, swallowing, and regulating her body temperature—all on her own. All exactly as she'd planned.

After Ellie was delivered and rushed out of the operating room, my doctor told me it was time to deliver our son. In the emotion of the moment, I'd almost forgotten. Dr. Macer asked me if I wanted to see him after he pulled our lost son out of my body. I wasn't sure. Did I want to see my baby's face, or would that only make it harder for me to forget? A good mom would say yes, because a good mom would have the strength to grieve for her lost son. A good mom would be able to set her weakness aside and show up for her child. That was what motherhood was all about, right?

I shook my head and said no. I didn't want to see my son. In that moment, I didn't have the strength. In that moment, I made a decision that made things easier for me. In that moment, I was selfish. I thought that if I didn't see his face, maybe I could convince myself on some level that he was never real, that his life and sudden death didn't really happen, that he never really existed. In that moment, in that first act of motherhood, I failed my child.

My line of drugged-up reasoning for not choosing to see my son worked for a few hours. I was solely focused on stopping the severe chills that had been the side effect from the epidural and on the positive reports Chad reported back to me from the NICU. Things were looking up. My daughter was healthy, and I had survived the experience. And then the social worker walked into my hospital room and brought me back down to the reality I was so desperately trying to convince myself was just a horrible illusion.

The law stated that any parent who had given birth to a stillborn child was required to answer questions from a social worker. This intruder asked me if my son's death was caused by illegal drug use or negligence on my part. She needed to know if his passing was caused by anything I did or didn't do during his nine months in my body. I gave standard answers to her standard questions but it got me thinking about the not-so-standard questions that were not listed on her form: Was it responsible of me to get pregnant so quickly after a bone marrow transplant?

Was my body not strong enough to support him and his growth? Was my mixed blood type, the unintended result of only converting halfway to my brother's immune system during the transplant, the cause of his little heart stopping? Was the combination of O-negative blood type from my brother and my original O-positive blood type creating an electrical current that interfered with the beating of his heart? Was this idea that I could defy the odds and have a baby or babies just an idealistic dream that was reckless and greedy? Had I done this to my baby boy?

Aunt Karol had told me while I was pregnant that guilt was like an anchor to any mom's heart and that the best moms had figured out a way to shed the guilt so they could be free and, therefore, act as their best selves for their children. Although I see what my aunt was saying, the guilt I felt within the first three minutes of being a mom sent me deeper than any anchor could ever reach. My new mom guilt caused by my selfishness sent me torpedoing down to the furthest depths of the dark part of my soul.

Ellie came home from the hospital exactly five days after she was admitted to the NICU. Her acid reflux seemed to be the only sign of her being born before she was ready. You were waiting for us when we returned home. I could see you through the screen door—your large, lanky body swaying side to side, propelled by the powerful wag of your tail. Tom gently carried Ellie into the house. I carefully and slowly leaned down to kiss the top of your head, my C-section incision still sore and painful. I lowered myself into the white lounge rocker in Ellie's nursery and Tom lowered Ellie into my lap. You gently approached this tiny person, already familiar to you in so many ways, and put your wet black nose on her cheek—the Riley Rose baptism.

No kisses were given, just an acknowledgement and a promise that you'd accept this little miracle into your love and care, and you'd protect her because she was your own. You already knew that this little human would be no threat to you. Your place within our family and hearts had been firmly cemented. Tom then walked to the other side of the nursery and placed our son's ashes onto the shelf above the television. Our baby boy had come home too.

Those first few days home as a new mom were awkward. Motherhood didn't feel natural to me. I watched videos to teach me the basic things, like changing a diaper, that I'd assumed every woman on the planet knew how to do for her baby. I tried to breastfeed but produced no milk. I was unable to calm my screaming daughter and powerless to bring my son back to life. My two children were home in the nursery I'd so carefully designed, and nothing was as I pictured it would be.

My inability to help my children caused me to distance myself. I spoke less and numbed out with reality TV and election news more. My son had broken my heart, and my daughter was breaking my spirit. My life felt completely out of control. And then there was you. There you were, offering me courage to take in this new life in this new house with this new normal.

Nothing fazed you, not the screaming baby, nor the baby we never met. You filled the space where the second crib should have been with your large napping body and never minded watching me open a twin gift from a friend who had not yet heard the news. You were steady, solid, safe. You could hold my heart while my children could not. You were the great reminder that life went on.

As the days passed, Ellie's screaming became more bearable. Tom and I discovered the large bouncy ball that seemed to give her the comfort her body needed so she could swallow her formula. That in turn filled her tummy so she could sleep and therefore, so could I. I'd been keeping my distance, protecting my already weighted-down heart. I didn't want her to hurt me, and I did not want to hurt her. How could I be a good mother to my child when I was broken?

And then, one day, the world shifted.

Because she reached for me.

My daughter reached for me. She recognized me and wanted me. This little miracle human was asking for me, trusting me, needing me. She chose me. Even after failing her brother, my daughter still trusted me and wanted me. And chose me. And so, I chose her.

With the one reach of her little arm, my maternal instinct broke through the depression, and my natural mothering ability began to flourish. I quickly made up for any initial emotional distance with absolute and total immersion into my daughter. And even with my laser focus now on being the best mom possible to my healthy baby girl, you didn't worry, Ri, that my love would transfer from you to my human child. You always trusted that your purchased real estate in my heart would always be yours—my heart would just need to grow more square footage to make room for the new, human child love. And grow, it did.

I liked to think during those months spent together in Ellie's nursery that our little boy was watching over us. I even sometimes liked to think that you and Ellie could see his spirit. I think he appreciated that I didn't have the strength to return the rug I'd picked to match the blue and pink colored nursery. I think he was proud of his black and white sonogram picture, framed and standing by his ashes. I was no longer trying to erase our son's memory. Even though I will never know the features of his sweet face, deep in my heart, I know the features of him—the child that will never be on this Earth but was certainly of this world.

Now, as I sat in the white lounge rocker in the nursery in the front of our Pasadena home, I closed my eyes and felt Ellie's heartbeat against mine as she peacefully slept in my arms. I listened to the sound of my old friend Reba connecting me to the outside world, and I looked at your body and saw you physically next to my feet. I raised my eyes to the shelf above the TV and looked at the urn containing my son's ashes. I wanted to look away, but I didn't. Instead, I held my gaze steady and allowed the tears to well up in my eyes without rushing to wipe them away. My heart didn't feel the enormous pull of mom guilt that Aunt Karol warned me about. It didn't feel wrong or bad or selfish. It just felt like the love and loss of a grieving mother.

# CHAPTER 8

# The Story of My Closet

Dear Ri,

Our time was no longer ours. We were no longer the controllers of our daily destiny. We were living someone else's life. Ri, you and I were being fully controlled by a diaper-wearing dictator with the cutest freaking smile we'd ever seen. Unfortunately, that smile didn't come out of hiding often during those first few months. Our captor usually only showed her "mad" face, which left us scrambling to find anything we possibly could to pacify her.

We were parents. This was parenting. Tom, you, and I had officially been called to a higher purpose. We were now forgoing our own desires and instead giving our energy and time to a little being who depended on us all the livelong day for survival. The magnitude of this dependence was as exhilarating as it was terrifying. It also felt strangling. When I became your mom, at least I could count on your predictable two-hour midday nap and paw on the leg to tell me when it was time for dinner. A car ride always made you happy, and a trip to the dog park checked the "good mommy" box for the day. This little human, however, was unpredictable, complicated, and always needy. But, man, was she cute.

The impassable wall around my heart that I'd built during the transplant and with losing our son was being slowly torn down brick by brick, smile by smile, gurgle by gurgle, tail wag by tail wag. But for every two bricks that came down, an orange cone of caution would be placed squarely in front of the new space. My heart was too raw to expose too much too fast.

After surviving a bone marrow transplant and the loss of a child, my body was well versed on separating from emotion so that it could survive. It was survival of the fittest, and I was still standing. I'd found a strategy—protecting my heart. And it was working.

By this point, I knew enough about parenting to know that my ability to parent and my daughter's ability to develop a healthy attachment depended on me leaning in and feeling the love for my daughter and the satisfaction that motherhood brought to my life. When the three of us were together in the nursery, we enjoyed that open air of my unguarded affection. When the three of us went out into public, the orange cones went up, barricades surrounded the area, and no one could get too close to my heart. Outside of the protective walls of the nursery, we were exposed and unprotected and that felt...unsafe.

Ri, I wish you could've been in that first Music Together class with Ellie and me. Ellie was nine months old and screaming a little less when I felt ready to get out of the house with her. She seemed to love the *Reba* theme music, so I decided she must be musically inclined. A music class seemed like a good, safe place to test the waters outside the walls of our safe-haven nursery.

Class day arrived, and per usual we arrived five minutes late. I parked my car in the shade and popped open the back window so you could listen from the parking lot. The class had already begun. Ellie and I walked into the room, and the music (literally) stopped. Damn—we were late.

After surviving the teacher's disapproving glare, I found a spot in the circle of moms and babies. I copied the more seasoned moms and crossed my legs so I could place Ellie in my lap. I tried to mimic the hand motions of the teacher and swayed to the rhythm of the songs. I felt like such a phony.

Ellie seemed to love every second of the class, which in turn made me so glad that I was willing to forsake my authenticity and give way to singing about frogs going Blah! and making the corresponding silly face—All. Day. Long. My child was happy. I had done well. The feeling was euphoric.

The class was a raging success—for my daughter. For me, not so much. Walking in late felt like being blinded by a spotlight. It took me a minute to notice or observe anyone or anything around me until I'd gotten settled and the adrenaline and embarrassment from the late arrival had worn off. Once my eyes had adjusted to the scene around me, I began to observe the other moms in the circle. They seemed to have a particular vibe: "this is what a good mom, an on-time mom looks like," which they shared with each other in the form of knowing looks throughout the class. They knew the songs and knew that you weren't supposed to grab the instruments until the END of class. They wore Juicy Couture velour warm-ups and Tory Burch flats. It was like a uniform! The more I observed, the more fascinated I became. Even their babies were dressed in similar outfits. These must be the local housewives, and I was observing them in their natural habitats.

Once I had stopped staring, I looked back down and smiled at my daughter with her large hot-pink bow and her southern smocked dress. I then looked at my maternity jeans (why would anyone ever want to go back to the non-elastic waistband?), Old Navy V-neck sweater, and faded gray New Balance tennis shoes and realized with striking clarity that we most certainly did NOT fit in. If Ellie and I stood a chance with the Tory Burch posse, we would have to get a new uniform.

Class ended, and we made a beeline for the car. You were waiting, as you always were. I gave you a quick kiss on the forehead and strapped Ellie into her car seat. I put our new CD into the CD player because our teacher had told us that we would get the most out of the class if our children heard the music as much as possible. I was thinking of driving straight to Nordstrom to buy the required housewife uniform but knew Ellie had to get home for her nap.

Shopping to fit in would have to wait.

The songs on the music class CD were horrible. Truly, truly horrendous—like nails on a chalkboard. I didn't want to get another strikeout with the music teacher, so I grinned through the pain. My chosen musical education for my daughter of Led Zeppelin and Guns N' Roses would have to wait for another day. With "Trot Old Joe" and "Train is a-Comin'" fumbling out of my car speakers, we drove home and put Ellie down for her nap. And then I walked to my closet.

My closet was small, but even still my clothes didn't take up much space. My few pairs of shoes hung on the shoe rack attached to the door and my two purses sat on the chair by my bed. My head scarves hung from the doorknob. For the past two years, I'd either been in a hospital or pregnant (or both). I went from being a cancer patient to carrying a child.

I had a few months off in between, but those months were spent recovering, rediscovering, redefining. I had come out of a potentially life-ending situation only to then create a new life. And Ri—this new life, this new child, this new world—I HAD to get this right.

Exhausted from the morning, I sat down on my bed. You jumped up and settled down next to me. I succumbed to my body's lack of energy and put my head on the pillow. I tried to sleep, but my thoughts were too loud. The strangest memory popped into my head: my eighth-grade graduation dance.

The dance had been held in the junior school cafeteria. All my friends were planning to go. And the word was, so were the cute boys. I had the biggest crush on one boy in particular and was desperate to get his attention. I'd heard all the cool girls say they were wearing jean shorts with a patterned ruffle at the bottom and a sleeveless silk shirt that matched the ruffle. It was the "new" look and, since they were wearing it, the only look I wanted was to match.

A few nights later, we all showed up to the dance wearing The Look. Many of us had on the same ruffled shorts and matching top, because how many different patterns can Dillard's sell? But it didn't matter. We matched. We conformed. We all "fit in."

I've thought back to that moment so many times over the years. In high school, I began to rebel against the "in" thing and tried to pave my own path (as much as one dared when they were sixteen years old). I became my own person with my own style and was fiercely protective over my newfound freedom. How silly was I to think that wearing the right outfit at an eighth-grade dance would gain me friends or popularity or the attention of a cute boy?

My crush never did talk to me the night of the dance. We did, however, start dating my sophomore year. I guess being my true self paid off.

So then, Ri, why now would I want to run to the mall and buy the housewife version of the ruffled jean shorts with the matching top? Hadn't I learned my lesson all those years ago? Maybe, but motherhood in this new city in this new state in this new music class was my eighth-grade dance all over again. My old gray Yukon with the Texas license plates with the big goofy yellow Lab hanging his head out the back already screamed that we don't belong here, so was I really willing to seal our fate with this group by rebelling against the fashion as well?

Hell to the yes. I sure was.

I liked my maternity jeans because they weren't tight around my C-section scar, and I loved my worn-in gray New Balance running shoes because they reminded me of college, and I really loved my old ratty V-neck sweater from Old Navy because it was comfortable and hid the elastic waist of my maternity jeans, which brought us full circle.

Eighteen months prior, I would've said that I liked my sweatpants and comfortable tops because they allowed for easy access to the CVC line that was sewed onto my chest, just above my heart. My comfortable clothes made it easy for the nurse to hook up my medications to any one of the three tubes coming out of my chest that led to the veins leading directly into my heart.

My knit hats were handmade by other cancer patients and kept my head warm in the freezing hospital temperatures. My head scarves provided a pop of fashion when I ventured outside of the walls of MD Anderson and always drew a sympathy compliment. And I wasn't ready to give any of those up.

My closet told a story. To me and to those who knew me, my clothing choices were those of a Texas girl who went to college in the south, had a damn good time, then moved to New York City and continued the party until getting serious and going back to school, only to be taken out because of a stage IV cancer diagnosis. My fashion told the story of a marathoner-turned-cancer-patient who diverted her intense focus from medical school and running to saving her life. My sweatpants hanging next to my maternity jeans showed a survivor-turned-mother who fought like hell for her own life and then offered life to another. The diaper bag sitting next to the fanny pack used to carry around the chemo and IV pump told the story of a mom who knew all too well how quickly all the good could be taken away, and who wasn't going to waste one single day on anything that wasn't truly, authentically, honestly real and meaningful—and that meaning had been found in health, marriage, and motherhood.

Exactly one week later, the three of us pulled back into the music class parking lot, determined not to make the same mistakes. I parked under the shade tree and popped open the back window for you. I unstrapped Ellie from her car seat, held her tightly in my arms, gave you a quick pat, and turned toward the building.

Ellie and I walked into music class seven minutes late. Who the hell cared? We found a spot and ignored the irritated look from the mom who had to scoot over a whole two inches to make some room for us in the circle. My gray New Balance came dangerously close to her shiny Tory Burch flat. I laid Ellie on her back and placed her on the floor in front of me. She smiled up at her mom, and I smiled back at my little angel. THAT was what mattered. THAT was what it was all about. THAT was why I fought like hell and that was why I was forever changed.

As the weeks passed, some of the Pasadena housewives started talking to us. We even made a friend. This friend mom never wore the Tory Burch uniform, so maybe she admired my rebellion. This mom and I became as close as two people could become, meeting post-transplant and post the loss of a child. As much as this mom cared and tried to understand my past, she wasn't there. She could never know. No one could. And that was OK.

My past and my story belonged to me and me alone. Even with the best-meaning friends and family, no one was there with me twenty-four hours a day, seven days a week. No one felt the physical pain I felt from the chemo or the emotional torture of not knowing if I would live or die. No one understood the abandonment one felt when they went from being the center of attention and being treated like an infant, to then being turned loose back into the real world and told to go live your life. But that life we knew when we went into the hospital no longer existed. So what life did we go "live"?

Turned out, my new life started again with you, Ri, and then led me to Ellie. I went from being the infant to raising an infant. I turned the spotlight from me to my daughter and then, in music class, onto both of us. Until that first day of class, I hadn't been ready to expose myself or my daughter to the outside world and the harshness that world could sometimes bring.

The three of us were happy at home, breaking the bricks around my walled-off heart. True, I was raising a little human who was fully dependent on me, but I was also raising my infant self with my infant immune system into a new life and a new role—being Ellie's mom.

Choosing to keep with my closet and the clothes that hung in it was my choosing to keep with my story. Cancer was a part of me. The son we lost was a part of me. My pain and fear were a part of me. Some was too fresh to fully accept, but with each brick that fell down, one more ray of pain was allowed in.

It was OK that no one could ever understand the massiveness of my past. I shared what I could with my new friend and kept the rest for myself. And if I ever felt the gap between me and the other housewives was too great to bridge, I could always walk back to my car with the Texas license plates, pop open the back window, and look deeply into your knowing eyes so I could be reminded that being fully seen can sometimes end with total acceptance.

CHAPTER 9

# Tommy Rose

**Dear Riley,**

I was struck by how many times a friend would come to me to share something painful that was going on in their life, but before diving into the conversation would preface it by saying, "I know I shouldn't complain to you, because compared to what you've been through, this is nothing…" But, Ri, isn't all pain…something?

And what exactly were those friends referring to when they mentioned my pain? Was it The Cancer, which yes, gave me a wild ride but possibly left me stronger for it? Were they trying to measure my perceived pain inflicted by The Cancer with their current pain caused by "ordinary" life events? Because, Ri, if that was the case, I desperately wanted to tell them that it really was okay. Yes, my life was in danger. Yes, The Cancer scared me and made me sick, and it sucked at times, but The Cancer also gave me a lot of love and comfort. The Cancer had picked me up off of the wrong path and had deposited me into a life as a wife to Tom and a mom to you and Ellie. The Cancer saved me. The Cancer led me to happiness.

My Pasadena mom friends met me after The Cancer, so they only knew what I shared with them. I didn't put The Cancer in a negative light. It was shaded already. So, I tried to shine away the shadows. My hair had grown back, and my scars had healed. The Cancer and I had parted ways as friends, so I had no grievances to voice. No, I think when my friends tempered their pain in comparison to mine, they must've been referring to the unbearable heartbreak brought by the loss of a child.

After we lost Ellie's twin, we lost three more babies. One was a natural miscarriage at nine weeks. The other two babies had no heartbeat at the twelve-week check-ups. Two DNCs were performed, and two more urns of ashes were added to the shelf in Ellie's nursery. Our failed attempts to successfully transfer embryos and have them grow to term inside my damaged body had turned my maternal desire for another child into a primal urge.

Every day with Ellie was true glory, but I wanted more. I NEEDED more. I had to have what had been taken from me time and time again.

My singular focus in life became giving Ellie a sibling. Unfortunately, my strong will was ill-paired with my flawed body. Yes, The Cancer was gone, but my body was way weaker than those of most other thirty-one-year-olds. The chemo had taken a chunk of me, and I was starting to wonder if this missing piece was in fact the missing ingredient in being able to carry my children to term.

The anxiety over having another child came together with my worry regarding my mortality, which in turn fed my desire to give Ellie a sibling even more. I was living in a Category 5 hurricane of fear and uncertainty. My bone marrow transplant had, maybe, left me "cured," but I was still being scanned regularly, which told me that the doctors were still looking for "something." What if that something turned into everything?

With each insufferable loss of each child, I channeled my distress into frantic action. The ink on my baby's death certificate was not even dry before I was already asking my fertility doctor how long I had to wait until we could try again. Death was looming all around me. No time to think or feel or process. Feelings wouldn't give me another child. I had to take action. Baby steps. Long lunges. Full on leaps. Just get one foot in front of the other. And then…

God made the impossible possible. I got pregnant. Naturally. With a boy.

Thomas Neely Rose was born on December 15, 2009. Five and a half weeks prior to his due date, my weekly check-up with Dr. Macer revealed my son's heart rate to be double what it should've been. I was rushed over to labor and delivery at Huntington Hospital, only to be told by the neonatal specialist that my child was in heart failure. If we had any chance of saving him, he had to be delivered—immediately. Within seconds, ten nurses in yellow surgical robes swarmed around me and started preparing me for surgery. I remember seeing a sea of yellow and hearing the fetal monitor alarm screaming into my right ear. Lord, please, please, please don't take this child from me. Please don't take yet another sibling from Ellie.

Tommy was delivered and immediately given to a team of doctors. I didn't hear crying sounds. I didn't know if my child was dead or alive. I closed my eyes and tried to picture something, anything that would give me some stability, some comfort, some peace. Ri, I pictured you.

I thought of you and tried to imagine what you were doing. You were home with Ellie. The two of you were probably together in her room. She would've been pulling on your ears and tail, and you would've been letting her. For her second birthday, she'd been given a plastic Mickey Mouse drill that she loved to use to try to "fix things" around the house. The previous week, I'd walked in and found her drilling up your nose. She was trying to "fix" your boogers, and you let her try.

Tommy's first EKG to test his heart was abnormal. It wasn't functioning properly. Lord, please…

My little boy weighed a hearty seven pounds and zero ounces and had been able to take a bottle without a problem. His lungs seemed to be breathing on their own. These were very good signs. But his heart…

The second EKG was more normal than the first. Lord, please don't stop yet...

The third EKG came back normal. Holy hell. Lord, thank you.

Tommy and I met twenty-two hours after he was born. Death had been so close, yet we'd once again narrowly avoided its reach. As much as I wanted to fall into the joy of this new child, the residual fear guarded my heart. I was too well aware of the precariousness of life. If I leaned into this joy, it would hurt more when it's taken away. And in that moment, the losses I'd suffered seemed as real as the new life I was holding in my arms.

Tom drove Tommy and me home five days after our son was born. Ri, just as you'd been with Ellie, you were waiting for us behind the screen door. You sat patiently as we introduced Ellie to her new baby brother before letting you come give Tommy your first big sniff. His little pink face scrunched up when your wet black nose touched his cheek for the first time. He let out a little grunt. Ellie wanted another turn with her new brother, so you stepped aside. Life as a family of five had begun.

The five of us had five blissful weeks. We snuggled and cuddled and counted our blessings. You alternated napping spots between the two nurseries while I balanced differing nap schedules. Our family was complete. My heart was soaring. And then, as if it had been patiently waiting for the perfectly cruel occasion, The Cancer reappeared.

## CHAPTER 10

# The Lump

**Dear Ri,**

Carrie Geller was getting married. There are few friends for whom I would leave my five-week-old newborn son for even a few hours, let alone two whole nights for a wedding in a different state—but it was Carrie, and Carrie had been my person all throughout college, my friend who'd always innately understood me on every level. We first met as college freshmen at Vanderbilt and continued our four-year journey together, always by each other's side.

Our bond began over waking up with moral hangovers after a drunken night at a fraternity house and moved into traveling Europe together during our semester abroad in Italy. I counseled her through boyfriends, and she talked to me for hours about the pros and cons of my life choices. And she always knew that if she looked around the bar after midnight and couldn't find me that I had "pulled a Caroline" and left without saying goodbye. Even with all the training in college, I never could stay out late.

Ri, before you, Carrie was my safe place. She understood my quirks, and I understood hers. We knew when to give each other space and when to envelop the other in a bear hug. I'd met her fiancé and adored him. Carrie and I had waited for Jeremy for too long for me to miss out on Carrie's once-in-a-lifetime occasion.

With the wedding quickly approaching, I realized I had a million things to do. Mom was flying out to stay with the three of you while Tom and I traveled to Houston. I needed to make lists, mix bottles, wash burp cloths, stock up on your dog food, find a dress that fit five weeks post C-section, and of course get a spray tan. In addition, I wanted to give a toast at Carrie's rehearsal dinner, but I needed it to be spectacular. I had so much to say but wanted to make my words count. Carrie was too special not to have the perfect delivery.

In the midst of all the chaos, I had to find time to brainstorm this important speech. In the past, running had been my time to think and organize my ideas, but as The Cancer, you, Ellie, and Tommy entered my life, my running had become walking and my walking had become strolling. The power-walking moms now easily passed us on the sidewalks.

In an effort to come up with the perfect words for Carrie, you and I put Ellie and Tommy in the double stroller and headed out for our leisurely stroll. I knew I should've been taking advantage of these few quiet minutes when all three of my children were content to look at the beautiful nature all around us, but my mind kept drifting to all the other things I needed to do before we flew out the following day. Would that long black dress fit me? Maybe with Spanx... Did I need to pack exercise clothes? Oh right, I'd not yet been given the all-clear to exercise post C-section. What about Ellie's play group? Did I let my Pasadena housewife friends know we'd be missing? Wasn't it our day to bring snack?

Thankfully, you'd hit the doggie equivalent of turning forty—you were beginning to mature and calm down but still had a wonderfully playful side. You never pulled on the leash but instead pranced along with your tail held high in the air along the side of the stroller, almost as if saying, "Yep, this is MY family." You only broke stride when the neighbor's cat showed up for yet another game of "chase me if you can." That mischievous cat always taunted you into thinking you could actually win.

As we strolled, I reflected on my friendship with Carrie and tried to recall our more memorable moments together. Recalling specific details was slow going, because as soon as an idea came into my mind I'd be pulled away from it by something happening in the stroller. Ever since Ellie had been born, having a complete thought without being interrupted by a need from my daughter was a rare treat. Ever since Tommy was born, complete thoughts were nonexistent. I was starting to recall a memorable night in Italy and our dancing to the techno music in the bar with… Tommy screeched with excitement at the passing French Bulldog walking on a leash crusted in shiny jewels. Ellie turned toward her baby brother and tried to soothe him by giving him a "love pat," which was much more of a love whack. It was quiet again. Back to the toast. What memory had I been about to recall?

Our flight was in less than twenty-four hours. I still hadn't fully checked off one item on my to-do list, but my spray tan appointment was in half an hour. Everything else would have to wait until I got back. The four of us returned home from our stroll, and I began the process of putting Ellie and Tommy down for their naps. Ellie was on a sleep schedule and went down for her naps after just one read of *Goodnight Moon*. Tommy usually fell asleep mid-bottle and would sleep for a solid hour and a half. He was such an easy baby. With both kids asleep, I changed into my baggy, don't-care-if-this-gets-stained spray tan clothes and grabbed my purse. I knew you'd want to come in the car, so I looked for you in one of the two places I was sure to find you—Ellie's or Tommy's nursery. Sure enough, you were sound asleep on the rug beside Tommy's crib.

My entire day thus far had been one big rush to the next, but when I opened the door and saw the two of you asleep, side by side, my day slowed. I stopped. I took a breath. And I paused. I fell into that beautiful moment.

My two boys—sleeping so peacefully. You guarding Tommy as you always did, and Tommy—my second little miracle baby, happy and healthy—sleeping in his crib. I watched his chest as it rose and fell with each breath. I saw his little mouth open ever so slightly with his chubby arms stretched up above his head. I reminded myself that he was here. Tommy was alive. He'd made it. My thoughts were interrupted by your loud snore. It seemed to lull Tommy into an even deeper state of sleep.

From the moment Tommy had been born, he seemed so content with life. It was like he knew the deal and gladly accepted. Being born into this family, with this mother, with her body, just meant things might've been a little different. He may have had some heart issues, and we may have needed to go to the doctor more than most, and I may not have been able to get in the sun or eat oysters—ever—and he may not have been able to go on a play date if his friend had even a slight sniffle, but we were OK with that. Tommy had chosen us, and I liked to believe that his uncomplicated temperament implied he was at peace with his decision.

After waking you from your midday slumber, you and I jumped in the car and drove to the spray tan salon to get that natural Southern California girl tan. I'd told Mom we'd be gone thirty minutes, tops. I wanted to be there when the kids woke up from their naps.

I'd never been to this particular spray tan lady before, so I felt that first time awkwardness. Where did I go and where do I stand? Did I completely undress, or did I leave on my underwear? Would she be chatty (please, no!) or would she be focused and efficient? I prayed for the latter, as I didn't have the time or energy to give to anyone living outside the walls of our Pasadena cottage.

The spray tan lady introduced herself to me and told me to undress completely. I walked into her room and froze. Glaring back at me was a full-length mirror. Oh dread. I'd not yet wanted to look at my five-week post-pregnancy body in a full-length mirror, especially with bad overhead florescent lighting. But the trip was the following day, so like it or not I had to do what I had to do. I always felt better with a spray tan. It made me feel more like my pre-baby self. Not to mention it always seemed to give the illusion of making me look ten pounds lighter.

Once I was completely undressed, I took a deep breath and prepared for the worst. I slowly turned to look at myself in the mirror. My baby belly was slowly shrinking. OK—could be worse. My arms and legs were less swollen. Could be better. My face was less puffy, but cheeks were still a bit chubby. Okay, Caroline, not so bad. Things could definitely be worse. With a dark enough tan and a… I was cut off mid-thought. My heart stopped. My blood turned cold. I felt dizzy. Please, Lord, tell me I didn't just see what I know I just saw. I had to sit down. No time. I fell hard down to the floor.

Standing in front of the full-length mirror in the spray tan lady's room with the horrible florescent lighting, I'd seen what had been there for most of my pregnancy but had been hidden by my large pregnant stomach—I had seen The Lump.

The first time I was diagnosed with The Cancer five years prior, lumps were all over my body, but the largest and most prominent lumps were in my groin. I had two symmetrical, acorn-shaped lumps on either side of my bikini line. My bikini wax lady in Brentwood had expressed concern, but I dismissed her as being a hypochondriac. Once I understood that this Swedish waxer was, in fact, correct, I began to check my bikini line for lumps regularly during my first remission. That was how I found The Cancer when it came back the second time, just three short years ago. And that was now how I knew in my soul of souls that The Cancer had come back—again. I slowly picked myself up off the floor. I somehow got dressed, made it to the sofa in the waiting room, and pulled out my cell phone. I emailed my local doctor in Los Angeles and put a red flag by the subject line. I knew he was in clinic that afternoon—and I knew this was an emergency. I kept it short and to the point. I wrote,

> *Dr. Forman—I just found a large lump in my groin. I am very worried. What should I do? Caroline*

I pressed send.

And then I waited.

At some point, I decided to get up and walk to the car. On the way, I called Tom and told him what had happened. He told me to stay where I was, that he was on his way to meet me. I got into my car and turned on the engine. The words my uncle had spoken in my moment of despair so many years ago ran through my head—baby steps. One foot in front of the other. I took a breath. I turned on the radio. I checked my hair in the mirror. I pulled my phone out of my purse.

I checked my email.

I had a new message from Dr. Forman.

> *Caroline—I'm in clinic. Come out this afternoon. I will see you when you arrive. Dr. Forman*

I snapped back into life. Okay. I was getting a plan. I had told two people—the two people who could help me the most in this moment. Tom would be there to support me emotionally, and Dr. Forman would be there to order the necessary medical tests. I was beginning to feel more in control, more in my body. The plan to expose The Cancer was in motion.

I called Tom and asked him to meet me at City of Hope. Then I called my mom and told her that I had an appointment with my OBGYN that I'd forgotten about and would be home later than expected. No need to worry anyone until the truth had been confirmed by something other than my intuition. Thirty minutes later, Tom and I were sitting in Dr. Forman's waiting room. Dr. Forman's nurse met us and took us back into an exam room. Three long minutes later, Dr. Forman walked in and looked at me with concern-filled eyes. I showed him The Lump and watched his eyes as the concern washed out and a tidal wave of fear flooded in. He now knew the truth as well but ordered a CT scan to confirm the nitty-gritty.

The first opening for a CT scan was not until the following evening, so Tom and I changed our travel plans. We'd miss the rehearsal dinner Friday evening, but by flying in on Saturday morning we'd be there for the main event. I called Carrie and told her that I'd found a lump but was sure it was nothing. Just to be safe, we needed to do this test, and that would put me in a day late. I didn't want to worry my friend, but I also knew she would see right through my effort to be nonchalant.

The wedding was amazing, I think. Truth be told, I don't really remember the details. Tom and I danced with the bride and groom, but my glee was forced, and my dance moves rigid. I looked around at my college friends dancing happily together in one large circle of innocent bliss. As much as I wanted to relax into my terrible dance moves, my heart was home in the nursery with my babies and The Cancer had my joy in a straitjacket. I was in purgatory and wouldn't be able to calm down until I knew where and how it was using my body yet again.

Tom and I landed at LAX the following afternoon. We were walking through baggage claim when the voicemail notification popped up on my phone.

> *"Caroline, it's Dr. Forman. I got your CT results, and it's not good. Your lymphoma is back. This time it's wrapped around your spine and is dangerously close to infusing into your spinal fluid. This could have devastating consequences. We need to start treatment immediately. Please call me as soon as you get this."*

I wanted to call Dr. Forman back. I really did, but I also just wanted to put my phone down and pretend like I hadn't heard one word of the reality of my situation. I wanted to go home and love on my babies and wrap my arms around your big, furry neck and feel that love flow from your body into mine. I needed to be recharged before I could be taken back down. Ri, I couldn't call him back, because once I did, everything would be forever changed.

Tom made the call for me. We were sitting in my car on the top level of the Parking Spot at LAX, smelling the nearby In-N-Out burgers and fries mixed with jet fuel. He put the phone on speaker. Dr. Forman answered after the second ring.

Tom, Dr. Forman, and I spoke for an hour and a half. We all cried. We all laughed. We all silently prayed.

An hour later, Tom and I pulled into our Pasadena driveway. I saw your large body standing in front of the front screen door. Your tail was wagging furiously, and your alert ears fell into a relaxed and joyful state. I jogged up the red brick sidewalk and opened the front door. You met me on our front doorstep and buried your large head into my legs. I folded my body down over yours. I heard my babies in the living room a few feet away, but I needed this moment with you. I needed your strength. I needed your reassurance. I needed to be weak before I could walk through that door and be strong.

Ever since finding The Lump, I knew my cancer had come back. And those closest to me knew it too. Tom knew the second he received my phone call. Dr. Forman knew when he read my email. You knew it as soon as I returned without my spray tan. Carrie knew when I told her I wasn't coming to the rehearsal dinner. I knew everyone was terrified and felt responsible, almost as if I'd let them down.

For the forty-eight hours of knowing without knowing, I'd been strong. I didn't break down. I didn't openly cry. I couldn't have, because I had to be strong for everyone else. But I was about to walk into my home and look at my two babies, the two humans who needed me to be strong the most. How could I hold them knowing I may not be able to hold them for much longer? How could I give them my love if they were at a high risk of losing it, of losing me? Was it cruel to fall even deeper in love if we were possibly about to lose each other? Was it easier if they didn't ever really know their mom? Was it easier for me if I didn't ever really know my children?

I watched Tom as he brought the luggage in from the car and gave Ellie her gift from the Houston airport. He seemed to understand that

I needed this time with you. You sat down, and I sat down next to you. You felt my sadness. We sat together on the front step for a long while. You lowered your head into my lap.

I began to think about the day we first met. I thought about our first walk together. I pictured the first night you trusted me enough to sleep on the floor next to my bed. I thought about your life before we met. Ri, I was so damn proud to be your mom. I thanked you for trusting me and for sticking with me. We'd come a long way together. I'd never imagined our journey would bring us back to that place. We'd been together for five years. For some dogs, that was half a lifetime. In the beginning, I was your savior—but as I felt your wet nose against my leg, I realized you were now becoming mine.

I looked at you through my tears. Ri, how was I going to walk through that door? I didn't have a clue. I didn't know how I was going to do any of it, all while being my best self for my children, who deserved the best version of me. The anxiety was overwhelming. I was falling into the abyss of uncertainty. Then, with the simple act of placing your paw lovingly across my arm, I was pulled back into the present. You raised your head and gently held my gaze. I took a breath.

I was alive. I was here. I was with you. You were with me. My children were in the room behind us. My strong and loving husband was getting dinner ready. My mom's steadfast love was caring for all of us.

The only thing I knew for certain was that there, on that front porch step with your paw across my arm and your gaze fixed on mine, it was all about that one moment—and together, in that moment, we were okay.

## CHAPTER 11

# Finding Francis

Dear Ri Rose,

In the weeks following my third diagnosis, I kept asking myself—was this my fault? Could I have done more? Did I not eat the right foods? Did I not eliminate all toxins from our home? Did I get rid of our microwave too late? Did I forget to throw away all plastic containers? Did I wait too long to switch you to organic and raw dog food?

During my first transplant, I immersed myself in every cancer book I could find. I became knowledgeable on alternative cancer treatments and ways to supplement them with the Western medicine approach. I became a firm believer that there was room for both holistic and conventional treatments and that the two could complement each other. I knew the damaging effects the chemo had on my body, so I became an expert in rebuilding my body with supplements and began to treat food as medicine.

I eliminated chemicals from our home and only bought organic food. The Saturday farmers market was added to our weekly schedule, and I even toyed around with making my own bread. Living a clean life gave me a sense of control in a time when the conventional treatment had stopped, and I was in the "hopefully this worked" stage with my Western doctors. But, Ri, did I do enough?

Despite my best efforts to keep The Cancer out of the fighting ring, it had come back for more. Three days after speaking with Dr. Forman, Tom and I flew back to Houston to meet with Dr. Andersson at MD Anderson. We needed as many brilliant doctor brains working on this treatment plan as possible. The problem was that I'd already done the only potentially curative treatment with the first transplant, and it had clearly failed. Our options were limited. Dr. Andersson knew of a clinical trial that combined protocols from Johns Hopkins, Fred Hutchinson, and MD Anderson. They were allowing sixty-eight patients to join. I joined as number sixty-six.

The plan was to start chemo immediately at City of Hope in Los Angeles, so I could stay close to home. I would try a chemo regimen referred to as ICE, which required five to six rounds. Then, after we had shrunk The Cancer as much as possible, the five of us would then move to Houston for six months so I could undergo a second bone marrow transplant. Dr. Andersson was very clear about the risks of this second transplant. He made sure I understood that there was a 40 percent mortality rate and that, even if I survived, my body would never be the same again. I signed the release form before I had time to contemplate the magnitude of these words. What other choice did I have?

Tom and I returned to Pasadena and began making a plan. I was scheduled to start chemo the following day at City of Hope, so we had very little time. One thing was clear—we needed help with the kids. The ICE chemo was rumored to be nasty and could make people crazy sick. The first round would be administered inpatient over a three-day period. Three days away from my babies. But Tommy was only six weeks old…

Upon understanding the reality of my situation, I reluctantly agreed to begin the search for a nanny. Never in my wildest dreams did I think I'd be looking for another person to take care of my precious angels. I mean, goddamn it. This wasn't how my life was supposed to be. I should be a bad-ass surgeon and insane marathon runner. I should have summited Kilimanjaro and, who knows, maybe even Everest. I was supposed to be strong and healthy and invincible. Yet here I was in a world where "supposed to" translated into the great reminder that I was glaringly mortal.

The Cancer had already taken away my intended career and all athletic accomplishments but now, with the prospect of hiring a nanny to take care of my children, it was taking away all my remaining value. Admitting that I could no longer take care of my children was admitting defeat. And it pissed me off.

Since Tommy was still so young, his days and nights were consumed with sleeping and eating. Ellie was entering the terrible twos, but she'd counteracted that stereotype and was the happiest, most fun-loving two-year-old in Pasadena. She took great pride in helping with her brother, and when she got bored with him, she turned to you. The two of you would spend hours on the floor of her nursery. She loved to "read" to you and dress you up as a princess. One day, she even painted your paw nails bright pink. That nail polish stayed on your feet for weeks.

Shortly after returning to Pasadena, Tom and I began the nanny interview process. We spoke to a few candidates before I went into the hospital for my first round of ICE. I turned each of them away. They weren't the right fit to take care of my children. Three more candidates came to my bedside in the hospital to interview for the position. I sent them each away within the first ten minutes. We interviewed twenty-two candidates in total, and I said "no" to each and every one of them. They were either too experienced or not experienced enough, too over-eager or not eager enough, one had bad breath, one wore a horrible perfume, one candidate wore all black and another all white. At the end of the day, I couldn't accept any of them holding my children in their arms while I was away. I wanted to find "perfect," but no one even came close.

I was getting sicker by the day. The ICE kicked my ass. My ego had convinced me that I would have a much easier time with this chemo than all the other cancer amateurs, but I was quickly humbled as the sickness began almost immediately. The chemo made me violently ill, so anti-nausea medication was given. But that gave me horrible headaches, so pain medicine was given. And the pain medicine made me ill, and we were back to where we had started. And that was how it went—for a very long time.

As I grew sicker and sicker, Tom grew more and more anxious. He was trying to be a present dad to his two very young children and at the same time a husband to his very sick wife. Our need for help had reached a critical level.

As Tom was seriously contemplating hiring a previous candidate that was very qualified and, if I'm being honest, very lovely, God sent us an angel. A good friend had heard about our desperate search and had a thought. Her nanny's sister lived in Pasadena but worked in the Palisades. The drive across town going to and from work was an hour and a half each way and was becoming unsustainable. My friend's nanny's sister needed a job closer to home, so she suggested we meet.

It was a Sunday afternoon in late January. I was sitting on our sofa near the front window. Tommy was sound asleep on my chest, and Ellie was serving us "lunch" from her toy kitchen. You were napping by the front door.

A little red Ford Focus drove up and parked on the street directly in front of our house. Francis stepped out of her car, closed her door, and calmly, slowly walked up our red brick sidewalk. I didn't feel my skin crawl. I didn't feel my insides turn upside down. I hadn't already made a mental list of ten reasons why she wasn't the right fit for our family. Tom opened the door and introduced himself. Francis stepped into our front room and paused. She looked down at you on the floor across her intended path. This wise woman didn't try to step over you but instead bowed her head while saying, "Hello, Señor." She didn't change her voice into an artificially higher pitch or use her arms to reach out and invasively touch your large head. It was almost as if she knew she hadn't yet earned the right. Some part of this wise lady knew that to get to this family she had to get through you first. She was hired on the spot.

Francis started working for our family one week after I had finished my first round of ICE and two weeks before I was scheduled to go back in for round two. We met when I was bruised but not battered. We entered into a delicate dance of who would do what without overstepping or interfering with the other. I learned to give, and she learned to take. I fell in love with her quiet presence. Francis never tried to impress us by taking Ellie or Tommy out of our arms or picking them up from their cribs when they awoke from a nap. She knew I was their mom and was happy to support me in that role. Francis did all the things that would've otherwise taken my time and energy away from my children and allowed me to focus on being a mom and fighting The Cancer.

I spent every minute I had with the three of you. Nothing else seemed to matter. Life outside of our cottage and City of Hope evaporated. As I grew weaker, our daily walks stopped. I hired a dog walker. He came highly recommended and seemed to really love showing up in the mornings, leash in hand. I assumed your walks together were going well until a week in, when the highly recommended dog walker came in and told me that he could no longer work for us. When I asked him why, he explained that for the past week you'd walked with him to the end of our short block and then stopped. You wouldn't go any farther. He tried everything he could think of to try to get you to continue the walk and hoped that with time you may change your mind, but he finally realized that you were just not going to walk with him, or—as I like to say—without me. So your highly recommended dog walker fired us. And I kind of loved it.

Instead of walking, we began napping. You snuggled your large body up to mine, and we both stayed in bed together until we heard Ellie or Tommy call for us. As my weight dropped, your weight rose. You went from a lean 111 pounds to a solid 137. We were doing the best we could.

You were happy, Ellie and Tommy were safe and well taken care of, Tom was finding a healthier balance, and my battle with The Cancer was progressing through the first phase—and we all had each other. And, for those few months, that was good enough for me.

## CHAPTER 12

# Motherhood Swirled with Chemo

**Dear Ri,**

The months leading up to my second bone marrow transplant were Heaven swirled with Hell, motherhood swirled with chemo. Just like my favorite chocolate and vanilla swirl yogurt flavor, the two were equally present in every single tasteful moment. And you, Ri Rose, were the blissful Oreo topping that made any flavor taste ten times more delicious.

Our roles had officially shifted. You were now my caretaker in every way. You asked for nothing and gave everything. You kept us laughing with your desperate love of food and tennis balls and all the creative ways you would think of to obtain both. After about a year of living in our Pasadena cottage, you'd somehow lured the UPS man into bringing you treats every time he dropped off a package. For years after, every time you'd see a UPS truck, a steady stream of drool accumulated at the corners of your mouth.

You'd become a beloved and respected member of our community who impacted many people with your loving and goofy personality. Even my friends who didn't care for dogs always acknowledged and thanked you after they came by to drop off a homemade casserole for our family dinner. Your role as our family's keeper was never unseen or unappreciated.

Your devotion to our family was evident in your eyes with every gaze we shared, even over the clumps of long brown hair covering the white-tiled bathroom floor. The ICE chemo had caused my hair to start falling out after just one round. I was relieved. In the life of mothers and toddlers, this would simplify my day: one less thing on my list of things to worry about.

You were relieved because the hairdryer was still a major source of fear for you. You never forgot the inhumane pain you endured when the horrible people burned you with the grooming dryers after hours. Anytime you heard Tom or me say the word "shower," you hurried to the back corner of our garage and violently shook until you knew that either all hair had been dried or my hair was pulled back into a wet ponytail. Even though I knew the hair loss was imminent and the alleviation was real, seeing the hair that had taken me three and a half years to grow back loosely covering the bathroom floor filled me with a sense of awe. The hair loss reminded me of The Cancer's incredible strength and determination.

My friendship with my housewife friend, Jill, from music class had stayed strong. Jill wasn't an animal lover, and you sensed that. You never asked her for attention, but after a few months she gave it to you anyway. One day, I caught Jill kneeling in front of you, gently patting your head and speaking soft words into your relaxed ears. Her kids considered you their dog, and with time Jill began to understand the powerful love of an animal.

Not long after knowing you, Jill adopted a rescue cat named Nacho. And then Tirza adopted Frida. And then Violet adopted Barney. As I said, your impact on those around us was far-reaching.

Jill's daughter, Abby, and Ellie had been born three days apart. We then ended up pregnant at the same time with our boys, Tommy and Cooper. Our due dates were a few weeks apart, hers closer to Christmas and mine a few days after New Year's. Jill had texted me on December 14th and told me she'd been sent to the hospital and was in labor. I read Jill's text and thought, *I'm so glad that's not me.* We both gave birth to our sons the following day.

Jill became my most trusted friend in Pasadena. I spoke to her about my innermost fears while she listened and gave honest advice. I told her how much I worried that The Cancer would have a permanent impact on Ellie and Tommy. I'd read a few child psychology books and understood the importance of the first three years of life. The "Zero to Three Movement" had proven that birth to three years old was a critical period for human brain development and that any sort of deprivation during that time could lead to lifelong cognitive, emotional, or even physical issues.

Jill recommended I go see a renowned child psychologist. This doctor had co-written many books with a world-famous child development expert and came highly recommended. She had a very full practice and only took on the most "serious" cases. I left her a voicemail, and she called me back an hour later. Apparently, I qualified.

One week later, I walked into her office for our appointment. The child psychologist was wonderful. For the first time, I was sitting with someone who not only deeply understood the density of my mom guilt but also had ideas for ways through. I explained that I would be away from all three of you while I was an inpatient during the transplant and that I worried about the impact that would have on Ellie and Tommy. This psychologist explained that, yes, it would have an impact. However, there were concrete things I could do to minimize the damage.

Because of their differing ages, the emotional imprint would be different for Ellie than it would be for her little brother, resulting in differing needs. Consistency in caregivers would be of top importance for Tommy, while Ellie would need information, honesty, and comfort. Tom, Francis, and Mom gladly stepped into the role of consistent caregiver, while Tom and I gave Ellie the information and honesty in an age-appropriate manner and could comfort her whenever we were able. I knew you would be there to offer the comfort when I could not.

Per the psychologist's suggestion, I made a book for Ellie. It was titled *Ellie's Book from Mommy*. This homemade project contained pictures of the two of us from the past two years. I tried to explain how much I loved her and treasured all of the fun times we'd shared together. You were in almost every picture, as almost every memory included you too, Riley Rose.

I then tried to explain in the picture book that Mommy had a big, BIG germ bug in her body that would need some really big, strong medicine called chemo to fight it. The medicine would make my hair fall out, but that was okay because that meant the medicine was working. I included pictures of my bald head from treatments before she'd been born. I explained to Ellie that in a few months' time we'd move to Houston together as a family and that I'd need to go into the hospital for a few weeks. I emphasized that she'd be surrounded by so much love from her daddy, Tommy, her grandmother, grandfather, uncle, Francis, and other family while Mommy was away.

When I wrote this book to Ellie, I had to be very careful. I couldn't promise her that everything would be OK. I had to be honest, and the truth was I had no clue how our story would end. I didn't know if my daughter would leave Houston with a mommy or with only the memories of one. I had to focus on the few things I did know to be true, no matter what happened in that hospital room. I knew she'd have Tom. I knew she'd have Tommy. I knew she would have uncles and grandparents and cousins and aunts from both Tom's side of the family and from mine, who wouldn't hesitate to step in and give my children whatever they may need. And, Ri, at the end of the day, when all the noise was silenced and all the uncertainty had settled, I knew my Ellie would have you.

A few days after my hair started to fall out, I called Audi. She'd been cutting my hair in Pasadena ever since it grew back long enough to be cut, so for about the past two years. The child psychologist had strongly suggested that I take Ellie with me when I shaved my head. She thought it would be important for Ellie to see that it was my choice, and it would help her to feel involved in the process in some small way.

Ellie and I walked into Audi's salon on a Tuesday afternoon in mid-February. Ellie sat in my lap as my trusted hairdresser fastened the black cape around my neck. We both stared straight ahead into the mirror that reflected back the eyes of an innocent child topped with the eyes of a more jaded and wounded mother.

Audi pulled out the clipper with the number three clipper guard. She asked me if I was ready. I said yes. She asked Ellie if she was ready. Ellie's wide eyes stared straight ahead into the mirror and made eye contact with mine. I gave her a reassuring smile. Ellie nodded. Audi pressed the power button. The quiet hum of the electric clippers filled the silence.

The clippers sheered the sides of my head before moving to the top. My total time spent in Audi's chair was less than five minutes. Ellie's focus was on the bushels of long hair that covered the floor. With each row of hair that fell off of my head, I grasped a little bit more control. My bald head looked tough.

Without my hair, I'd chosen to step into this recurring role of a cancer patient. My baldness represented my showing up for the fight. The Cancer thought that taking my hair would create a weakness, a despair, in its opponent, but I'd turned the tables. I didn't give The Cancer a chance to take my hair and my dignity away from me. I took it for myself.

Ellie didn't say a word on the short car ride home. The sound of the still-present music class CD came through the speakers. "Trot Old Joe, trot Old Joe, you ride better than any horse I know…" From my rearview mirror, I saw you stand up from your spot in the back of my Yukon. You turned your body around, reached your head over the backseat, and put your nose next to Ellie's face. I saw the corners of her small mouth turn upward toward a smile. I saw love move, actually pass, between the two of you—and it felt like hope.

When we got home, we turned on the TV so we could watch *Reba*. Ellie didn't dance to the theme song. I sat down to give Tommy a bottle. Ellie stayed on the other side of the room. She looked at me as if she didn't know me. She looked at me like I was a total stranger.

Halfway into the second episode, Ellie crossed the room and sat down next to me. She was careful not to wake Tommy, who was now sound asleep in my arms. She looked up at me with her big green eyes. I gently smiled back at her. Then, very slowly, she reached her hand up to my bald head and passed her hand back and forth across my scalp.

She rubbed my head like this for a while before taking her hand away and asking, "Mommy, will your hair always be this short?"

"I don't know, sweetheart."

"I like long hair."

"I know, my angel. I do too."

"Did the big germ bug do this to you?"

"No, cutie, the really big, strong medicine that is trying to get rid of the big germ bug did this to me."

"Why, Mommy?"

"Because it means the medicine is working."

"I'm mad at that big germ bug."

"Me too, sweetheart. Me too."

Ellie thought about this for a few moments before she looked at me and said, "Well, Mommy, no matter what, I still love you a whole lot."

"I love you a whole lot too. I love you so much, my angel."

So, you see, Ri, here was what The Cancer didn't take into account when it picked a fight with me for the third time—the game had changed.

Same fight, but different opponent. I wasn't the same person I'd been the first or even the second time we entered the ring together. I was now a mother to two innocent young children.

The Cancer didn't realize it, but my resolve had strengthened, because that third time I wasn't only fighting for my life but for my children's lives as well. Unknowingly, The Cancer had made the mistake of challenging the love of a mother. Game fucking on.

## CHAPTER 13

## My Lifeline

**Dear Ri,**

Well, game on almost turned into game over. With one strong blow, The Cancer had floored me, and I couldn't get up. I was lying on my back, staring up at the lights swirling above me, willing myself to get back in the fight. All I had to do was stand up. This wasn't supposed to happen. It was too early on in our match. Thus far, The Cancer had been the one to deliver the punches. I'd tried to dodge every stinging impact. Come on, Caroline—get up! Stay in this fight. Don't let The Cancer have the gratification of raising its arms in victory over your lifeless body. The crowd was chanting my name. The referee was counting: six, seven, eight...

I wanted to stand up but couldn't get a breath. My lungs felt like they were filled with cement. I felt trapped beneath the severity of the situation. Slowly, the lights on the ceiling began to come into focus. The room quieted. The referee standing above me lost his black stripes, and his shirt turned into a white lab coat. My boxing ring morphed into my hospital room. Once again, I struggled to take a breath. I felt an intense burning deep in my chest. Confused, I looked back to the figure in the white lab coat for an explanation. In my daze, I could only make out a few words. Dire. Critical. Double. Pneumonia.

Before this unexpected knockout, our plan had been to do six rounds of ICE chemo before flying to Houston for my second bone marrow transplant. Now that The Cancer had compromised my lungs, we all knew my body could not handle the sixth round of ICE, so my doctors declared my pre-transplant chemo to be complete.

The double pneumonia could have easily taken my life. By the time the infection hit my lungs, no one knew if my body had the strength to overcome the bacteria. I was given the strongest IV antibiotics available, and after a week and a half they started to work.

With the immediate fear of death passing us by in the rearview mirror, the doctor's worry became the impact this had on my body and our treatment plan. My body was now much weaker than they had anticipated it being at this point. They had wanted to eliminate as much of The Cancer as possible before my transplant, but I also had to have enough strength left to be able to handle the upcoming pre- and post-transplant chemo, as well as all the challenges that were sure to come during the recovery. In their medical predictions, the doctors forgot to consider the toll that being a mother to an infant and a toddler could have on one's body. The combination of motherhood and chemo had deemed me an "unusual case."

I had spent two weeks in the hospital at City of Hope with pneumonia. Dr. Forman and Dr. Andersson both agreed that at this point the best plan was to get to Houston as soon as possible for the bone marrow transplant. The five rounds of ICE had reduced The Cancer, but as soon as the chemo stopped, The Cancer would seize the opportunity and grow back—fast. Our window was small, and we couldn't wait. The problem was, I was weak—VERY weak. Commercial air travel wasn't an option.

My dad called in a gigantic favor and the next day we were all boarding his friend's private plane at the Burbank airport. Tom and Francis had packed everything we would need for the next six months:

baby bottles, formula, anti-nausea medication, diapers, your leash, Ellie's favorite stuffed animals, head scarves, princess costumes, bibs, your favorite dog food, burp cloths, Tom's laptop and the work files he would need to work remotely for the next six months, the Chuckit!, tennis balls, masks for me to wear in any public spaces, swimsuits for the kids, and Saran Wrap and tape to cover my PICC line when I showered. We were ready.

We all walked together onto the tarmac. The air smelled of jet fuel but not In-N-Out this time. The roar of the engines filled our ears. You stopped walking. Your ears fell flat against your head, and your tail was tucked tightly between your legs. I felt your shaking body lean into my legs. I leaned back. You looked up at me. I looked down at you and smiled. You took a step forward. At the sight of the "little white plane," Ellie squealed with delight and ran up the stairs. Francis carried Tommy onto the plane. You and I carried each other.

We entered the cabin and found our flight attendant asking Ellie if she wanted to watch *The Little Mermaid* or *The Lion King* on one of the many TV screens situated throughout the cabin. I wanted to enjoy the luxury but found I was unable to settle into the experience. I was too deep in my fear.

The three-hour flight flew by. With my arms too weak to hold Tommy for more than a few minutes, I asked Francis to feed him a bottle. The gentle hum of the engine lulled them both to sleep. Tom and Ellie enjoyed a buffet of chicken fingers, sandwiches, and fruit followed by freshly baked chocolate chip cookies. You and I lay down together on the long, narrow sofa. Our two bodies fit together perfectly.

Dad was waiting for us on the runway when the plane pulled up to the private terminal in Houston. It should have been such a baller moment, but as soon as the door opened and my frail body appeared at the top of the steps down to the tarmac, it was anything but. Dad helped you and me down and gave us each a long, deep, hard hug. I saw him whisper something into your ear. You pushed the top of your head into his thigh.

After the bags were loaded and the seatbelts buckled, Dad drove us to our new home. Our "Houston House" had been a massive team effort. Uncle Paul's father had passed away a while back and had left his home to his son. Uncle Paul had fond memories of growing up in that house, so he didn't want to sell it, but Aunt Karol wasn't sure if she was up for the renovation.

As they were deciding what to do with the empty house, Mom had called with the news of The Cancer. By this point, Aunt Karol and Uncle Paul knew the drill. They knew we would be in Houston for many months and that now with children added to the picture we would need our own place to stay. A plan was hatched. After weeks and weeks of hard work and gallons and gallons of love, Mom and Aunt Karol transformed this empty, older home into a fully functional residence, replete with cheerful drapes and sippy cups.

Mom had agreed to move to Houston for the duration of the transplant. Even though Tom and Francis were both on board to help, we knew it would take a village. Chad, Dad, Aunt Karol, Uncle Paul, Gigi, Cousin Kelly, Cousin Paul and his wife, Katie, were also ready to fill in wherever they could. My second mom growing up, Rosa, drove over from San Antonio and moved into our Houston home with us. Chad and Dad would visit on the weekends. Mom and Dad's dogs, Sam and Abby, came along to keep you company. We had our village.

We were still on schedule. I had made it to Houston within the ideal timeframe. Before I could be admitted to the hospital for the pre-transplant chemo, I needed to meet with Dr. Andersson so he could order scans and yet another bone marrow biopsy. These tests would determine just how much of The Cancer had been killed off by the ICE chemo. I was also scheduled for many different "baseline" tests, which would be our basis of comparison post-transplant. Basically, they wanted to be able to look back and see how much of a toll this upcoming transplant was going to have on all aspects of my body.

Tom and Chad went with me to see Dr. Andersson. After so many years together, we had grown very close to this respected doctor. I was always happy to see his reassuring face when he opened the door to my exam room. Once the hugs, handshakes, small talk, and test scheduling had been sorted out, Dr. Andersson once again explained the transplant protocol (aka game plan) to Tom, Chad, and me.

Now that the transplant was days away, the details suddenly seemed much more important. This clinical trial required me to start my pre-transplant chemo one day after being admitted to the hospital. I would once again be in an inpatient room on the eleventh floor, the hospital floor reserved exclusively for transplant patients. I would be allowed minimal pre-approved visitors. We couldn't risk a germ bug finding its way into my hospital room and infecting my soon-to-be nonexistent immune system. The stakes were too high, as infection was the number one cause of death during transplants, and unfortunately kids were the biggest carriers of germs. Ellie and Tommy wouldn't make the approved visitation list. Neither would you, Ri.

My pre-transplant chemo would last five days, otherwise referred to as day −7 through day −3, a backward countdown to transplant day. The nurses would come in at 4:30 in the morning to hook up my chemo cocktail of the day. The infusion would last for three hours. Dr. Andersson would check on me each morning during his rounds and again in the evening, if necessary. Blood would be drawn every morning before the chemo was hooked up, and the lab results would be given to me during my doctor's rounds. Having done this once before, I understood the grave importance of these lab results. They would be the only number separating me from life and from death.

After the five days of pre-transplant chemo, days −2 and −1 would be "rest" days. Curious about the rest days, I asked why I would have two days off.

"Ahh, because we need extra time to make sure the chemo kills off every last stem cell in your immune system, so it can be a clean slate for your brother's donor stem cells."

Chad looked at me seriously. "Dr. Andersson is saying that we need extra time to kill off your not-so-great cells to make way for my awesome cells." Laughter. This was Chad's way—he could bring laughter to even the scariest moments.

"OK, so basically, I'll have this super-strong chemo come in and wipe out my immune system as I know it and then will have two days of rest so that the killing of my cells can continue. Why do y'all call them rest days when it seems to be the complete opposite?"

"You always do ask the questions none of my other patients have ever asked."

"Yeah, her first transplant with my cells made her crazy smart." Chad couldn't help himself.

"You're a funny brother," Dr. Andersson humorlessly replied in his thick Swedish accent.

"But, seriously, why do you call them rest days?" I asked again.

"We call them rest days because those are the two days the patients will need to be able to summon all their strength for what is to come."

The room was silent. Tom looked at me. Chad looked at the floor. I looked up toward the ceiling. After a few moments, Dr. Andersson resumed his explanation.

The five days of chemo and the two cell-killing, strength-summoning "rest" days would bring us to day 0, Transplant Day. This would be the day that would be considered the first day of the rest of my life.

Transplant patients tended to adopt the date of their transplants as their new birthdays, because with this new opportunity at life we were reborn with new bodies. I remembered this day from my first transplant, both mine and from looking into other patients' rooms while on one of my many walks with my IV pole around the nurses' station. I remember seeing cakes delivered to the patients' hospital rooms and party hats worn by the pre-approved visitors. Everyone sang "Happy Birthday" while the new cells were being infused into the previously broken body that was now, in theory, being made whole. I remember watching those celebrations and thinking it didn't feel right.

My family had also seen the celebrations on transplant day and offered to do the same. I kindly and graciously refused. Actually, it probably sounded more like, "No way. I don't want any celebrations and anyone who does try to celebrate will be taken off the visitor list." I was determined to keep my original birthday. I did not want to erase the body that had brought me to this point, the body that had beaten cancer twice before and had even given me two healthy children. It felt like a betrayal to erase all of that and start over. We had come this far together. I was not going to abandon my greatest ally in favor of cake and party hats. We would win this fight against the foreign invader together.

I remembered my first transplant day as being incredibly anticlimactic. The donor cells were carried into the room in a red medical cooler by a team of doctors no one had ever seen before. They hung the bag of bright-red donor cells on the IV pole and programed the IV pump to the correct flow rate. The doctors stepped back as we marveled at the medical miracle that was happening before our eyes. The cells infused over a half-hour period. All the while, the patient felt like a caged animal in a popular zoo exhibit—on display, with no escape from the attention.

Once the last red cell was infused, the bag was unhooked, and the medical team excused themselves and went back to their laboratory somewhere in the basement. The patient and their loved ones looked at each other with the same question: That was it? That was the brilliant medical procedure that was supposed to save the patient from this cancer that was biting at the bit to take over and end things? What happened next?

No one would be able answer that question.

Since we had been through this once before, our expectations were in check. We didn't have many questions. As Dr. Andersson once again explained transplant day, I no longer envisioned fireworks and rainbows. I understood the importance and significance, but more importantly I understood what was to come next. Or at least, I thought I did.

As Dr. Andersson had told us many times, the big difference between this transplant and my previous one was the post-transplant chemo. I didn't have any additional treatment after my transplant day four years ago. With my first transplant, starting on day +1, all I had to do was rest and recover. Not this time. This go-round, I'd have a slight reprieve on day +1 but, starting on day +2, more chemo was coming, and this chemo would be, by all accounts, no joke.

This post-transplant chemo would be the element that gave this second transplant a 40% mortality rate. This chemo starting on day +2 was going to damage my body in such a way that I'd never fully recover. This chemo would take me to the edge, and it was going to be up to me to fight my way back. During the first transplant, much thought and attention had been given to balancing the treatment with my quality-of-life post-transplant, but the only goal I was facing was survival. Life post-transplant would have to be addressed when and if that time came.

The post-transplant chemo would last for four days. It seemed counterintuitive to me to administer chemo after my body had just been given these infant stem cells that were supposed to find their way into my bone marrow and build a new immune system. Wouldn't the chemo kill off those all-important cells? Apparently not. The clinical trial research was finding tremendous benefit with this chemo protocol. This was the "magic bullet" that would save my life—if it didn't kill me first.

Once Tom, Chad, and I felt as comfortable as we could possibly feel with my upcoming schedule, we turned to the piece of this equation that had been slightly overlooked on my part, but that was pretty much the cornerstone in my being able to even have this potentially curative treatment—my brother.

The donation protocol for the first transplant had required Chad to inject himself with a crazy-high dose of medication that would stimulate the stem cells in his bone marrow to overproduce. Stem cells, the basis of our immune system, would transform into red blood cells, white blood cells, platelets, and so on.

Chad followed the instructions and injected himself with the medication multiple times a day for four days in a row. The resulting side effect was extreme bone pain that lasted seven days. The stimulating medicine had found its way into my brother's bone marrow and was asking the marrow to work beyond its capacity, therefore causing the marrow in the bones to throb with overworked aches. Chad couldn't sit or sleep for days. The only relief was found in walking, so for seven days, instead of sleeping, he walked and he walked and he walked.

Ri, I remember those nights lying in bed in Aunt Karol and Uncle Paul's house. Your twitching, dreaming body was stretched out next to mine. I was awake, staring at the ceiling, trying to calm my racing thoughts. What was about to happen to me? Will I survive? Will it work? Will I ever again have a normal life?

The rhythmic sounds of your deep breaths had just begun to lull me to sleep when I heard another rhythmic sound: creak, creak, creak. Someone was awake. Someone was walking down the bedroom hallway toward our room. The sound coming from the hardwood floors continued to grow louder as the visitor approached. Then the creaking faded as the unknown walker retreated in the opposite direction.

This pattern of the creaking growing louder then softer continued for hours as my brother walked up and down the hallway, trying to ease his insufferable bone pain. Back and forth, up and down, one step at a time. I wondered why he didn't turn on the TV in his adjacent bedroom to help pass the time instead of pacing. Surely a good VH1 *Behind the Music* would get his mind off of some of the pain. Why wasn't he taking advantage of middle-of-the-night reruns? Ahhhh. Of course. He didn't want to take the chance of waking me up.

Growing up, Chad and I had a fairly typical sibling relationship. His being three and a half years older but four grades ahead of me in school created a significant gap between our lives. I idolized him and his friends and lavished any scraps of attention thrown my way. I knew how to infuriate him and delighted in getting any reaction out of my big brother. He in turn knew how to get me back and by the time he turned sixteen and started driving me to school had figured out the perfect way.

Chad was a junior in high school when I was in seventh grade. The junior school started fifteen minutes earlier than the high school, which meant that, in theory, Chad would have to leave fifteen minutes earlier to get his sister to school on time. He, however, paid no mind to my earlier start time and reasoned that if he was being nice enough to drive me to school every morning, I shouldn't complain about being "a few minutes late."

Every single morning of my seventh-grade year, I was ready and waiting by the front door on time. And every single morning, Chad would come down the stairs exactly fifteen minutes late, walk into the kitchen, pour himself a cup of black coffee, and walk toward the front door with a grin on his face while purposefully avoiding my fuming glare. He would then walk to the passenger side to open the door to his black Ford Bronco for me before slowly walking around to the driver's side.

Once in the car, Chad always glanced into the backseat to make sure his backpack was still where he left it from the previous afternoon (his motto was that homework was totally and completely unnecessary) before finally turning on the ignition. First things always first, he had to pick the right song. Chad was a true lover of good rock 'n' roll, and he knew I shared his love of Guns N' Roses, so he usually chose a song off of *Use Your Illusion I* or *II*, or on a good day, off of *Appetite for Destruction*. No matter the weather, the windows were then rolled down and the music was turned WAY up. With one hand jumping between the stick shift and the wheel and the other holding his cup of strong, black, "absolutely necessary" coffee, he somehow managed to back out of our driveway and turn onto the street toward his friend's house.

Every morning was like Groundhog Day. I'd always look at the clock on the dashboard and watch the minutes tick by with no worry from my brother. 8:14. The tardy bell would ring in one minute. Hooooooooonk.

Chad laid his hand on the horn until he saw the front door open. That was his loud and not-so-subtle signal to his football friend (and the neighborhood) that the ride to school had arrived.

The front door would open. Cape would appear and then walk out of his house and toward the passenger door. It would've been so much easier for me to get in the backseat, but Chad always insisted that I stay in the front. Once Cape had crawled around me and into the backseat of Chad's two-door Bronco, we resumed our drive to school. I'd glance at the clock. 8:16. I was officially late, again.

The two-lane curvy road that led to the junior school was Chad's version of a racetrack—his one free hand navigating quickly between the gear shift and the steering wheel. This was the point in the morning where, every single time and on the exact same curve, Chad would yell out, "Motherfucker!"

Cape and I would feign looks of concern and ask, "What's wrong?"

Chad would reply, "I spilled my damn coffee!" The coffee would, every time, spill onto his jeans along his left thigh, just below his left hand, which always held the black and absolutely necessary coffee.

At exactly 8:29, fourteen minutes after I should've been in class, we'd screech into the drop-off line at the junior school. With the windows still down and Guns N' Roses blaring at a deafening level out of the speakers, I'd throw open the door and run toward my classroom, which just so happened to be the classroom closest to the drop-off line. It also just so happened to be the room belonging to Señora Peraza, who preferred to keep the windows to her room open, giving everyone in the class a full view of my late arrival and, by the end of the year, a complete retrospective through the GNR musical library.

On mornings when Chad and Cape were in an especially good mood after a big football win, they'd add to my mortification by honking and yelling after me, "Have a wonderful day!" For an entire year, I arrived at school fifteen minutes late with hair looking like I had just jumped out of a wind tunnel and cheeks that were a deep shade of scarlet red, stained from embarrassment. In total, I missed twenty-seven hundred minutes of class that year. And I have my older brother to thank for my lack of Spanish verbal and comprehension skills.

While it was true that I may have only known "hola," "como estas," and "adios," my sacrifice didn't count for nothing. Chad filled my bilingual gap with something much more valuable—safety. The only way I was able to get out of his front seat every morning and run into class fifteen minutes late was because behind all the inconvenience was an intense and unbreakable sibling bond, rooted in the absolute knowledge that my brother would always, ALWAYS protect me. He'd protected me growing up, and he'd saved my life with the first transplant. And, even after all of that, he was being called on to lace up the gloves once again for the ultimate fight against my ruthless opponent. He'd been training for this his entire life.

Four years prior: Creak. Creak. Creak. All night long on the night before his stem cell donation process for the first transplant, the hardwood floor in the hallway outside our bedroom creaked under the weight of Chad's pacing. The shots were clearly working. The marrow deep in his bones ferociously ached and throbbed because it was being asked to produce a much higher number of stem cells than his marrow could comfortably hold. Since there were too many cells to fit in his marrow, the stem cells were starting to pop out into his blood stream, and that was what the doctors wanted, because now they could catch them.

The day after Chad stopped the shots, the doctors brought him into the apheresis room at MD Anderson. They put him in a bed and injected a very large needle in each arm. The doctors turned on the large apheresis machine located behind my brother's bed. I watched as his red blood left his arm and flowed through the clear tubing and into the big machine. The stem cells were extracted through a vigorous spinning process before the dizzy blood returned to my brother's body through the tube connected to the needle in his right arm. The doctors circulated Chad's entire blood volume six times through this amazing machine. It took six hours.

On Chad's day of donation, I was booked solid with pre-transplant appointments but had a twenty-minute break around Chad's fourth hour hooked up to the machine. I found the apheresis room on the seventh floor and searched for my brother among the sea of beds. After locating him in the back corner, I walked over to his bedside and pulled up a chair. How many times had he pulled up a chair to my hospital bed? He opened his eyes and saw me sitting next to his bed, staring at the huge needles taped into each of his arms. He carefully raised his right hand and lifted the earphone out of his right ear. I could just make out the opening guitar riff over the hum of the spinning of his cells. "Strutter." KISS. Of course.

Once Chad's stem cells had been collected, they were taken "downstairs" to be cleaned and frozen. When the time was right, these lifesaving cells would be thawed in a certain manner to coincide with the timing of my transplant day. The long donation had left him dizzy and weak. Huge bruises marked each of his arms from the supersized needles.

It took a few more days for the bone pain to subside, and he had a few more sleepless nights of pacing the halls. As I watched the technician take my brother's freshly collected stem cells away, I felt tears spilling on my cheeks. I hadn't been aware of the significance of that bag until I saw it in the hands of the unknown person who had been entrusted with safely delivering my life-saving cells to the appropriate person and place.

That bag of cells was the only thing that separated me from life or death. Those cells had come from my brother. And in that moment what struck me more than even the fear of the uncertain outcome of this risky transplant was that I knew for certain that those cells had been collected and frozen with pride and love inside each and every one of them.

I guess after having gone through the donation process once before, we assumed it would be the same the second time around. Tom, Chad, and I learned in our meeting with Dr. Andersson, however, that it would in fact be quite different. There would be no shots, no bone pain, no apheresis machines. Chad would come to MD Anderson in the early morning hours on the day of my transplant. He'd check in and be prepped for surgery. The doctors would put him to sleep, roll him onto his stomach, and then drill through his hip bones close to one hundred times. The holes made would be the passageway for the long needles that would pass through his hip bones and directly into his bone marrow, which once collected would be immediately cleaned and delivered to my hospital room.

On one level, I understood what Chad was about to experience. To date, I'd endured over thirty-six bone marrow aspirations/biopsies. I'd only had one hole drilled per side, though, not one hundred. I knew the soreness that I felt when I woke up, and I knew the bloody bandages that would need to be changed. I hated this for my brother, and I really hated that he wouldn't hesitate to do this for me, and I really, really hated that in order for me to live he would have to suffer.

Dr. Andersson then turned to Chad to go over some necessary pre-donation appointments. Because of the stress the donation procedure would put on his body, he had to submit to a boatload of tests before his surgery. I went with Chad to all his appointments, some we even shared. Chad wore a hospital ID band and received an MD Anderson medical record number.

Every time I saw him check in for an appointment or get stuck with a needle, I felt a heavy sadness, like The Cancer had dealt me a closed-fist blow to the heart. I was the patient, not my brother. Surely this was a violation of the rules of our fight, some sort of foul. I was the opponent, so keep the fight with me. The Cancer couldn't just pick a fight with everyone around me. It felt like a hit below the belt, but since there was no referee to call the foul, the match continued.

A few days later, after countless pricks and pokes and questions and monitors and wires and needles, Chad and I were officially ready. We'd completed all our testing and pre-transplant appointments. My hospital room was ready and waiting. My bag was packed. All that was left was to say goodbye.

Ri, you and I'd done this once before, but we both knew this time was different. I couldn't look you in the eyes and tell you not to worry. I couldn't say that everything would be okay. Instead, I asked you to take care of Ellie and Tommy. I told you they needed you. I promised you that I wouldn't give up and that I'd fight like hell. I told you that I loved you so very deeply and that you were the best risk I'd ever taken. I told you goodbye.

Then I walked into the library, where Ellie was watching Snow White and Tommy was playing in his play gym. I picked up my son and buried my head into his little shoulder. I inhaled deeply, begging myself never to forget the way his soft skin smelled. I smiled through my tears and told him that Mommy loved him very much. Then I told my little baby that I was just so sorry.

Never wanting to miss out, Ellie jumped out of her chair and came over to us.

"What's going on, Mommy?"

"Hi, sweetie. I was just saying goodbye to Tommy."

"Where are you going, Mommy?"

"Remember how I told you that Mommy would have to go into the hospital for a while to get that big germ bug out of my body? Well, it's time for me to go to the hospital."

"When are you leaving?"

"Right now."

"I don't want you to go, Mommy."

"I don't want to go, sweet girl. I want to stay here with you and Tommy and Riley. But I know I have to go so I can get better, and then we can have a lot of fun together once I get home."

"But I want to have fun with you now!"

"Me too, angel. But now I have to go. I want you to promise me that you will be strong. Take care of your brother. He'll need you to be a good big sister. Riley's here, and he's going to take care of you guys. Remember what we do if we ever get sad?"

"Wrap our arms around Riley's neck. His love always makes our hearts feel better."

"That's right. And Ellie—I want you to promise me one thing. It's very important. Can you promise me?"

"Yes, Mommy."

"I need you to promise me that you will always, always remember how much your mommy loves you. No matter where I am, I'll always be able to feel your love, and you'll always be able to feel mine."

"I promise, Mommy. I won't forget. When will you be back?"

Choking back a sob, I answered my little girl as honestly as I could and said, "I don't know."

"How can I plan our tea party if I don't know when you'll be home?"

"Well, sometimes we can't plan things. We just have to trust."

As if on cue, you walked into the room. Ellie saw you, and her face turned from worry to excitement.

"I can have a tea party with Riley! He loves crackers. He can take your seat."

"Yes, he sure can, my angel. He sure can."

# CHAPTER 14

# Nurse Jan

Dear Riley,

It was the 4th of July. In some other non-cancer universe, I was vaguely aware that the lake was full of people in red, white, and blue swimsuits celebrating America's independence and the freedom that came with being an American. Boats were being filled with gas and sunscreen was being applied. Music was turned up and beers were thrown down. The sound of WaveRunners zooming by filled my ears, or was that the IV pump as the rate of the drip on my meds was being turned up? Maybe if I didn't think about the world outside of my four walls on the eleventh floor at MD Anderson, it wouldn't be real. The ever-increasing pain meds were making the line between truth and fiction fuzzier and fuzzier.

"How's my patient doing today?" my chipper nurse asked as she skipped into the room.

I responded by slightly turning my head in her direction and pressing my thin lips together in a kind of "your cheerfulness is grinding my last nerve" way.

"Are you excited about the pole parade?" Nurse Cheery asked to no one in particular.

"The what?" Chad asked incredulously.

"The pole parade. It's a tradition on the eleventh floor. Every 4th of July, we give the patients red, white, and blue decorations and we let them decorate their IV poles. Then, at noon, the patients parade around the nurses' station. Get it? Pole parade!"

Oh no. Nurse Cheery had just hit Mr. Grumpy's limit. I knew Chad wouldn't be able to let that one slide. She had just served it up, and he couldn't wait to spike it down.

"Are you kidding me? This is a thing? Do people actually ENJOY this pole parade? You can just skip right over my sister's room when you're handing out the decorations. We will NOT be decorating any poles in this room. But thanks anyway." And then under his breath, I heard him mutter, "This is ridiculous."

Ri, I know it was wrong, but a half-laugh escaped my lips. I felt for Nurse Cheery as she backed out of our room, never to return again, but it just felt so good to laugh. The burst of emotion restarted my heart for a beat. I felt energy surge through my body.

It was the day before transplant day, otherwise known as day -1. The unspoken emotions were running high. My blood counts were bottomed out—straight 0.0s across the daily blood lab sheet. I literally didn't have one germ-fighting cell in my body. My entire life depended on the success of the following day. Chad was scheduled for surgery early the next morning. I knew his lack of holiday cheer was his way of mentally preparing. He had his pre-game face on. Freedom celebrations had no place in my hospital room, especially since I had none to celebrate.

I glanced across the room to the doorway leading into the hall. I saw flashes of patriotic colors streaming by like fireworks in slow motion. Apparently, the pole parade had begun. I couldn't bring myself to look away. Like a small child with a front row seat, I was mesmerized. Patient after patient, caregiver after caregiver, IV pole after IV pole, like floats proceeding down the designated parade route. Nurses cheered.

American flags waved. Medicine dripped. Patients smiled. I asked Chad to close the door.

I pressed the down arrow button on the side of my hospital bed. My body reclined into a flat position. For the thousandth time that day, I rolled my head slightly to the right so I could see the large canvas print proudly displayed on my window ledge. I smiled as I saw the picture of Ellie and Tommy lying across your big, long body. Ellie was caught mid-laugh. Tommy had his green Baba pacifier in his mouth, and you were looking straight into the camera, straight at me. I turned my head away from the windows and closed my eyes.

Ri, I knew how much you hated the 4th of July. The sound of the fireworks always sent you into the corner of my closet. The grand finale put you into a full-on panic. I remember our first 4th together. I was surprised at your fear and tried to comfort you by reminding you that you were free—free from the bad people who hurt you and free from pain. You were safe. You were with me.

Well, it was my turn in the corner of the closet. I hated that day. I hated not being one of those lake-goers whose biggest worry was how to keep their beer cold in the summer heat. I hated knowing that I couldn't be there to comfort you during the fireworks, and I hated not being able to be one of the patients outside my hospital room doorway, parading around and accepting gloved high fives from everyone they passed. But most of all, I hated living through a day of celebrating independence when my life was fully dependent on someone else.

I would only live because of my brother and his donation. I was at the mercy of my doctors and their brilliant minds. I would only regain a healthy immune system if my brother's cells gave me one. I would only be able to make it to the bathroom if my nurses helped me to the toilet.

Freedom? Independence? I'm with you, Ri. Those two words gave us no reason to celebrate.

The next morning was July 5th, 2010—transplant day. Chad was taken down to the operating room before the summer sun had even risen. The holes in his hip bones had been drilled, and his bone marrow had been harvested. Before Chad had even woken up from surgery, five people I'd never seen before carried my brother's bone marrow into my hospital room. Their names and undoubtedly impressive titles were stitched into their white lab coats in matching navy blue thread. White Lab Coat Number 1 read off the numbers listed on the soft clear bag that contained the bright-red marrow. White Lab Coat Number 2 verified the numbers on my hospital wrist band. White Lab Coat Number 3 confirmed the flow rate entered into the IV pump. White Lab Coat Number 4 was busy taking notes. White Lab Coat Number 5 looked in my direction and gave me a strained smile.

I heard the familiar squeak as Tom rose from the Murphy bed. His beard was getting longer by the day. There had been no time for shaving, no time for him to do anything for himself. I could tell he was exhausted. He was trying to be my caregiver and husband while also being present for Ellie and Tommy. He'd stay with me until the morning chemo was complete, and the doctors made their rounds, before driving to our Houston house to spend a few hours with you and the kids.

Our evenings were the time when Tom would fill me in on all the stories from the day—Ellie had a new tooth, Tommy was propping himself up on his hands and knees and rocking back and forth, you had buried your favorite tennis ball in the backyard, and no one could find it. I hated hearing these stories. They made y'all seem real.

White Lab Coat Number 3 asked me if I was ready. Even though I'd been through that same procedure before, part of me was unsure what to expect. I nodded. White Lab Coat Number 3 said, "Okay, here it goes. Good Luck." Luck? What was luck anyways? I was more and more unsure. I looked up at the bag holding the lifesaving bone marrow that had been in my brother's body not even an hour prior. The thick bright-red liquid slowly began to make its way down the clear IV tubing toward one of the three portals sewn into the left side of my chest.

I closed my eyes. I felt nothing. I heard nothing. No clapping. No cheering. No fireworks. Just…silence. The five white lab coats were speaking quietly amongst themselves. Tom squeezed my hand. White Lab Coat Number 1 said something to Tom. More silence. Then a jumble of soft footsteps as the white lab coats left my room. Tom put his hand on my head. I opened my eyes. The IV tube was solid red, solid Chad. I held my breath.

"Caroline, it's over."

Chad's voice came floating into my consciousness.

"You're now officially awesome."

I opened my eyes. How long had I been asleep? I looked over at my brother. He was sitting in a wheelchair. His face was paler than I'd ever seen it.

"You look awful," I told him.

"I actually feel great. I'm not sore at all."

Ahh. He was still high on the post-surgery drugs.

"I bet you do. Well, take it easy, because when the good stuff wears off, you're going to be really sore."

"Oh, I'll be juuuuust fine. I took enough hits in football to know how to handle a little pain."

Even though I knew the pain that was coming to him, I smiled. My drugged up, overconfident brother had just given me his new red bone marrow that was now becoming my new red boxing gloves. I now had the strength and protection I needed to deliver the ultimate punch against that relentless disease. I delighted in picturing myself introducing The Cancer to my brother's cells and seeing the fear on The Cancer's face as it prepared to be knocked the hell out.

I don't remember day +1. That rest day existed only in the number written on the dry erase board across from my bed. My day nurse updated my board daily with the correct date, the number of the day in my protocol, and any goals we may have had for the day. My goals had started out as: walk five times around the nurses' station, take a shower, discuss labs with doctor. But they'd turned into: sit up, breathe into tube, press nurse call button faster when throwing up.

The nurses continued to emphasize the importance of getting out of bed to walk the halls, no matter how horrible I felt. Sometimes my walks were just hanging on to Tom's neck and allowing him to drag my body along with my IV pole down the sterile hallway. Our walks took us by a long white wall, blank except for a singular framed photograph of a mountain peak surrounded by yellow wildflowers. This decorative photo was meant to raise patients' spirits, a reminder of the beauty and the light we were fighting to see again. After the pre-transplant chemo, whenever we approached that long white wall, I chose to keep my eyes focused on the white tiled floor until I knew the framed photograph was behind me and it was safe to look up.

The pre-transplant chemo had eaten holes in my esophagus. That was a problem for two reasons: I couldn't swallow any solid foods, and every time I threw up (which was all the freaking time), blood would come up and through the holes, causing me to lose too much blood. The pain was unbearable. The doctors had ordered a dose of Dilaudid to be automatically infused into my breaking body every fifteen minutes. The nausea was being controlled by regular doses of IV Ativan. The biggest mercy those two drugs gave me was the gift of total memory loss for hours, sometimes days at a time.

The post-transplant chemo started on day +2. My nurse came into my room at 4:30 a.m. She was covered head to toe in protective medical gear. Not one inch of her skin was exposed. I felt like an alien being studied by scientists. Her mask covered most of her face. Through the darkness, I couldn't see her eyes.

By day +4 of my post-transplant chemo, I was gone. My soul had left. I was hovering above my defeated body. The chemo had killed off all remaining fight. I no longer cared who won. I no longer cared about anything.

I began imagining my funeral. How many people would show up? Would you be allowed in the church? What songs would be played? It would have to be something different, something…me. I think "Patience" would be my song choice. I could just barely hear Axl's voice above Duff, Izzy, and Slash's melodic guitar riff. Would a gospel choir singing "Hallelujah" be too over the top?

I knew you were at home, waiting for me to walk through that door. I knew you were taking care of Ellie and Tommy, but you needed me to take care of you. I felt my maternal bond with my children coming apart like an unraveling rope. I'd told them about the invisible string that would always be connecting our hearts, no matter where we were or what we were doing, but that string was fraying, holding on solely by primal love fibers.

Just like the celebratory lake-goers on the 4th, if I didn't think about the three of you, maybe you wouldn't exist. Maybe my world in that hospital room was too separated from outside life. Maybe what happened in there had no effect or impact on anything or anyone not inside that room. You'd all be fine. It would be hard at first, but it would get easier. Ellie would hopefully have a few memories of me. Tommy would have pictures.

I'm sorry, Ri, but I just couldn't do it. I loved you but it wasn't enough.

My heart existed solely to pump blood. All emotion had been killed off by the poison they kept putting in my body. I fought. I promise I did. I fought for us—for Caroline and Riley. I fought for Tom and for my children and for the future memories I wanted to be there to witness. And I fought for me, for the scared little girl inside who wanted to survive and keep living. But I wasn't able to fight hard enough. The Cancer outlasted me.

I felt water on my pillow. Was the chemo leaking? I turned my head and felt a tear fall off my cheek. The still darkness of the early morning sky filled my sterile room. I felt Tom's shaking hand on top of mine. I looked up toward the soul-killing medicine and saw a figure beginning to come into focus. It was Nurse Jan.

"Caroline, it's me. It's Jan. Honey, can you hear me? Just squeeze my hand if you can hear me."

Squeezing required too much effort. My hand remained limp.

"Sweetie, I'm going to ask you something right now, and I know it's not what you want to hear, but I need to know. Are you still in this with me? Are you still willing to fight? I need to know, because I need to hang this last chemo bag, but I don't want to hang it until I know that you are in it with me.

"Three days ago, we made a pact. I promised I'd be here with you each day of this post-transplant chemo, and you promised you wouldn't give up. I know what this has done to your body. I see it on your lab reports, and I see it on your face. But I also know that you are a fighter, and I know how much you love Ellie and Tommy. And I know you also have Riley. Tom and I are right here with you. Caroline, hon, you have too much to live for, so do this with me. Please squeeze my hand and let me know you're still in this fight."

Ellie. Tommy. Riley. Earlier last week, Nurse Jan had stood in front of my large canvas print and asked about each of you. She knew your names. She knew Ellie's favorite book was *Goodnight Moon* and that Tommy couldn't fall asleep without his monkey blanket. Nurse Jan had a yellow Lab named Cody, so we traded funny dog stories. She knew I called you Goofball and that your greatest fear was the hairdryer. Nurse Jan had seen you. She'd seen my children. And she'd seen me.

Jan was now sitting on my bed. She was holding my hand in her own blue latex-covered one. I halfway opened my eyes. I saw Jan's compassion-filled eyes above the yellow protective mask that covered the rest of her face. The chemo was still hanging on the IV pole, waiting to be infused.

Tom's voice filled my head.

"Babe, I know you can do this. You have to do this. Please, Babe, please, do this for me, for us, for our family."

"Caroline, dear, I can only imagine how you feel right now, but, honey, your husband is right. You can do this. This is your last dose of this chemo. Just let me start this infusion, and then I promise, no more chemo. I'll stay right here by your side until it's finished. I'll be right here with you."

*I'm sorry, Ri. I tried. I really did. Please forgive me. Take care of Ellie and Tommy.*

I was talking to you, Ri, but I guess that, in my drugged-up, meshed, dream-like hospital room reality, I had spoken my truth out loud. The tears I had cried for the future with you and the kids and Tom that I was saying goodbye to fell onto my pillow. Now, all I had to do was nothing—keep my hand relaxed, don't tighten my fingers—and it would all be over. All I had to do was resist the reflex to squeeze back...

I looked into Jan's eyes. I found compassion. I looked into Tom's teary eyes. I found love. I felt my heartbeat. I felt my lungs fill with air. I looked at the canvas print. My heart surged. Goddamn it. I loved you all too much. I couldn't give up. I wanted to so badly. I wanted to make the struggle disappear. My plan to be your guardian angel had been a good one. I'd made peace with the idea. My floating soul above my sick body had already taken on wings; I just had to keep floating upward.

Jan's eyes had brought my soul down closer to its human form. Tom's eyes had brought it back into my body. Ri, your eyes, full of unconditional love and infinite wisdom, reconnected my soul and my heart. The choice was no longer mine. Maybe it never was.

There I was, alive and present in my body. All I had to do was hold on and pray. I had to let the medicine and The Cancer consume my body so I could build it back up. I had to feel so I could fight.

Nurse Jan asked again if I could squeeze her hand.

Chad's cells. Red boxing gloves. Delivering punches. Never giving up.

Tom. Ellie. Tommy. You.

Baby steps.

I squeezed Jan's hand.

## CHAPTER 15

# Mommy's Tennis Ball

**Dear Ri Rose,**

Do you remember that morning at the Brentwood dog park when Dixon and Keiko tried to play tug of war with your tennis ball? I was chatting with my dog park posse while trying to keep up with your intense focus on the tennis ball. Friends and laughter surrounded us in both the human and canine form, but you wanted nothing to do with anything or anyone except me and your beloved ball. I had to laugh whenever a new dog would trot up to you and you wouldn't even award them a sideways glance. Your eyes darted from me to the ball, me to the ball, me to the ball, just waiting for me to lift the plastic Chuckit! so I could maximize my throwing distance while keeping my hands germ-free.

It was like any other spring morning in Brentwood. The air was crisp, even though the marine layer hung heavy in the sky. I had my coffee in one hand, Chuckit! in the other. Anne was asking Chris about his love life or lack thereof while we watched Keiko trying to hump the new Goldendoodle who wanted nothing to do with this pound puppy.

Parker, the English Mastiff, had just run into the park, slobber flying in all directions, before plopping down at our feet exhausted. Your pals had given you friendly backside sniffs and you pretended they didn't exist. My southern hospitality gene cringed a bit, as it did every morning when you dismissed everyone around you, but the mother gene in me was beaming with pride.

My Chuckit! arm had begun to get tired when you dropped your ball at my feet. As I'd done for the past hour, I glanced down at your ball and had started to lower the Chuckit! when Dixon and Keiko appeared out of nowhere. Keiko distracted you briefly by trying to mount you while Dixon seized the moment and grabbed your ball in his mouth. Since you were twice the size of Keiko, his effort to latch on quickly failed, which gave you the opportunity to run after Dixon. Dixon's tail stood tall with pride. He wanted you to chase him, wanted you to engage. You see, Ri, that was how dogs played. That was what was considered fun for the canine species, yet you wanted no part in this canine carnival. You just wanted your ball back.

Once Dixon realized his final attempt at friendship had failed, he stopped running and waited for you to approach. You did so cautiously, unsure of the next move. Dixon stood very still. You came within two feet of your opponent and stopped. Neither of you moved a muscle. You locked eyes. No one blinked. No one looked away. You took one step closer. Dixon didn't move. I held my breath.

You took another step before turning it sideways to reach into Dixon's mouth to reclaim your ball. Dixon's tail began to wag. Yours didn't. You both gripped the ball and refused to let go. You began to shake your head. Dixon tightened his grip. You stepped backward and shook harder. Then harder still. In your final attempt, you shook with all your might until Dixon released his grip on the ball. You stumbled backward with the ball in your mouth. Keiko ran circles around the two of you and began to bark. Dixon turned his attention to Keiko and began to chase his willing friend. You stood frozen for a few seconds before you slowly turned around and cautiously returned to my side.

You held the ball in your mouth until you knew it was safe. Only then did you drop it at my feet, your intense stare returning to your face. I lowered the Chuckit! and threw the ball.

As I sat in my hospital bed, I found myself thinking about that morning. My eyes were darting between the canvas print of you and the kids to the white dry erase board displaying my daily goals: you and the kids, getting up to walk, you and the kids, completing my breathing exercises, you and the kids, hanging on one more day.

Weeks had passed and my blood counts remained 0.0. On day +14, I had developed a fever. Everyone had tried to conceal the seriousness of the situation from me, but there was no hiding that kind of worry. We did everything we could to overcome this foreign invader, even though I had no immune system in place to fight. My doctor prescribed high-dose IV antibiotics, and I prayed. I felt like a shell of a human, but at least I was feeling like something.

As the days passed with no improvement in my blood counts, fear, along with my newly renewed desire to return to my previous life, return to you, grew exponentially. It was the classic case of wanting what I couldn't have. The Cancer had my tennis ball—the image portrayed on my canvas print, you and the kids—and was holding on tight.

And then...

On day +18, Nurse Jan delivered the good news. "Hon, I have your labs, and I think you're going to like today's results."

Tom practically flew across the room and grabbed the daily blood results sheet out of Nurse Jan's hands.

"Your white count is 0.3! Babe! It worked!"

0.3. Three tenths of a something. It was a seemingly small number, but to us it was everything. 0.3 was the number that told us that Chad's cells had found their way into my bone marrow. My brother's cells had made themselves comfortable and gotten to work. His cells grew and multiplied and divided and then differentiated themselves into all the important components of a functioning immune system. 0.3. Hot damn. Ri, we did it.

Wait—we did it. It worked. This was good, right? It meant I'd live. It meant I'd be able to eventually come home to you and the kids. It meant our journey together wasn't over. Tom was jumping around the room while taking turns hugging Nurse Jan and me. I was happy, I think. It was just that…knowing I was going to live meant knowing that the pain and suffering wasn't over. It meant that it might even get worse before it got better. It meant that my perfectly imagined funeral was going to have to wait. It meant I was going to have to put on my big girl pants and finish what I'd started.

My blood counts rose exponentially each day. By day +23, I was able to do a full lap around the nurses' station. By day +26, I stopped throwing up. The holes in my esophagus slowly began to heal. My first bite of solid food was on day +27. On day +28, I allowed my eyes to brush past the framed photo of the snow-capped mountain, surrounded by the yellow wildflowers. I entertained the possibility…

After six and a half weeks in the hospital, I was told I was being discharged. The doctors said I could go home to sleep at night, but I'd need to return to the outpatient transplant floor each morning at 8 a.m. so I could do labs and be hooked back up to the IV and all the necessary fluids and medications. But I'd have my nights and evenings with you and the kids. My eyes darted back to the canvas print—you and the kids, my tennis ball. I was getting it back. And I was terrified.

The car ride home was quiet. Tom was just as focused on the road as he'd been the day we'd driven both our newborns home from the NICU. The sun hurt my eyes. All the cars seemed to be moving so fast. The sound of a horn caused me to jump in my seat. I felt anxious and nauseated. I began to sweat. The physical exertion of leaving the hospital and sitting upright for the ride home was a complete and total shock to my system.

We turned onto the street of our Houston house. I knew my canvas print, my tennis ball, you and the kids, was waiting for me. The difference was that the three of you wouldn't just be an image frozen in time. You'd be real beings in motion, and that required me to be a being in motion, and that would require energy I knew I didn't have.

The time had arrived. It was the moment I'd been waiting for, the moment I'd been fighting for—maybe even living for. I'd pictured that moment a million times in my mind. I saw myself walking through the front door and having you run between my legs. I saw Ellie running up to me and jumping into my arms and talking a million miles a minute about all the things she did while I was away. I saw Tommy's eyes light up when he saw me for the first time.

He'd reach out his little arms and squeal for his mommy to hold him. I'd hold my babies, one in each arm, while telling them how much I loved them and that I'd never leave them ever again. And my dream was about to become a reality.

Tom put the car into park. He came around to the passenger side to open my door and help me out. He put his arm around my waist and supported me as I walked up to the house. I looked through the glass windows on either side of the front door. No little faces pressed up to the glass. I stopped. I needed a moment, needed a breath. I closed my eyes and filled my lungs with the heavy and humid Houston air. Better. I opened my eyes. I couldn't help but look again to see if any eagerly awaiting small faces had appeared in the glass windows. No faces, just one wet black nose. Just you.

I took the last few steps in one giant leap. My hand closed around the doorknob, and I flung the heavy wooden door open. And just like that, you were against my legs and my body was folded down on top of yours. I sank to the floor and wrapped my arms around your neck.

You shook and pawed me over and over again. It was better than I'd imagined because it was no longer pretend—it was really you.

I heard Ellie before I saw her. She was running down the staircase yelling, "Tommy, Mommy's home! Mommy's home!" Her bright-pink bow bobbed on top of her head as she ran as fast as her new smocked dress would allow. Never before seen gold beads hung around her neck. Her hair was longer and blonder. Front teeth had fully grown in. This was not the child I'd left almost two months prior. I was scared to hug her.

Ellie ran up to me and stopped short of giving me a hug. She wanted to show me her artwork from her week at a summer nursery school. Wait—she went to nursery school? I tried to feign interest in her finger painting, but all I wanted to do was wrap her up in my arms. Could I just reach out and touch her? Would she allow that or yell, "Stranger danger!"

Before I could decide what to do, Francis walked into the room holding Tommy. My little six-month-old was now eight months. His entire body was so much larger than I remembered. He was sucking on a piece of fruit. I didn't even know that it was safe for him to have fruit. Francis was singing an unfamiliar song to him, and he was sloppily clapping along. When he saw me, he stopped clapping. I put my arms out to hold him. Francis had just begun to pass him over to me when a loud wail filled the room. His arms reached up and wrapped around Francis's neck. He had a death grip on her and wasn't going to let go. In that moment, my son had no idea who I was.

Ellie was still talking. She was now showing me how she was tall enough to ride you like a horsey. As always, you patiently waited until she was on to the next thing before plopping down on the marble floor.

"Mommy, come with me. Come with ME, Mommy! I have a surprise for you! Daddy helped me and Tommy sort of helped, but he can't really do anything so really, it's my surprise."

Ellie reached up and took my hand. I shuddered at the touch. It seemed so familiar and yet so jarring all at the same time. She pulled me into the dining room. I looked up and saw the "Welcome Home, Mommy" homemade banner hanging in front of the antique mirror. A plate of cupcakes had been set out on the table. Ellie beamed with pride.

"Do you like it, Mommy? It's for you. It's your welcome home party!"

"Oh, sweet girl, I absolutely love it. Thank you so, so much."

"If you like it, why are you crying?"

"Well, these are happy tears. I just missed y'all so much and am so happy to see you!"

"We missed you too, Mommy. Sorry that Tommy isn't happy to see you. He just only wants Francis or Kiki or Dad. He'll probably want you too, someday."

"That's true. He probably will want me someday."

I sat down at the table. I felt you lie down on top of my feet. Ellie was busy telling everyone where to sit. I looked over at Tommy. He was staring at me with his big blue eyes. I smiled at him and held out my arms one more time. He didn't respond. Minutes passed, or maybe it was seconds. Then, slowly, cautiously, he reached his arms out for his mommy.

Being in the hospital was so much easier than being home. Being an inpatient meant being cared for by others, home meant caring for others. For weeks, I'd been free to focus only on myself while all my immediate needs were met by the doctors, nurses, hospital staff, and room service menus. All I had to do was push my nurse call button or pick up the phone and dial zero. Home didn't have that nurse call button. I WAS the nurse call button.

"Mommy, Tommy took my stuffed animal!"

"Mommy, can you come outside with me?"

"Mommy, want to have a tea party?"

"Mommy... Mommy... MOMMY!"

It was like a version of Chinese torture. Ellie's innocent voice pierced my heart. She wanted so much from me, so much that I couldn't give her. I didn't have the energy to mediate a dispute between my two children. I didn't have the strength to go outside. I couldn't bear to sit through a tea party. I couldn't offer my body, only my heart.

"Sweetie, Mommy doesn't feel well. Maybe we could just sit and read a book?"

"You never feel well. Forget it. I'll go ask Francis."

And this was how it went, day after day.

A friend had written me a "welcome home" card and offered up her encouragement by reminding me that God wouldn't give me more than I could handle. Well, I called bullshit. It was too much and I couldn't handle any of it. I was exhausted. I'd been keeping Tommy's monitor by my bed at night so I could hear him when he woke up. I was determined to be the first face he saw in the mornings. I treasured those few moments together in the early morning. My little boy was still groggy from sleep. We would sit together in the white lounge rocker, just the three of us. You always woke up and followed me into the nursery. The sunlight was just starting to peek through the curtains, and the house was blissfully quiet. And then…

Tommy would wake more fully and feel the hunger pain in his stomach. His face would crumple, and the cries would come as suddenly as a Texas summer thunderstorm. His cries would wake Ellie and Ellie would wake the whole house. All at once, Tom, Mom, and Francis would be up and swarming like bees around me.

Francis would try to heat up Tommy's bottle. Tom would try to get Ellie's breakfast ready. Mom would make my sack lunch of the only foods she knew I could tolerate to take to the hospital. I would realize I was running late for my daily infusion. Tommy would be taken from my arms. I'd leave the house and drive myself back to my safe place.

By the time I arrived home, the bedtime drill would already be in full swing. My children had become used to me not being a part of the evening routine. I felt like that kid in the eighth-grade cafeteria trying to find a spot at the cool kids' lunch table. I found that the best chance I had of inserting myself into this pattern was to wait patiently in the white lounge rocker for one of my children to allow me to read them a bedtime story. I tried to anticipate what story they might enjoy but always came up short. I never knew the funny way Daddy would say the characters' names or the goofy voices he used while reading aloud. I thought only the lamp should be turned on, but apparently the room required full overhead lighting.

Ellie no longer slept with certain stuffed animals but absolutely had to have never-before-seen stuffed zoo creatures. I never knew how to comfort Tommy when he cried. Our rhythm was out of sync. I felt like an outsider with everyone—except with you, Riley Rose.

Two weeks after being home, Dr. Andersson surprised me by saying I could take Sunday off from my infusion and stay home all day. I know he thought he was giving me a luxurious gift, but I panicked. All day at home? But what about my eight hours of "other people are taking care of me" time? Who would give me my warm blankets and ask *me* how *I* was doing? Was he sure I could miss a day of my blood counts being checked? Shouldn't I come in, just in case?

The first Sunday at home began in the same manner. Tommy cried and I greeted him with a smile. He grew hungry and woke the whole house. Ellie wanted me to take her to the zoo and was despondent when I told her I couldn't. By 8 a.m., I felt like a total failure.

I was tired. So. Very. Tired. I wanted to sit downstairs with Ellie and Tommy but had already used up my daily quota of energy. I slowly climbed the stairs, my heavy anchor of mom guilt seemingly trying to pull me back down toward my children with each step. You helped me carry the weight of my shame by following me up the stairs.

I shuffled into my bedroom and closed all the curtains. I pulled down the covers and crawled back into bed. You jumped up and gingerly stepped over me to your normal spot next to the side of my too thin body. I closed my eyes. I felt your muzzle fit between my chin and shoulder. Like a puzzle piece, we still fit together perfectly. I seemed to be a mismatch with everyone around me, except with you. We were still Caroline and Riley, Riley and Caroline.

I spoke to you out loud, or maybe it was a prayer clothed in a one-sided conversation.

*Ri/God, everyone seems to want so much, to NEED so much from me, yet I have nothing to offer. I can give them nothing except my unconditional love from afar. I have that to give because that is what I have been given, by you, Riley Rose.*

My thoughts drifted back to my days of riding horses. I counted the minutes until the dismissal bell rang at 3:30 and I could run to the school pick-up line. A day of being around teachers, friends, and people in general had drained me. I needed real connection. I needed to be filled up, recharged. I needed Brimstone.

Every single day, Mom would pick me up from school and drive me straight to the barn. And every single day, Brimstone would be waiting. The two of us had turned into quite the little pair on the horse show circuit, winning class after class and even earning a state ranking in our division. Of course, I loved hanging all the blue ribbons up outside his stable door in the beautiful wooden barn, but more than that I just loved Brimstone. I loved putting my forehead to his and feeling happy. I loved that he never judged me. I counted on the fact that he would be happy to see me no matter what mood I was in or how tired I was or what I looked like. All he asked was that I show up for him and, in return, he showed up for me.

Ri, you reminded me of Brimstone. You were even both physically similar, with your white coloring and your big black noses. You both had an endearing goofy quality that people were drawn to. You both were beloved by those who had the privilege of getting to know you, and I felt the pride of knowing you'd chosen me. You both had earned my trust, and I'd earned yours, and you both were the only two creatures I knew for certain would never let me down. Despite our best efforts, humans hurt each other. Animals, on the other hand, never do.

God, please tell me. How was I going to do this? Would I ever be strong enough to be able to give my children what they needed, what they deserved? Would they have emotional trauma from this past year and need intensive therapy? Would Ellie grow up and go through a rebellious Goth stage and wear black lipstick? Would Tommy be angry and bitter and hate me forever? Was that what I fought for? Would we all have been better off if I'd not squeezed Nurse Jan's hand that day when it would've been so easy to just let go? Did The Cancer take away all chances of happiness for my family?

I felt your lungs expand next to my legs. I felt your heartbeat against my arm. Your nose muzzled in closer. I looked at you more closely and saw you had your tennis ball between your paws, the ball we both fought so hard to win back. And I noticed you were content. You were happy in that second, because right then, right there, we were together, and we were okay. We were okay.

Ri, was I dying? Being there, in that bed at home in the Houston house with you by my side, I realized that I was NOT safe. I may never feel safe ever again. Remission didn't mean cured. The Cancer and death were hand in hand, lurking in the shadows of my fearful soul.

As if in acknowledgment of this looming threat, you adjusted your position by placing your head onto my stomach. And that was the thing, Ri. You saw it, you felt it, and you fell into it. You acknowledged it. You accepted it. You accepted me.

The battle with The Cancer had been me staying in the ring and fighting like hell. But, Ri, I was tired. I needed to step out of the ring and gather my strength. I needed time to be honest about the reality of my life. As much as I wanted to be, I was no longer in control. Maybe I never was. I knew I had to surrender and accept my limitations, but how did I relinquish control while staying in the fight?

When I did gather my strength and get out of bed, I knew I would come face to face with the people I loved the most in the world. I would put on a smile and tell everyone I was doing well, because that was what they wanted to hear. That was what they NEEDED to hear, and I would give that to them. I looked down and saw some gray whiskers surrounding your nose that I hadn't noticed before, and I had the thought that you were dying. Maybe we were all dying. Maybe that was the point, to acknowledge it and then use that truth to live our best damn lives.

Ri, for you, there was no yesterday, no tomorrow, just the here and the now. You had fully accepted what was lurking in the shadows and were at peace with whatever happened. I wrapped my arm around your back. I heard the kids' voices downstairs. Guilt rose up until your breath knocked it down. Who knew what tomorrow would bring?

I didn't even know what the next half hour would hold, but I guess for that moment all I really needed to know, all I really was able to know, was that we were all okay.

I closed my eyes and fell into a dreamless, restful sleep.

CHAPTER 16

# Deepest Level of Right

Dear Ri Rose,

"Mommy, I'm scared," Ellie said as her grasp on my arm tightened.

"I know, sweet girl, but your friends will be so happy to see you," I replied, trying to reassure my nervous three-year-old.

"Are Will and Tara going to know who I am?"

"Your friends will remember you. I promise."

"Promise?"

"Pinky," I replied as I held out my hand to link our pinky fingers, our way of committing our promises to each other.

Here I was, a thirty-three-year-old mom with a four-month-old immune system walking my daughter into the first day of her new year of preschool. Of course, the rest of the kids had already been in school for months while we were in Houston.

"Can Riley come in with us?" Ellie asked with imploring eyes.

"No, angel, but he's happy waiting for us in the car."

"Okay, but maybe I should rub his head so I can be super brave, just in case."

I tried to hide my smile. "I think that's a great idea. Let's go rub Ri's head."

Ellie slowly released her grip on my arm and walked around to the back of my gray Yukon. The back window was popped open as it always was when you were in the car, Ri Rose. I lifted Ellie up so she could reach her little arm through the large opening. You calmly looked up at us and moved your head a little closer so Ellie could reach you. I held on tightly to her waist as she stretched her arms out a little farther before lowering her hands onto the top of your head and starting to rub in a circular motion.

"Wow, Mommy. That really works. I feel braver already."

I lowered Ellie down from the back of the car while giving you an appreciative wink and once again took her hand in mine.

After shouting, "Bye, Goofy! Thanks for the courage!" Ellie guided me toward the brown wooden gate that separated the parking lot from the inside of the preschool.

As I reached up to pull the child-proof lever on the top of the gate, I happened to glance back over my shoulder. A little girl and her mother were standing near my car. The little girl's cheeks were red, and her eyes were puffy from crying. Her mother looked across the parking lot and made eye contact with me. I knew exactly what she was asking. I gave permission with a slight nod of my head. The mother then reached down and lifted her little girl up into the back of my car so her child could also rub your head. And, thus, a tradition was born.

Having you become the "good luck charm" of the preschool parking lot helped me feel less guilty about Ellie and Tommy missing the first two and a half months of the school year due to our time in Houston. I know, I know. Ellie was only three, and Tommy couldn't even walk yet. Worrying about Ellie missing a few months of the half-day three-year-old program and Tommy missing two mornings a week of the infant/toddler class might seem silly. But to me, in that period of time, it felt like my absence had deprived them of one of the most important and formative years of their lives.

Much to everyone's great surprise, most of all my own, I had chosen the one preschool in Pasadena that was the antithesis of the conservative and traditional nursery school I had attended as a child. I was used to smocked dresses with tights and shoes with buttons. We were taught to sit still, to raise our hands, and to always color inside the lines. We walked in a line and got in trouble if we got our dresses dirty. Choosing Pacific Oaks for Ellie and Tommy was one of the most rebellious things I'd ever done.

When Tom and I toured the Pasadena preschools while I was still pregnant with Ellie (apparently, I was already late getting her name on the waiting lists), we made the normal rounds through the local church preschool programs. We listened to the schedules and the rules and the expectations placed on two-, three-, and four-year-olds. I smiled, nodded, and joined the other parents in trying to impress the admissions committee. And I left each tour feeling like I'd been placed in shackles. This wasn't the path I wanted for my children.

And then I heard about Pacific Oaks. I was at the house of one of my newer friends. This new friend had seen me driving around town with my back window open and a large Lab casually hanging out in the back. She introduced herself to me in the Target checkout line. I immediately knew I loved her style. She invited us both over to her house the following week.

You were supposed to play with her dog while my new friend and I had a glass of wine and got to know each other. I knew exactly how that doggie play date would go so was not surprised at all when you completely ignored her eager black Lab and instead chose to sit by my feet at the grown-up table. Her human children were home and impressed me with their confidence. My new friend equally impressed me with her parenting style. She valued her kids' opinions and their individuality. I asked her where her children went to preschool. She picked up the phone and arranged my tour.

I loved Pacific Oaks from the get-go. The entire parking lot was shaded by gorgeous trees, which meant I could park in any parking space and you would be cool and comfortable for hours. The school was in a lovely old neighborhood of Pasadena. Each class was based in an old Craftsman-style home with a large, low-fenced yard extending out from each house, and so the classes were called "yards." Shady Lane, the quaint main "street," ran through the middle of the yards.

Walking into this campus felt like taking a deep breath of peace, love, and acceptance. I looked at the kids. They were dirty. They were wet. They weren't wearing their shoes. And, Ri, they were HAPPY. Teachers were called by their first names. The sound of music was coming out of most of the houses. Kids were digging tunnels in the sand and adding water to see how they could connect the canals they created. Teachers were down in the sand with the kids and encouraging them to think about problem-solving in creative ways.

I saw all skin colors, all hair types, all different family configurations. Many kids had two moms or two dads. Some kids even had one parent with an egg or sperm donor. And you know what? I knew, beyond a shadow of a doubt, that I'd found my people.

By a miraculous stroke of luck, we were accepted to Pacific Oaks. Ellie started the infant/toddler program when she was nine months old. Coming from my traditional nursery school training, I was expecting our two hours twice a week to be filled with educational and informative tidbits for both the infants and the caregivers. The program started at 9:30 a.m., so I dressed Ellie in her monogrammed bloomers and matching top that tied in the back. We arrived at exactly 9:25. We were the first to arrive. 9:40—three other caregiver/child combos had arrived. Finally, by 10:00, most of the class was present, but nothing had happened. We were all just sitting on the floor, watching our infants crawl toward different objects and put them in their mouths. Sherry, one of our teachers, came and sat by me. She quickly introduced herself while never taking her eyes off the drooling child before her.

"Wow, isn't it just fascinating?" Sherry asked.

"Isn't what fascinating?" I replied with confusion.

"Just watching them, seeing what they gravitate toward and observing their little brains in motion."

What?

"Yes, it's...fascinating. But, Sherry, when does it start?" I asked.

"When does what start?"

"The class."

"Oh, well, this IS the class. We just learn so MUCH from these little beings."

Oh. My. Lord. What had I gotten myself into? Maybe there was some value in learning to color in between the lines.

And you know what, Ri? Fast forward two years from that first day to the day in the parking lot when you became the unofficial Pacific Oaks good luck mascot—I got it. I totally, 1,000 percent got it. As my one other traditional-turned-hippie friend Susan likes to say, I now drink the Kool-Aid. I am in—hook, line, and sinker.

Coming back from Houston was tough. I left Pasadena weak and broken and flew back five months later "all put back together." But, Ri, here's the thing. When I left Pasadena, my body was weak and broken, but my heart was still whole. When I returned home, my heart had been broken and my body was far from being put back together.

Everyone was so eager for me to be better, for me to be okay, that they willed me to be healed. They wanted me to be better. They needed me to be cured.

In Houston, I'd looked frightful. My skin was gray, and I was basically a skeleton. My scarves slid off my smooth, bald head. I hunched over when I walked because standing up straight had taken too much energy. My kids had rarely bathed, and our use of electronics skyrocketed. I'd been hanging on by a thread, just trying to survive. But see, in Houston

I was a cancer patient. I was sick. I had an excuse. However, in Pasadena, I wasn't.

I forced myself to get dressed. I wore stylish knit hats that stayed in place. I stood up straighter when I saw someone approaching. My kids were still dirty, and the screen time was still double what it should have been, but I hid it well. I perfected my smile and my reply of, "I am feeling great!" In Pasadena, I gave the outward appearance of being better, being recovered, being strong. If only that had been true.

Most of my Pasadena friends welcomed me back with open arms. They asked how I was feeling and then invited me out to drinks. But not my PO friends. They welcomed me back then asked when they could bring dinner. Albeit, a vegan dinner, but that made me love it even more.

See, Ri, these friends from PO knew Caroline the Cancer Patient. They knew the Caroline who wore whatever the hell she could throw on before leaving the house. They'd been there with me in infant/toddler as I rocked my four-month-old baby in my cancer-ridden arms as I watched my two-year-old playing with the wooden blocks. They sat with me as we observed our infants learning to crawl, and they sat with me now as I observed my own infant immune system learning how to fight. They were with me in the trenches and knew that it was impossible to dig oneself out alone. They let me be whoever I needed to be and that allowed me to begin to heal. The Pacific Oaks culture of understanding and acceptance was more than just a philosophy. It was their way of life, and I was all-in on loving it.

Ri, all my life I've done what I have thought others wanted me to do. I've studied hard and worked hard and played hard. I've gone to the right schools and made the right grades and worn the right clothes. I never got a tattoo or an inappropriate piercing (well, excluding that one time in Cancun when I got an upper ear piercing and a hot dog for the price of one, but since I don't remember it—and my piercing got infected, forcing me to take it out the next day—let's just say that doesn't count).

I think something was happening to me, Ri. I was learning that there were different "levels of right," and that when I chose the deep-down right, the right that I couldn't deny, I chose that school. I chose those people. I chose my kids. I chose Tom. I chose us. I chose me. It was now about my kids and their futures, and you know what? It was also about me and finding the community in which I would feel safe enough to be able to try on my true authentic self. Somewhere, somehow, listening to and honoring that deepest level of right had given me the insight and courage to say no to the conforming and yes to the finding my own sweet way.

And do you know who I have to thank for that? You. See, you weren't exactly the Lilly Pulitzer kind of breeder dog that one would normally bring into the family. You were a little rough around the edges, but you know what? So was I, and so were my children. And I was so damn proud of that fact because having a little bit of texture meant you were courageous, you were independent, you were celebrating the perfect being God made you to be. So, thank you, Ri, for paving the way for different. I still have not gotten that tattoo I've always wanted, but I did do right by my kids by putting them in a place to learn love and acceptance. For that, Ri Rose, I say thank you.

I walked over to the sandbox where Ellie, Tara, and Will were digging a path for the toy tractor.

"Ellie, are you going to be okay if I leave you and go home to check on Tommy?"

"It's OK, Mommy. We still have to put all this sand into the big truck."

"Oh good, sweet girl. That makes me so happy. Have so much fun. I'll see you in two hours."

"Okay, Mommy. Bye!"

As I was walking back toward the brown gate that led to the parking lot, I felt a tightness in my throat. Tears were welling up in my eyes. I loved that school so much, and it felt so amazing to be back. I knew my daughter was in the most loving environment and with the most amazing teachers, but I still couldn't help but feel that for the past five months I'd deprived my precious little girl of love: both the school's love and mine.

I opened the brown gate and walked over to the back of my car. You were there, patiently waiting. You looked up at me with a questioning expression. Through my tears, I told you she was great, that she didn't cry at all when I left. Satisfied, you lowered your head and resumed your nap. I stood there for a moment before reaching my arm into the back of my car and rubbing your head.

CHAPTER 17

# Bravo and Babas

**Dear Goofball,**

Ri, I think I may have failed my three-year-old son. Tommy's dentist wanted me to take away the pacifier, but I couldn't bring myself to do it. Tommy was a great napper—he loved his bed, zero complaints. When it was 1 p.m. and time to get in his crib, his pacifier, Baba, was waiting for him, and he knew his crib was the only place he was allowed to have it.

Nap time was sacred. The ritual of it, the quiet of it. Tommy was so utterly comforted by his big blue Baba, like everything was right in the world. I loved to watch his little red cheeks cave in with each hard suck and puff back out on the relax. The Baba was Tommy's version of my beloved Bravo reality TV. Immersing ourselves in the comfort of our Babas seemed to be the only time we would truly relax into two hours of tranquility.

And I knew from experience, when Baba went away, that peace would definitely be threatened. Goofball, I'm pretty sure you remember the day when we were in Texas visiting my parents and I decided it was time to take Ellie's Baba away. She was three and a half and by all accounts too old for a pacifier. I told Ellie that it was time to say goodbye to her Baba. I may have also told her that it was the kids who kept their pacifiers past age three and a half that grew up and had to wear braces for the rest of their lives. Not my proudest parenting moment, but sometimes the Invoking Fear tactic was the best way to get results.

Ellie thought about her Babas (while most likely pondering a lifetime of braces) before telling me she'd made a decision. She was ready to give up her Babas, but she didn't want to throw them away. Instead, Ellie was going to give them to her grandfather, Hoppy, so he could take her Babas to work at the hospital and pass them out to all the sick little boys and girls who really needed them.

So, the next morning, Ellie woke up before my dad left for work and gave him a Ziploc bag full of her Babas. Dad accepted the collection of used pacifiers and assured Ellie they'd help many little children feel much, much better. I held my daughter's hand as we watched Hoppy carry the bag of Babas with him out the door. I felt Ellie's hand shaking a bit in mine. I turned to give her a hug, but she pulled away and went to lie on the tile floor next to you.

I was prepared for a morning filled with tears of regret, but Ellie surprised me with the speed at which she forgot about the missing Babas. The rest of the morning passed uneventfully.

And then…it was nap time.

I was exhausted, as I always was after a few hours of life, and needed my two hours of restorative quiet. So I told Ellie it was time for her to get in bed for her nap. Ellie followed my direction and put on her PJs before climbing into bed. And then…the screaming began.

"I can't take a nap! I miss my Babas! I can't sleep without them! I'll never be able to sleep ever again!" And so it went for an hour and a half. Ri, I tried. I really, really tried to hang in there so Ellie could tire herself out to the point of falling asleep in my arms, but my daughter's strength and determination were matching her generosity of spirit, which compelled her to give away her Babas in the first place, and she did NOT back down. She wore me down until I finally said, "Okay, I won't make you sleep, but I do need you to lie here quietly for the next hour so that Ri and I can go lie down and rest."

"But, Mommy, what am I going to do for an hour? There's nothing to do in here."

"Well, you could sleep," I suggested.

"But I TOLD you. I can't sleep without my Babas."

"I know, sweet girl, but I'm giving you a choice. You can either sleep or you can lie here quietly while I nap."

"But I don't want to do either of those things."

"I understand that, but these are your choices."

"But, Mommy, it's not fair! I miss my Babas! I want my Babas back! I need them more than the sick boys and girls. Oh, why did I give them away? Mommy! Please get my Babas back!"

I had a choice to make. I could be the good mommy who stood her ground and taught her daughter that sometimes life was just not fair, and that even though I wished it was, better to learn that hard lesson sooner rather than later. OR—I could be the bad mommy and hand over the remote to the TV, so she could watch a few shows in blissful silence and allow me my sacred quiet time.

Without much hesitation, I handed Ellie the remote.

The two-hour midday quiet time for Mommy and Ri and the two-hour electronic screen time for Ellie was born. In my moment of weakness, I'd started a pattern of excessive screen time for my young child so I could have my two hours in the middle of the day in bed, with you and Bravo. I was putting my oxygen mask on first so I could assist my younger passengers. I knew I was doing the right thing for me, but I couldn't help but think that I was sacrificing my daughter's developing brain in return for my health and happiness.

One of my hesitations about taking Tommy's pacifier away was because I feared the same thing would happen for him. His body-strengthening nap time would be replaced with potentially brain-damaging excessive electronic time. After failing in this department so miserably with Ellie, I was at least honest enough with myself to admit that I wouldn't even really try to do better the second time around. Hadn't the damage already been done?

But maybe too much time spent on electronics wasn't the worst thing in the world. I was killing it in other areas. I'd made the homemade vegan sugar-free flax seed muffins for snack last week. Ellie had seaweed in her lunch box yesterday. I'd been to the farmers market twice in the past month and had even started to buy raw milk for the kids. I'd tried some bone broth and bought a bread maker to bake our own bread. No matter that no one in my family ever ate a bit of this good-intentioned nourishment, I was putting it in front of them. All this effort to provide healthy food for our bodies had to count for something.

By this point in my children's lives, I'd accepted the fact that I was not a "normal" mommy. By trial and error, I'd discovered the undeniable fact that my energy level was that of an eighty-year-old woman. I'd tried the kids' museums and after an hour was back home in bed. The zoo was fun for the first half hour, which was about the time my energy tank hit empty. Over time, my kids began to accept that their mommy didn't do the things other mommies did because she needed to rest. And bless their little hearts, that was just what they did. They accepted it.

Their cooperation, however, didn't relieve any of my mom guilt. I was well aware of the fact that while my kids and I were home in bed with TVs and iPads turned on for hours at a time, other moms were out with their kids at a park or museum or some other child life-enhancing location. I developed such shame over this 1 p.m. to 3 p.m. mandatory rest/electronic time that I began to approach this two-hour window with anger—at myself and anger at my body.

Why, by lunchtime, did I always feel like I'd just pulled an all-nighter? I had no more energy left to give. If I pushed it and stayed to eat lunch on Shady Lane with Ellie's preschool friends and their moms, my throat would inevitably begin to get sore and scratchy, the sure sign my body would give me that it needed a break. Why couldn't my children and I stay and play with the normal moms and non-electronic-addicted kids after school? Why were we forced to come home and screen-time up?

Ri, you and I both knew the answer, and it was unfortunately simple. You and I understood that The Cancer may have left my body, but it hadn't left my life.

And then, God revealed a little bit of truth to me through my friend Mona. I'd just undergone sinus surgery number four and was home enduring this particularly painful recovery. It was around 2:30 p.m. on a sunny spring afternoon in Pasadena when the doorbell rang. My initial thought was—crap! I hope that didn't wake up the kids! But then I remembered that no one was actually sleeping. It took six months to finally take the dentist's recommendation, but Tommy had finally given all his Babas to the garbage truck, so we were all in the middle of "quiet" (AKA screen) time.

When you heard the doorbell, you barked while jumping off the bed. I usually didn't get out of bed for anyone or anything during my two hours with the Real Housewives, counting on your deep bark to scare away any unwelcome guests, but Mona knew you well and wasn't fooled by the threatening sounds coming from inside the house. The doorbell rang a second time. Ugh. I begrudgingly got out of bed. You moved to the side so I could open the front door.

"Hi, friend. How ya feeling?" Mona asked, standing on the front porch with a small brown paper bag in her hand and grin on her face.

"Hey, Mona. I'm okay. How are you?"

"I'm great. Listen—I've been thinking of how to help you recover from this surgery and all those lethal antibiotics they put into your body. You know they're just eating up all your good bacteria, so you need to replenish the good stuff. I spoke to my lady over at the health food mart, and she was able to find a SCOBY mother, so I brought it to you!" Mona exclaimed as she handed me the small brown bag.

"Huh?" It was all I could think to say.

"Now, listen, it's really important to remember to remove the SCOBY baby layer off the top when you brew a new batch of kombucha, so it doesn't merge with the SCOBY mother on the bottom. At our house, we keep our babies and mother in glass jars in the kitchen. It's super easy."

"Wow. Yeah. That's amazing. I've been wanting one of these, umm, babies. That really was so thoughtful of you. Thanks, Mona."

"It's the mother, not the baby. And really, no problem at all. I gotta run and get the kids to their Mandarin lessons, but I'll check on you tomorrow. Bye!"

And with that, my friend was already back in her car and on her way to the next activity for the day.

I reached my hand down and steadied myself against your back. I needed to sit down, but instead of turning around to walk back inside, I walked outside and sat in the chair on our front porch.

Goddamn it, Ri. I knew my friend had the purest of intentions, but that Scooby whatever baby thing had made me feel like the most horrible person and parent in the world. While my friend was out there doing everything right, I was in there doing everything wrong.

Her kids were probably going to grow up to be well-adjusted, trilingual, musically inclined, athletic scholars who became politicians or doctors or human rights activists, while mine were on the track to become video game connoisseurs. I'd tried so hard to do the right thing, but somehow I ended up feeling like a total and utter failure.

Ri Rose, I was absolutely terrified that Ellie and Tommy were going to see me in bed two hours a day and think that was normal. I worried they were going to grow up and do the same. I was scared they'd model their behaviors after mine and not realize that I was doing it because my body was not a normal body. They didn't understand that their mom HAD to do this for her health because she'd been through years and years of crazy stuff being done to her body and was anything but normal. But you know what? I was maybe most afraid that they'd understand.

How did I tell my kids that their mommy could and couldn't do certain things because their mommy's body was different from everyone else's body? How did I stress the importance of putting my health first without alarming them? How did I rid myself of the guilt I felt for failing them in so many ways? My children had so readily accepted my shortcomings. So, Ri, why couldn't I?

In that moment, sitting on our front porch with you now at my feet, I listened to the background noise of Mary Poppins singing out of the TV and telling us to, "Feed the Birds." I heard Ellie and Tommy's shared laughter. They must be watching that children's classic together. My intense frown relaxed. I loved it when they chose to spend quiet time together, resting in the same bed, watching the same movie. And sometimes that shared movie-watching experience led to playing on the rug together, which led to Ellie reading a story to Tommy, which led to them cooking in their play kitchen. So, one not-so-great mommy parenting thing led to creativity. It led to connection. It led to good. It led to right.

My thoughts drifted to dinner. What to make for dinner—the never-ending question. I considered dusting off my bread maker that was sitting on a shelf in the basement. Maybe I could roast some of those organic veggies that had names I couldn't remember or find a new recipe for a vegan casserole I knew my kids wouldn't touch. The homemade sushi rolls with brown rice had been a major flop, and my roasted zucchini soup made in the Vitamix was thrown out after the first bite.

Our neighbor's dog barked, and you lifted your head. Just as quickly, you lowered it back down onto my feet and took a deep breath. I heard a garbage truck in the distance and wondered if that was the truck that had taken Tommy's Babas away. I looked out across our front yard and noticed the colorful blooming flowers.

The grass in our front yard was greener than I remembered. The birds were singing in the trees above. I closed my eyes and felt the sun on my face.

Tommy and Ellie had been hesitant to give up something that had helped soothe and comfort them, but they did, because they were growing up and it was time to learn new ways of self-care. I could relate. I'd tried many self-soothing methods in my lifetime, yet none had seemed to really work—and then I met you, Riley Rose. You and I entered into a life together and had kept our unspoken commitment to one another. We continued to show up for each other every single day. I gave you a home and food and love. In return, you gave me comfort and a safe place to land.

Mary Poppins told us to "Feed the Birds." Well, maybe I'd start by feeding my family, feeding our souls. Sometimes, Ri, when I was reminded of what really mattered, I stopped trying to be something or someone I knew I wasn't. After bending down and giving you a kiss on the top of your head, I stood up. I turned around toward our house, walked into the kitchen, and opened the freezer. Frozen chicken nuggets. Perfect.

CHAPTER 18

# God, Please

**Dear Riley,**

Did you ever think about God? And I'm not talking about the Bible or what you believed to be true but about God Himself? What did you think He looked like? Had you ever pictured Him? I'd always thought of Him as some larger-than-life, Zeus-like character—half His body invisible below the white clouds He surely sat atop while waving his lightning bolt Godly wand.

As I sat on the curb next to the stinking garbage bins that had been rolled out for pick-up in front of our house in the pitch-black early morning hours, awaiting my Uber to take me back to the Emergency Treatment Center, I wondered—who was to say that God wasn't up in Heaven drinking a beer and smoking a Marlboro Light?

God and I had always had a pretty good relationship. I met Him in junior high when I started going to Sunday school with my friends, because all the cute boys went to church, and we wanted to casually run into them. As I listened to the teachings of the Bible, I was interested and wanted to learn more. High school led to Bible studies and weekend retreats.

I was starting to understand God in the way He was being taught to me by the Christian teachers of a God-fearing community. I was repelled by the ever-apparent Christian hypocrites who veiled gossip in the form of a prayer request but at the same time was drawn to something inside me I knew to be true and real and BIG.

Somehow, even in the midst of all the Southern Baptists preaching their fear of an eternity spent in the fiery depths of Hell, I felt my God was different. I felt pulled toward compassion and forgiveness. I believed my God rooted for us and understood who we were, imperfections and all. I believed He smiled if we decided to spend a Sunday morning in nature rather than squirming on a wooden pew. I believed my God was love and acceptance of all and felt that love was incredibly personal and unique to only the two of us.

When I went to college, I put my relationship with God on the back burner, but I noticed He kept popping up when I least expected, never letting me forget what we shared. My time in New York after college began my quest for absolute control over everything in my life, and since living in accordance to God's will meant "Letting Go and Letting God," I looked the other way.

Medical school and marathons felt safe to me, controllable. I knew God was there, but I told Him I was just fine doing things my own way. So, seeing that I was on a path of my own making and not of His divine choosing, He knocked me over the head with a sledgehammer by introducing The Cancer to my life.

I knew the natural reaction was to sometimes be angry with God for these tragedies, but, Ri, I never was. My true self that I buried deep down inside was thankful, so very thankful for the escape. I believed my God had given me a heaping dose of His love. I kept trying to convince myself that I was devastated to have to drop out of med school and deeply distressed to have to step away from my running. I told everyone I was strong and would fight this thing so I could get back to living life. But as the chemo rounds progressed and my body and soul were worn down more and more, light was shed on that true self that lived in the depths of the deepest part of my soul. That soul exposure allowed me to accept the warm blankets with a smile and rest with gratitude. I went on walks to The Rock and prayed. I began to look upward.

God must've known that after my first battle with The Cancer, I'd not quite learned my lesson, so He did what He had to do by bringing The Cancer back again and then yet again. My true self understood The Cancer was there to stay. Just as God gave me Tom, you, Ellie, and Tommy, God also gave me The Cancer as a permanent member of our family. And I understand that it was not to punish me but to serve me. The Cancer was the vessel with which God shed light on my truth.

Ri, as I sat there on the curb in front of our house, holding the ice pack to my head, watching my Uber app telling me my driver was arriving, I said a prayer. It was the only prayer I had been saying lately. God, please.

My driver arrived, and I stood up. I turned back toward our dark house. Tom and the kids were still sound asleep. I didn't see the need to wake them. I saw you watching me out the window. I climbed into the backseat of the Honda Accord. Without raising my eyes or the ice pack from my forehead, I mumbled hello to David—my four-and-a-half-star-rated driver. I felt his concerned eyes checking on me through the rearview mirror.

Without traffic, the drive from our house in Pasadena to the Emergency Treatment Center at City of Hope took thirteen minutes. My eyes were tightly shut the entire way. The ice helped a bit. My facial muscles were exhausted from grimacing in pain for the past four hours. My stomach was raw from throwing up.

I didn't have to open my eyes to know where we were on our route. I'd done that drive too many times. I knew every turn by heart. Slight veer to the right, we were exiting the highway. We came to a complete stop. We must have been at the first stoplight. We crossed the train tracks. Just under a minute left. We took a left. Almost there. The driver turned into the entrance. I knew he'd slow to a stop. We were at the guard gate.

"Name?" I heard the guard ask.

"Caroline Rose," I said as loudly as my pain would allow.

"Are they expecting you?" the guard asked through the window.

"Yes." They were always expecting me, I wanted to say.

"Okay, then. Do you know where you're going?"

Like the back of my hand. "Yes, sir," I managed to answer.

"Have a good night," the guard said to us before I felt the car accelerate toward the main hospital building.

"You should see some sliding doors behind the large fountain at the end of this road," I told the driver. "You can pull up there and let me out."

"You got it. Do you need any help out of the car, ma'am?" the driver asked.

"No, thanks. I've got it." Like hell I did, but no point in letting David know that.

When I felt the car slow to a stop, I lifted the ice just enough so I could open the car door. I avoided looking toward the front seat. It was easier to pretend that person didn't exist. I mumbled a "thank you" to the driver and closed the door. Then I began my walk of shame back to the Emergency Treatment Center. God, please.

It had been six years since my second transplant. Ellie was in first grade, and Tommy had entered kindergarten. By all accounts, I should've been back to my old self, but Ri, as I walked down the hallway toward the gray door labeled ETC, I felt like my old self was gone forever.

The pain was all-encompassing. I steadied myself against the wall. Almost there. I took a few more steps and stopped in front of the large steel door. I looked to the right and saw the call button. All I had to do was press for admittance, but I couldn't do it. I felt tears soak the ice-filled paper towel I had pressed against the front of my face. Pressing that button led to help and relief from the atrocious pain, but pressing that button also meant I was failing. It meant I was not doing things right. It meant I was not in control.

I paused for a few minutes before I did what I always knew I would do. I pressed the button. I waited a few seconds before I heard Nympha's familiar voice over the speaker.

"May I help you?"

"Hi, Nympha. It's Caroline."

"Oh, okay." The door opened.

I slowly walked through the door, keeping my eyes diverted toward the ground. I heard the familiar beeps of the machines and rings of the nurses' station phones. I saw Nurse Jeff as he was delivering meds to a patient and smelled the soothing scent of the sterile hospital environment.

I waited for Nympha by the scale.

"Hi, Rose." The ETC nurses always called me by my last name. It had been that way ever since my first visit to the ETC seven years prior. I never had the heart to correct them.

"Hi, Nympha. It's really bad this time."

"Okay, Rose. Let's get your weight, then you go to Room One."

I stood backward on the scale. Everyone knew never to tell me my weight. Just because I was a cancer patient didn't mean I wasn't still vain.

Marissa came in and took my vitals. Nympha called the on-call doctor. Due to my frequent trips to the Emergency Treatment Center, orders for my "sinus migraines" were clearly listed in my chart, but the nurses were still required to call the on-call doctor for the final okay.

I asked Marissa for a pink vomit tray. She brought it to me just in time. It was pretty much just stomach acid by that point. She brought me a box of Kleenex. I hadn't realized I was still crying.

I raised the back of the bed up to a sitting position. Lying back hurt too much. I pressed the ice harder against my head and tried to listen. I hated being alone in the room, not knowing what was being said about me at the nurses' station. Shame filled my entire body.

What if the nurses and doctors thought I was a wimp and just couldn't handle pain? What if they didn't believe me when I told them that my pain was a ten out of ten? What if they thought I was making this stuff up? It was impossible to prove invisible pain.

Sitting in that room in the ETC, waiting for Nympha to come back in with the final approval from the unknown doctor, was the time my anxiety peaked. I felt naked and exposed, totally open for judgment. I'd fought so hard for my health, for my life, but not for this life.

But was I asking for too much? Should I have just been grateful that I was granted a life at all?

"Caroline, I am Doctor Santera."

"Hi."

"It says on your chart that this is the ninth time this year you have been to the ETC for a…sinus migraine."

"I haven't been counting, but that sounds about right," I said with closed eyes and my face still scrunched up in pain.

"And I see in your chart that our pain management specialist doctor and your primary doctor have agreed on a medication regimen to be given to you when you come in for one of these…sinus migraines." The judgment in her voice was palpable.

"Yes, that's right," I replied through clenched teeth.

"Yes, that's what I see, but that's a lot of medication."

Oh, no. Here we go.

See, Ri, what this unfamiliar doctor didn't understand was that while I was an inpatient for my second transplant, the doctors had hooked me up to a high-dose pain medicine drip every fifteen minutes for six weeks. After each of my previous five sinus surgeries over the previous five years, I had been given strong pain medication in recovery and during the few days spent post-surgery in the hospital. My tolerance wasn't normal, and my body had been able to handle double or triple what a "normal" thirty-eight-year-old woman weighing—well, I don't know how much I weighed—could've tolerated.

"Well, I'm not comfortable giving you all of that. I'll just start with a little Toradol, and let's see how that works."

"Did you see my chart? My two doctors, my oncologist *and* my pain management doctor, agree and have clear notes in my chart!" My voice was becoming frantic.

"Yes, I saw the notes, but this is my decision."

Dr. Judgment was standing her ground, but who was she to act like she knew what I needed? I bent forward into sobs. Nympha entered the room to start my IV.

"Nympha, you know me. You know I'm not making this up. Please, can someone just help me?" The pain worsened with the prospect of relief taken away.

"Rose, just try to relax." It was the only comfort Nympha could offer.

"Why won't you treat me according to the notes in my chart that were written by the doctors who know me?" I asked.

"Because I can't see your pain. If you had a broken leg that I could see on X-ray, then I could treat you accordingly," Dr. Santera replied.

"So, you are saying that if you could see proof of my pain, you would believe me. But since you can't see it or since I can't prove it, you don't believe me?" I half screamed, half whispered in response.

"That is correct," Dr. Santera said through gritted teeth.

"I want a new doctor. I don't know who you are, and you don't know what I've been through. I want a new doctor, please!" I pleaded through sobs.

"I'm the only doctor on call for the night. The new doctor comes in at 6 a.m."

"What time is it now?" I cried out. I was unable to lift the ice from my forehead to look at the clock.

"Rose, it's 5:05 in the morning." Nympha had just given me a shred of hope.

"Fine. I'll wait for the new doctor. And just so you know, you are a horrible, horrible doctor!" I yelled in an unsuccessful effort to defend myself in some small and fruitless way.

God, please.

Fifty-five minutes passed. Nympha brought me more ice packs and fresh vomit trays. Marissa covered me with warm blankets, and both nurses asked about my kids.

"How did Ellie do in her bike rodeo?" Nympha wanted to know.

"She did fine." Although I greatly appreciated Nympha's attempts at distraction, I was in no mood to talk. The pain was too horrific.

"Did Tommy have fun at his Chuck E. Cheese birthday? I remember you were here the same night."

"Yes." That was certainly not a memory that would make me feel even the slightest bit better. Having to leave my six-year-old's birthday party so Francis could drive me to the ETC was a memory I hoped to never remember again.

Nympha left to get me a fresh warm blanket. I pulled my knees up closer to my chest. I heard the urgent announcement for a code blue being called over the PA system. The patient in the room next to me turned on the TV. I wished they would turn it down. I heard my door open.

"Rose, good news. Dr. Eddie called. He okayed your orders. We will get you relief."

Thank you, God.

Ri, I really, really wanted to do my recovery from the second transplant better. But I was struggling, and I knew it. I felt like every time I got one of my sinus migraines that the countless surgeries had yet to fix, a piece of my soul was chipped away. With each IV they started and every injection of pain medicine they pushed, I slipped away a little more. I reminded myself of the magnitude of the transplant I agreed to six years prior and that, compared to most of the other patients who went through the same insanely intense regimen, I was considered the star patient, the golden standard. I knew in my mind I could have never expected to be my old self, but I couldn't accept being this new self, either.

I was totally and utterly not in control.

God, please.

I was tired and discouraged and ashamed. I knew The Cancer was in my life to stay and I was trying to find a way to co-exist peacefully, but we hadn't found any common ground. I felt it keep threatening to destroy me while I in turn wanted to destroy it. I wondered if I would ever get to a place where I'd be able to pull up a chair for this unwelcome family member and invite him to our table. Would we ever be able to break bread together and share a glass of wine and toast to our insane journey?

My goal had always been perfection, but, Ri, that time I had to admit that I wasn't going to be able to do my recovery in a way that even came close to perfect. I was going to get sick, and I was going to need help. I was going to continue to need to push that nurse call button. That didn't mean every day would be a struggle, but it also didn't mean it would be easy. I was so ready to feel good, to feel happy, to feel free.

God, please.

God had given me so many incredible things, so many blessings. When I took the risk and brought you home, I imagined God cracking open a beer and toasting the journey He knew we would take together. I believed that when Ellie and Tommy were born, He cried tears of joy and danced to some classic rock. I may have pictured Him with shaggy brown hair and maybe even a super cool tattoo, the ultimate trendsetter. I knew in my truth that God was on my side and that He'd never do anything against me. I'd been trying for so long to shut it out, but as my numerous late-night Uber rides to the ETC had shown me, it wasn't working. I had to change my approach.

So, like my ever-changing image of God, maybe it was time I changed my image of The Cancer. I thought about welcoming it in a little more and showing a little love for what it had taught me and for the things I had yet to learn.

I wondered about listening to my God-given truth and calling a truce. I didn't think I was close to the point of pulling up a chair at the dinner table for my adversary, but maybe I could have agreed to entertain the thought. Who could know what might happen? Had it finally been time to let go and let God?

God, please…

## CHAPTER 19

# Hopeful Success

**Dear Goofy Riley Rose,**

"Wake up, Ellie! We're going to Disneyland!" I yelled as I ran into Ellie's room on a Wednesday morning in February.

"But, Mom, it's a school day," Ellie protested as she opened her eyes and tried to process the sudden burst of information.

"I know, sweet girl, but you only live once, right? Come on! Get up! We have to leave soon if we want to beat the morning traffic."

"Mrs. Dole might get mad at me if I don't go to school today."

"I don't think missing one day of second grade will be the end of the world. I'll call your school and tell them you're out today. We don't have to let them know ALL the details."

"But, Mommy, isn't that like lying?"

I paused before answering. "You're right. It's never good not to tell the truth. I'll call the school and tell them that I'm pulling you and Tommy out for the day to go have some fun with Mom and Riley. Everyone at school knows that it's been a tough few months for us, so I'm sure they'll understand."

"So Riley's coming too?"

"Of course Ri's coming. He loves Disneyland as much as we do."

"Will his leg be okay walking so much?"

"I hope so. And if it's not, we can always take a break and get some ice cream."

And with that, Ellie slowly made her way out of bed and started to get dressed.

As I left the room to wake Tommy for this unplanned fun-filled day to the happiest place on Earth, I reassured myself that I was doing the right thing. I knew Ellie was right and worried that your leg wasn't completely healed from the surgery you had endured three months prior to fix your torn cruciate, but Dr. Wantanabe had assured me that you'd fully recovered.

I knew you didn't love Disneyland, but I had to ask you to come anyways. I needed you in your recently earned red service dog vest. You were part of the fun-filled day I'd imagined us having, maybe even the center of it, and I needed that day. The kids needed that day. And I didn't want to do it without you.

It had been five weeks since my sixth sinus surgery. The doctors had declared this outcome a "hopeful success." Just as all the previous sinus surgeries, no one really knew if this would help relieve my sinus migraines, but we were…hopeful. I was starting to realize that hopeful could sometimes be code for, "We have no fucking clue what's going to happen, but let's all keep our fingers crossed that whatever we did to you in the operating room helps you feel better."

Truth be told, no one really knew what or where my pain even was. I'd coined the term "sinus migraine" to try to put a label on my excruciating discomfort so others could have some understanding of what my body was experiencing. I tried to Google sinus migraines, but unlike The Cancer it was a much murkier answer.

And what kind of prognosis was "hopeful success"? Was that really even a medically appropriate post-surgical outcome? And if so, what was I supposed to do with that? For so many years, I'd been clinging to hope with a death grip, as if hope were my only chance to survive. I was intimately familiar with hope, and as much as it had saved me I was desperately ready to drop this aspiration as a prefix to my life's prognosis.

Pain had become a huge part of my life. I didn't dance with it every day, but when we did get our groove on we tangoed toe to toe. Pain led, and I followed. We'd established our own routine, and I couldn't seem to break out of our rhythm, even though I was desperate for a new dancing partner.

Aside from the agony my sinus migraines were causing, there was also the issue of the fungus. All kinds of different fungi were popping up in my upper sinuses. These fungi were funky and unusual and too close to the blood-brain barrier for comfort. If any piece of the fungus happened to cross from my sinuses and into my brain, well, no doctor ever finished that sentence, but I could imagine what the ending might have been.

Waking up on that February morning after being in bed recovering from yet another surgery for the better part of a month, I realized I felt…better. I only had trace amounts of pain. I didn't seem to have an active sinus infection. I wasn't overly weak or tired. I was just me, waking up beside you with a full day ahead of us.

And I wanted to make that day happy. I wanted to make it count.

I felt the chilly air fill the room as I opened the window next to my side of the bed. Ski week had been coming up, and I was still in a funk about not having a trip on the calendar.

One thing I'd been trying to get used to in Pasadena was the concept of having a ski week on the private school calendars. The students were given one week off in February, deemed "ski week," and another week off in March, for spring break. The labels put on these breaks created immense pressure to take your kids to the mountains for snowy winter family memories. I didn't even know if I wanted to try to plan a ski trip, but I knew I at least wanted the option. My Cancer, however, hadn't afforded me that choice. But now, my doctors were "hopeful." And I felt good. But I was sad.

My physical body and my emotional soul were on two separate playing fields. As my sinuses healed, my soul slipped. I was tired and losing the will to pull myself back up again. Everyone around me wanted me to be better, needed me to be better. I felt immense pressure to "get back to normal," but normal for me was a thing of the past, Ri. Normal would've been waking up and throwing on Lululemon pants before taking the kids to school.

My post-school drop-off time would have been spent walking the Rose Bowl with friends or attending the school parent forum discussions. If I'd been "normal," I'd have been working as a doctor or running errands or scheduling the kids' annual physicals or staying current on your heart worm medication. Normal would've meant a routine, a schedule, a life.

The adults around me had to have known how glaringly NOT normal my life had been since The Cancer had robbed me of that monotonous luxury, but you and I seemed to be the only ones able to admit the obvious truth, and that made me feel sad. It made me feel lonely. It made me want to go to the "happiest place on Earth."

I sat back down beside you on the vacant side of the bed. Tom had been on a business trip in New York City. I envied how much he traveled for work. Each flight he took added to my feeling of being grounded. After my most recent surgery, I'd approached Tom about the possibility of planning a ski trip over ski week. He'd explained to me in very practical terms that since we had just moved into our larger home in a beautiful area of Pasadena that we should be responsible and wait a bit before taking a big trip.

As you knew, Ri Rose, Tom's career was in finance. And not only that but his focus was on retirement savings. Tom was exceptional at his job and prided himself on our family's financial security. I, on the other hand, was making a living by balancing a life with the kids and The Cancer and prided myself on still being there on Earth with my health arguably intact.

Finance had no place in my "I lived, therefore I deserve it" post-cancer world. Why would I put money away for the future when chances were

I wouldn't be around to enjoy it? I wanted to take the trips and make the memories NOW, while I still could. Our marriage had become the yin-yang of responsible saving versus living it up and partying like it was 1999.

So, Ri, as I woke up that February morning feeling physically good but emotionally defeated by the unmarked emptiness of the upcoming white ski week squares on the school calendar, I decided to take life by the horns and enjoy it with you and the kids while I could. Disneyland was a short forty-five-minute drive away, and we had annual Southern California resident passes. I didn't think it would be too crowded on a Wednesday in February, and even if the lines were long it didn't really matter because we entered the rides through the special handicap entrance thanks to your service dog vest.

After earning your certification and trying on your vest for the first time, I knew that if anyone asked me about you being a service dog that, legally, they could only ask me two questions:

1. Is this a service dog?
   Umm…yes.
2. What service does he perform?
   Well, Ri, that answer was not as easy to explain…

The car ride to Disneyland on that sunny Southern California morning was filled with excited chatter coming from the backseat.

"Small World is my favorite. Can we do Small World, Mommy? But no roller coasters. I don't like the scary rides," Tommy said.

"I want to do the roller coaster in Tune Town, so you can wait with Riley while Mom and I do the roller coaster," Ellie argued back.

"I can't wait with Riley without a grown-up. I'm only in kindergarten!"

"But I want to do the rollercoaster!" Ellie exclaimed.

Seeing this was going nowhere, I interrupted by suggesting, "Guys, why don't we go see Minnie and Mickey in Tune Town? Y'all love asking them to sign your autograph books."

"Oh yeah! I love seeing Mickey!" Ellie squealed.

"Me too!" Tommy agreed.

"And Riley likes seeing Mickey too!" Ellie said. "Mickey always likes taking pictures with Ri. Oh, remember last time when we saw Goofy and wanted him to sign our autograph books but there was a really long line? He saw Ri and came over to meet him and asked what our dog's name was and I said, 'His name is Riley, but we call him Goofball! Just like you! Goofball and Goofy!' And he clapped his hands together and gave Ri a hug? That was so funny!" Ellie leaned back in her car seat as she clapped her hands in humorous joy.

"Yeah, that was so funny! Then Goofy gave Goofball that special button," Tommy said.

"Yeah, the 'Honorary Citizen of Disneyland' button, and he pointed for Mom to put it on Ri's service vest. Mom, do you still have that button?" Ellie asked.

"I do. It's actually right here. I won't forget to put it on before we get out of the car." I smiled as I recalled the memory.

Ri, you really were famous at Disneyland. It was not often that a 137-pound Lab-Great-Dane mix was seen riding Autopia or the Circus Train. After so many trips with you to Disneyland, we'd become immune to all the cell phone videos and pictures being taken, but I never could get used to overhearing everyone commenting about your enormous size.

As we pulled into the Mickey parking garage, I noticed you didn't stand up, eager to see where we were. You knew. And you weren't so excited.

After we parked, I pulled out the double stroller. I could tell that Ellie and Tommy were tired. I'd woken them up an hour earlier than their normal wake-up time so we could be at the front of the line when the gates opened. I didn't want them to miss one minute of this memory-making day. You waited comfortably in the back of the car until I asked you if you were ready.

You looked at me with your big brown eyes, and I took that as my cue to wrap my arms around your body and not so elegantly lift you out of the back of the car, our new routine in your increasingly older years.

The line for the tram was short, but the line for entrance to the park was long. Damn it. I thought I'd planned it perfectly. No matter. The day would still be great. You took the opportunity to lie on the chilly cement that the still-rising morning sun had not yet touched.

As we stood waiting for the gates to open, I noticed the little boy standing in line behind us. He was clutching his mother's hand and his eyes were laser-focused on you. After a few minutes, I saw the little boy drop his mother's hand and cautiously approach your resting body. Once he was beside you, he slowly squatted down to your level and reached out. As soon as his hand had touched the top of your head, the boy quickly drew it away, almost as if he'd been burned by your calm. His mom drew a sharp breath. I looked up at her face.

She answered the look of confusion on my face by explaining, "Oh, I'm so sorry. I didn't mean to startle you. It's just that my son is truly terrified of dogs. He is on the spectrum, and we've been trying to get him more comfortable around dogs, but he's always been too scared to even be in the same room with one."

The boy's mom and I both looked back down toward you and the little boy. He was now sitting beside you on the cold ground. You looked him in the eye, and he didn't look away. He once again reached out his hand but this time rested it lightly across your back.

I turned around toward the boy's mom. I noticed tears had sprung into her eyes. And she then said to me, "Your dog is truly special. What's his name?"

I felt that familiar tug in my heart. "Riley. His name is Riley."

"But we call him Goofball!" Tommy chimed in.

The boy's mother took a careful step toward you and her son and squatted so she was on your same level. She then spoke directly to you through her tears.

"Thank you, Riley. Thank you so much." Our moment was interrupted with Mickey's voice booming over the speakers, "Ladies and gentlemen, boys and girls. Welcome to Disneyland, the happiest place on Earth! We hope you have a magical day here with us today."

The entrance ropes had dropped, and the crowd began pushing forward like the mosh pit at the Guns N' Roses reunion tour. I gave the boy's mom a smile as she helped her son to his feet before trying to catch up to my own kids, who were now running ahead of us, while at the same time trying to balance the double stroller in one hand and your leash in the other.

After making it through the turntables at the ticket check and pushing our way through the crowds on Main Street, we relaxed into the morning. Ellie and Tommy told us which rides they wanted to do, and we obliged. You were such a trooper, Ri. That Peter Pan ride made my stomach queasy too. Some of the rides I knew would be too much for you. I blamed it on me.

"Kids, Mommy's tummy just can't handle the teacups. I get too dizzy, and then I get sick."

"But, Mommy, you always get sick," Tommy said.

Ellie spoke up in defense of my tummy. "Tommy, that's not nice. Mom's doing the best she can. It's okay, Mom. We can do Dumbo instead," Ellie offered.

"Oh, sweet girl, I'm so sorry. Dumbo makes me dizzy too."

"Dumbo makes you dizzy? Even little kids can do Dumbo. What rides CAN you do?" Apparently, Ellie's patience with me and my queasy tummy had run out.

"Let's go over to California Adventure. I love Radiator Springs, and so does Goofball," I offered.

"Yea! Radiator Springs! Awesome! Come on!" both kids exclaimed as they ran ahead.

As the day went on, I noticed more and more the limp that had returned in your gait. I hadn't seen that limp since we'd first met. You didn't approach your favorite rides with the same enthusiasm and even refused the churro you sniffed out of the trash late in the day while we'd been waiting in line for the restroom. I rhetorically asked you if you were okay. I knew the answer.

The car ride home was blissfully quiet. Ellie and Tommy fell asleep before we even made it out of the parking garage. The sun had sunk, and the moon had risen. We were all exhausted.

I'd kept us at the park until closing. Every time I'd started to admit that we were tired, I'd reminded myself that there were still memories to be made. It was as if a part of me had wanted to call it a day and be thankful for the fun we'd had, but another part of me, the stronger part, the primal part, had overshadowed my better judgment, pushing me, propelling me, forcing me forward. It was like I hadn't been in my own body, but in a frantic human form that was running out of time and had to do it all "right now" because now was all we had.

My nerves were shot from the hours upon hours of constant overstimulation, so I turned on my mellow mix and tried to relax into the drive. I thought about the ski trip we wouldn't be taking and the memories that wouldn't be made this year in the snow and felt relief. Had it really ever even been about the skiing, or was it the rabid urgency to give the kids something special, something memorable, something they could hold on to after their mom was gone?

Ri, that was what I'd prayed for—I'd prayed to live. So, there I was, living, but was that what living with The Cancer looked like? Did I have to wake up on the good days and pull my kids out of school and run us ragged in an effort to fit in enough joy to make up for all the other days, to make up for the bad days, the days filled with pain and sinus swelling and infected mucus?

I rubbed my eyes as my exhaustion set in. I felt the familiar pressure under my cheeks as I rubbed a little too hard. I sighed as I thought about the toll that day of memory-making fun would have on my body for days to come. Any "normal" mom could've bounced back with an extra cup of coffee, but I knew I'd be in bed for days paying for living. Everyone had so badly wanted to believe I was good, cured, all better. They'd told me I'd been brave and called me a hero. But, Ri, if that was what a heroic life looked like, then no, thank you.

At least I finally understood that my sinus migraines were a side effect from The Cancer and nothing I did wrong. For the first few years after my second transplant, I'd felt tremendous guilt every time I'd feel the pain set in, thinking that I either hadn't done enough or that I could've done more to stop it.

As the years went by and the long-lasting effects of the chemo became more apparent, the doctors had been able to determine that the incredibly strong pre-transplant chemo had literally eaten away the inner lining of my body, including my mucosal membrane in my sinuses. So, along with inducing early menopause and a wide variety of gastrointestinal issues, the side effects of the life-saving medicine also meant that my sinuses were unprotected and exposed. Once a germ found its way inside my sinus cavities, without the necessary protective inner lining, it would be stuck and become a full-fledged infection. My lack of sinus defenses paired with my weak immune system created the perfect sinus storm, and there was nothing any of us could do to stop it.

Ri, I understood that it was just part of my dance with The Cancer and the price I'd paid for life. I thought back to earlier that day when we'd ridden Ariel's grotto ride. The four of us had crowded together into one little moving shell as the silver safety bar lowered. You'd ducked your head under the metal bar and sat down on top of my feet. The shell had moved slowly forward before turning around and descending downward, giving the appearance of going "under the sea." We'd seen Ariel's life with her father and Sebastian and the joy they all shared together while singing the familiar Disney tunes. Ariel and her family and friends were good. Their life was happy, but Ariel wanted more.

Our shell had then slowly moved forward and upward into a scary, dark scene. Ursula's voice could be heard telling Ariel that she could give her legs in place of her mermaid tail, and it would only cost her… her voice!

Ariel decided the sacrifice would be worth it, so the ride continued and showed Ariel above the sea, falling in love with her prince. As usual in fairy tales, the ending was happy, and Ariel got everything she'd wanted, both legs for walking and a voice for singing. Ri, you and I had both known that life was never a fairy tale.

The Cancer and I had made a deal. The day in Doctor Andersson's office, when I'd signed on the dotted line and agreed to the regimen for the second transplant, I'd agreed to give up a part of myself. The only difference was that, unlike Ariel, I'd had no idea what The Cancer planned to take from me. It needed something from me in order to give me the life I'd desperately wanted to live.

I saw the signs for the 110 North leading to Pasadena and knew we were getting close to home. The traffic was light at this time of night, so my mind was free to relax into deep thought. I smiled as I remembered the smile on Tommy's face when he saw Lightning McQueen, and Ellie's laughter at the show in Bugs Land. I frowned as I thought about the blister on Tommy's toe from all the walking and the burn on Ellie's face from being in the sun too long. The day had been good, but it also had been not great. And, Ri, I'd needed it to be great.

I thought back to the sweet boy and his mom, the people we'd met at the entrance gate. I remembered how the child reached out and touched you. I recalled the tears in his mom's eyes. That moment—Ri, that moment had been great. That moment had been real. That moment had been memorable.

I didn't even know if Ellie and Tommy would remember that day at Disneyland when they were older. Would it blur together with the many other trips they'd already taken there? Except for a blister and a sunburn, would anything from this day actually last? I wondered…would my life last? Would your life last?

I heard your sigh as you changed positions in the back of the car. "Almost home, Goofball. Almost home."

Ri, I was so sorry. I put you through that day at Disneyland because I couldn't stand the thought of not having you there with me. I knew you'd be sore for days and that you were getting too old for a day of rigorous walking. But I did it anyway. And in my selfishness, I sacrificed your physical pain to cushion my emotional discomfort.

To what service did you perform, that second question in the legally allowable service dog line of questioning. Well, Ri, I considered you as essential to my overall health as any life-saving medication.

I saw the Orange Grove exit and turned the car off the freeway. We stopped at the light. Your head popped up from the back. With a loud grunt, you collapsed back down onto your bed. I knew your leg was hurting you. You were in pain. And it was my fault.

The light turned green and we took a left toward our house. As we drove down the street that turns into the route of the Rose Parade every New Year's Day, I thought about pain: your pain, my pain, invisible pain, emotional pain. I thought about life: your life, my life, quality of life. I thought about sacrifice: your sacrifice for me, my sacrifice for you, the mom's sacrifice for her autistic son. I thought about pain and life, and I realized that, like Ariel's legs and Ursula's stolen voice, one couldn't have existed without the other.

In order to feel pain, you had to be alive, and in order to be alive, you had to experience pain. It was a fact of life. To live meant to be in pain. To have legs meant losing your voice. My choosing life was my choosing pain. My having said no to death was my saying no to peace. My dance with The Cancer was my dance with the struggle. I knew what I'd given up, but sometimes, in the midst of the struggle, it was hard to remember what I'd gained.

I turned into our driveway. You recognized the two soft bumps of the low curb and gingerly stood up. For the moment, your pain seemed to be better. I reached up for the clicker to open the gate. My sinuses weren't as sore. We pulled into our parking spot in front of the garage and turned off the car. Your tail was wagging, and your excitement to be home was palpable.

And Ri, that was the thing about pain. One moment it could threaten to take you down, sink you in all its agony. But then something would happen, or a new day would dawn, or you'd come up from under the sea and find the pain had lessened its hold over you and had made room for new life to fill the gap. And there was hope in that. There was inspiration in the Disney happy ending. There was life in believing in the magic of the fiction.

Life and pain, me and The Cancer, dancing partners to the end. And then there was you, waiting on the side of the dance floor in your red service dog vest, real and true in every way, in service to my heart.

You and me: Caroline and Riley, Riley and Caroline, still riding and dying to the end. Because, as we knew all too well, there was no riding without the dying.

The truth was that each day brought us closer to our last, but maybe, just maybe, if we could hang on to the hope of the happy ending even through the pain, we would be able to look back on our day at the "happiest place on Earth" and agree that it had been a very real and true "hopeful success."

CHAPTER 20

# Rose-Colored Glasses

**Dear Ri,**

Life was passing us by, and we were jumping in to participate as often as we could. Just as I was starting to pick up the pace, you were starting to slow down. Despite my best efforts to keep you forever young, there was no denying your limp, which was becoming more pronounced with each passing day. Our walks had become strolls up the street, and your favorite pastime had become observing from your shady spot on the front lawn.

To Ellie and Tommy, that was your normal. That was the Riley they saw; that was the only Riley that was. Even though my mind was desperately trying to acknowledge the passing of time and the inevitabilities that came with lost days, my soul refused the inevitable ending we were inching closer and closer toward.

Our midday naps had become more for you and less for me. Ellie and Tommy were in school most of the day, so their TV/quiet times were a thing of the distant past. While I was thrilled that their excessive screen time had been replaced with enriching classroom time and social interaction, I was also missing having them at home, having them with me, with us.

So much of their early childhood seemed like a blur. My fight with The Cancer had forced me to keep my head down so I could stay focused on beating my opponent, but in the process I many times forgot to look up to see what was right in front of me, two little humans vying for a piece of my time, a piece of my energy, a piece of my love.

In those deepest moments of struggle, I had intentionally kept Ellie and Tommy away from my pain. Maybe I pushed them far away from my battle to protect them from the enemy that was threatening to take their mother away from them. They had been too young, their innocence still shiny and new. I prayed that one day they would understand why I was absent from their lives in their youngest years. I desperately hoped they would somehow know that it was the choice I would've never wanted to make. Fate had made the choice for all of us. I needed them to know that I was only trying to survive.

Ellie and Tommy used to ask me to retell the story of how you and I came to be "us." The story of how we found each other morphed into one of pure comedy the more times it was retold, especially when Tom interjected his commentary. Over the years, you had worked your way firmly and deeply into your dad's heart, and it warmed mine to watch Tom talk about you and the memories we'd made together with such love and pride. You'd even become the screensaver on his work computer.

By this time, Ellie was in third grade and Tommy was in first. Their quaint private school was at the end of the street, a short five-minute walk from our house. You and I used to walk it with the kids, but we'd switched to driving for your benefit and sometimes for mine. I'd been doing so well, feeling so strong. I hadn't had a sinus infection or been out to the Emergency Treatment Center for two months. Sixty days of freedom. Sixty days of not slipping and falling off the tight rope that I walked in times of good health.

And then The Cancer reminded me of its permanent residence in our home.

I woke up in the middle of the night in tremendous, familiar pain. Another "sinus migraine" that came out of nowhere. And that had been one of the most frustrating things—I never knew when it would hit and derail all of our lives. The kids had become so used to Mommy having to go to the doctor. It had become normal, almost as if I were on a business trip.

Often, if I woke up closer to the morning hours instead of the middle of the night, they'd be in the car with Tom or Francis when I was dropped off at the Emergency Treatment Center on their way to school. No big deal. Mom was just going back to the doctor. Tell Nympha we say hi!

That particular time was really no different from all the others. Same symptoms. Same pain. Same middle of the night Uber ride while everyone else was still asleep. Same wet nose on the glass windowpane watching me leave. Same shame welling up inside.

On that particular visit, I spent eight hours in the ETC with an IV pumping me full of medications to relieve the pain and infection. I arrived at home midafternoon. You and I resumed our familiar place in bed with the Bravo housewives in the background.

I knew I didn't have much time before Ellie and Tommy got home from school. I wanted to be better for them, be able to put on my strong Mommy face, but I also knew I needed someone to be strong for me before I could give it back to them.

I felt your face lower onto my legs and saw your big brown eyes calmly looking up at mine. Of course. You'd give me that strength I so desperately needed.

As I laid my head back and closed my eyes, I began thinking about the story Tom and I had told the kids so many times, the story of Caroline and Riley, Riley and Caroline. But I also began to think about the people behind the story, the people at the dog rescue, the people that made "us" possible.

I'd always remembered the name of the dog rescue, so I pulled out my computer and searched for Ace of Hearts. Their website popped up immediately. I smiled as memories came flooding back. I clicked on the "Available Dogs" tab and stared at the pictures of the precious beings that had narrowly escaped death but weren't yet in their new lives with their new families.

I clicked on the "About Us" tab and began to read about the volunteers and then about the founder of this dog rescue. Her name was Kari. I clicked on her picture. I saw her lying on her sofa wearing a cowboy hat with her large bulldog, Hank, asleep on top of her.

I clicked on the "Volunteer" tab. Ace of Hearts was holding an adoption event that coming weekend and desperately needed help. I entered my contact information and added the upcoming event to my calendar.

Fortunately for me, Ellie shared my love of all things dog, so it was not hard to convince her to give up a Saturday to volunteer at the adoption event at a Petco in West Hollywood for the dog rescue that gave us Riley. In fact, there'd been no convincing at all. Ellie was thrilled.

Ace of Hearts was fostering sixty-five dogs of all different shapes, breeds, and temperaments. Each dog had been placed in a comfortable crate, either inside the store or outside under the shade trees. Ellie and I had been assigned to the dogs in the back of the store. We were to keep them company, give them treats, and make sure they always had water. If it had been over two hours, we were to find Jim and let him know that it was time for him to walk our dogs. Our instructions seemed simple enough, so Ellie and I headed to our section in the back of the store to meet our dogs.

As Ellie and I rounded the last aisle in the Petco, our eyes were immediately drawn to an extra-large crate in the back corner that contained two dogs—one very large bloodhound, Max, and a very small mutt, Hazel. Both dogs cowered in the back of their crate, their bodies wound together as tightly as could be. I watched as Ellie approached their crate. The two dogs retreated even farther into their back corner, now beginning to shake. Ellie found some small treats and carefully set them inside the large crate. Neither dog moved. Both stared at this small stranger with nothing but terror filling their eyes.

Ri Rose, you taught Ellie well. She knew what to do to comfort Max and Hazel. I stood back as Ellie walked to the side of their crate and sat down. She began speaking in a soft, reassuring voice, telling these two dogs that it was okay, that they were safe. I heard her tell them that no one was ever going to hurt them ever again and that they were going to go to a loving home. She promised Max and Hazel that they'd be able to stay together and that no one was going to try to separate them. In that moment, Ellie told these defenseless creatures what they'd wanted to hear and what she needed to believe.

And, Ri, that's the thing. In that moment in the back corner of the Petco in West Hollywood, I realized that in our times of total uncertainty and utter despair, we needed to believe we'd be all right, that we'd make it through, that we'd come out on the other side. We needed to believe we'd survive. But in order to survive we needed to have hope. And I didn't know if I trusted hope anymore. It had let me down too many times in the past.

For so many years, I'd clung to hope like you'd clung to your tennis ball. Hope was my safety net. If I'd kept hoping, it would eventually be okay, right? Wrong. The Cancer still came back. Then it came back again. I'd still lost Ellie's twin brother. And then I'd lost three more. I was alive, but I wasn't fully living. I was a parent but not always able to be a mother. I'd hoped for so many things, Ri Rose, yet still felt crippled by my circumstances. Was hoping in the face of the storm even worth it?

I turned my attention back to the purest display of youthful innocence one could witness in human form. My precious nine-year-old daughter had no way of knowing what would happen to Max and Hazel. We had no clue who would adopt them and if they would in fact actually be able to stay together. Would they go to a loving home or a home where they were given minimal attention and affection? I didn't know, and Ellie didn't know, but what Ellie did innately know was that offering blissful, idyllic hope to both the dogs and in turn to herself was the only way to survive the not knowing. I had to look away.

Ellie sat with Max and Hazel the rest of the afternoon. She answered questions to anyone who showed interest in adopting these two dogs and continually offered them tasty treats. Knowing Max and Hazel were in good hands, I helped other dogs in other areas but made my way back often to check in and see how things were going.

A few minutes before the end of the adoption event, I walked to the back of the store to check on Ellie and found Hazel curled up in her lap, sound asleep, and Max with his head resting on the floor near his new trusted friend's foot. When Ellie saw me, she looked up and smiled.

Knowing the event was coming to an end, I decided to make myself as useful as possible in the last few minutes. I began collecting dirty towels and refilling any empty water bowls. I refilled empty treat bags and folded up any now empty crates. I listened to the whimpers of the dogs not chosen as forever pets that day as I walked by their crates without stopping. I heard their cries, but I couldn't look because I knew there was nothing more I could do, and I couldn't face any more pain. I couldn't look into their eyes. I instead chose to look down at the floor.

After five hours, the adoption event officially ended. Twenty-two animals had been adopted that afternoon. Forty-three had not, including Max and Hazel. Ellie and I were starving. We decided to walk around the corner to one of our favorite restaurants. I'd anticipated a difficult conversation over dinner with my young daughter. She'd spent her entire afternoon consoling and holding the ugly truths of life in her lap. Part of me hated that she'd been exposed to realities that were difficult for even the strongest grown adult to grasp. I began to worry that I'd thrust her into a situation that was too heavy for her nine-year-old self to carry.

"Wow, I'm tired," Ellie said as we sat down for dinner.

"Me too, sweet girl. You worked hard today. I'm so, so proud of you. Did you have fun?" I asked, testing the waters.

"Mom, I had the BEST day ever. Thank you so much for letting me come with you."

Well, this was not the reaction I was expecting. "You're welcome. I loved having you with me. What'd you think about today?"

"Max and Hazel were the sweetest. I kind of wanted to bring them home with us, but I know they're going to go to an even more amazing home that's even better for them."

Huh? Her outlook was confusing to me, but I tried to play along.

"Did anyone you meet seem interested in adopting them?" Surely, I was missing something.

"No, no one wanted to take two dogs," Ellie answered.

"Did any of the other volunteers say anything about having anyone interested in adopting them?" I asked, still searching for the source of her optimism.

"No, I only heard one person say that they'd been in the rescue for a few months but that no one had been interested."

I paused to think. If I was hearing my daughter correctly, there was no shred of good news for Max and Hazel, yet Ellie was still beaming with the optimistic joy that these two dogs would end up with a Happily Ever After. I knew I could've either played along or turned that potentially sad situation into an opportunity to gently explain the harsh realities of the world we live in. I briefly weighed my options before responding.

"Well, I know you're right. Max and Hazel are going to have the best life together. I bet their new owner is looking at their picture online right now and calling Kari to schedule a time to meet them!"

Ellie's eyes lit up. "Yeah! I bet you're right! And I bet their new owner is so sweet and pretty. She may even have a daughter my age who will give them treats and sit with them and scratch Hazel behind her ears. Oh, and I bet they live on the beach, an off-leash beach so Max and Hazel can run around and play in the waves!"

I went with the fairy tale because it felt good. "Yes, and I bet their new owners have the softest dog beds in the world and let them sleep in their bed with them and feed them the yummiest dog food on the planet!"

Ellie looked up at the ceiling, smiling. Maybe she was asking God to make these wishes come true or maybe was thanking Him for already granting this dream. Either way seemed to be a happy ending to my hopeful daughter.

As our dinner was served and Ellie chatted on and on about her thoughts on what the world would look like if it were made of candy and what our lollipop castle would look and taste like, my mind wandered back to Max and Hazel. I pictured Max's eyes. I'd seen those eyes before. Ten years ago, those were your eyes, Goofball. Hazel was to Max what your tennis ball was for you. And I was your Ellie, telling you everything would be all right.

And like Ellie, I'd hoped. I'd refused to admit that your broken body may never heal, and I wouldn't accept that you may never trust. I'd trusted that things would work out with Landlord Jerry and his no-dog policy, and I'd chosen to believe that bringing you home with me that day was the right decision, even when all the initial evidence pointed to the contrary.

And then I thought about The Cancer and when it had come back for the second time, and then again for the third. I'd chosen to believe I'd beat it. I'd hoped I'd win the fight. True, I had moments when I'd wanted to give up, but I wouldn't have taken on the fight if I didn't believe I could win. When we lost Ellie's twin, a part of me had chosen to believe that he had never been real. When I felt the pain in my sinuses and saw the infected mucus rushing out of my nose, I told myself that it would get better, that I'd feel stronger, that life would get easier.

I told myself what I needed to believe in order to get out of bed and face each and every day, because if I'd allowed myself to turn my head toward the pain and look, really look at the reality, what would've been the point?

I understood when I looked at my brave and courageous daughter at dinner that evening that she was wearing a shiny and beautifully innocent pair of rose-colored glasses. I was well aware of the fact that she was making up a story about these animals that she could live with so that she could go to sleep that night with a full heart. I knew this because I'd seen her do it before when she went with me to visit you in the ICU.

It was a Wednesday, two days after you had collapsed early that Monday morning. I rushed you to Dr. Wantanabe and he immediately admitted you. You were the only dog in his practice that he refused to put into a kennel because he knew your past. Instead, he cleared a special area, and made a new ICU, just for you. He asked his nurse, Mary, to go to the hardware store and purchase cushioned floor pads and new blankets.

Dr. Wantanabe understood the anxiety you felt anytime they took you "to the back" of his office, so he'd given me permission to accompany you behind the wooden doors. Everyone who worked with Dr. Wantanabe knew you and therefore knew me as your person. I was Riley Rose's mom, loved by extension.

For the five days you were in the ICU, I was waiting outside the front doors when Mary unlocked them in the mornings and stayed until she relocked them in the evenings. The night nurse told me you refused anyone and anything while I was away. As soon as you heard the office staff arrive in the morning, you stared at the wooden door, knowing I'd be walking through as soon as it was unlocked.

I brought books and read while you rested and healed. Anna-Christine brought me coffee and kept us company. This dear friend and I had met at Pacific Oaks and had developed that kind of slow bond that seals the real deal, lasting friendship. This was my friend I could call if I needed to cry or if I needed a bottle of wine over lunch. She adored you and truly understood and admired the bond you and I shared. That was the thing about AC—she saw me. She saw us.

She saw how we authentically were doing without having to ask that seemingly ordinary and often infuriating social greeting of, how are you? Never one to gossip, this dear friend talked to us honestly about life, about things that mattered, about things that would last.

When Anna-Christine came to visit us on the morning of the third day, she knew I was struggling. She saw me sitting with my beloved Riley, on the floor of the ICU, for the third day in a row. She noticed you didn't lift your head in acknowledgement of her arrival. She paid attention to the new tube, which had been inserted into your nose. My friend handed me a coffee and without a word gave me a hug. I pulled away. I wanted to fall into her comfort, but not at the expense of the acknowledgement of the truth. I was clinging too desperately to the denial. I was surviving by believing you were going to be okay.

You hadn't eaten in three days. Dr. Wantanabe had tried cottage cheese with steamed chicken. That didn't work. He tried adding shredded cheese. You looked the other way. Mary asked me what your favorite food was, and I jokingly told her vanilla ice cream. Thirty minutes later, Dr. Wantanabe brought a large scoop of Trader Joe's vanilla bean ice cream to you in a large glass bowl. You closed your eyes.

Ellie came to visit you every afternoon after school. Anna-Christine drove her to us, so I didn't have to leave your side. The previous afternoon, seeing you were not eating, Ellie eagerly suggested we try pizza. Dr. Wantanabe overheard and loved the idea.

Your favorite pizza place happened to be one block away. Ellie and I called in an order, which Tom had offered to pick up for us on his way to come see you after work. Thirty minutes later, you had three hot and fresh large pizzas, each with different toppings to choose from. You closed your eyes. I'd turned my head away from Ellie and Tom's sight.

Ellie gave you a hug and told you that it was okay, that she knew you'd be ready to eat the pizza very soon. Ellie saw you there on the floor, too weak to even lift your head, and she believed. She believed that you would get better. Ellie was worried but stayed positive, because the lens with which she viewed that dire situation always stayed rosy, hopeful, distorted.

I went to bed that night without you by my side. Fear consumed me. My thoughts began to drift to the terrifying possibilities before I intentionally turned toward the house on Balboa Island we'd just booked for a few days that summer. You loved the beach, and I couldn't wait to see you digging your holes for your tennis balls in the sand. Denial covered in ocean waves. I fell asleep.

The next day, you were better. And the day after that, you came home. You were still barely able to stand up without help and still needed daily IV infusions. Our compassionate and loving friend, hiking partner, and crazy dog-rescue-loving friend, Lauren, came over daily for the next week. She put her old vet tech skills to work and stuck you with the large IV needles so your fluids and medications could infuse into your weak body. Over time, the medicine helped, and the food you'd slowly begun eating gave you strength. You were never quite the same after your stay in Dr. Wantanabe's ICU, but I chose to believe you were stronger than ever.

Sometimes I wondered, were we all just kidding ourselves? Would it have been easier to acknowledge the truth for what it was and accept what was happening to us and around us without trying to paint it in a cheerful light? Would being brutally honest about our reality have better prepared us for the inevitable heartbreaks that we knew were just around the corner? Would acceptance have saved us from future pain? Was continuing to hope only setting us up for more disappointment? Maybe not.

You see, Ri, I'd lived in that pain. I'd almost drowned in that heartache. I was acutely aware of the ugliest side of human suffering. But even when I was crushed under the weight of the misery, I still had hope. While I sat with you in your ICU, smelling the delicious scent of the untouched pepperoni pizza, I said a prayer and asked God to please heal your body. I asked God to please extend our time together so we could continue our journey of Caroline and Riley, Riley and Caroline.

I prayed because I hoped, and I hoped because if my prayers were answered, it would've all been worth it.

My thoughts drifted back to the present moment, the two of us in bed together, gathering strength, waiting for Ellie and Tommy to get home from school. I allowed myself to marvel at the journey you and I had taken together. We'd celebrated the highest highs and the lowest lows. We'd suffered alone until we found each other and then our suffering fused together and seemed lighter under the shared weight.

Over time, our optimism had dimmed, and our hope for a fairy tale ending evaporated. You and I both finally understood that life wasn't the effortless ride we'd wished for and that, in order to make it in the world, we'd have to fight, we'd have to hope, we'd have to love.

Ellie's and Tommy's voices filled the house. I heard their little feet on the stairs as they ran upstairs calling, "Mommy! Goofball!" Tommy came through the door first and jumped on the bed while Ellie walked in and sat down in her favorite chair. As I listened to my two children talking to each other about the scary fish tacos they'd been served for lunch, I smiled.

In spite of the past eight hours of my life spent in severe pain in an emergency treatment center at a cancer hospital, I smiled and for a moment felt happy.

I was filled with pure, enormous, crushing love. Because that was the thing, Ri. That was what I'd realized through the storm we'd weathered together. Hope got us through, and even though hope had let us down time and time again, to give up on hope would've been to give up on love, and we'd been blessed with knowing what Big Love felt like. It felt like that moment, right there, with you and with Ellie and with Tommy and with my marriage to Tom. And that, Ri Rose, was the point in all of it. That Big Love was stronger and greater than any cage you may have been forced to live in, any abuse you may have suffered, any pain or uncertainty you may have felt. That Big Love was even stronger and more powerful than The Cancer.

As Ellie and Tommy left my bedroom and went downstairs to get a snack, I took advantage of the quiet and closed my eyes. I thought back to Kari and Ace of Hearts. Finding your picture on that website didn't seem like it was ten years prior. How were you already eleven years old? How were you already living beyond your life expectancy? Please, Lord, grant me one more answered prayer…

I knew your end would come sooner than I'd ever be ready to accept. I understood my end was coming too, although my expiration date was more uncertain. I knew I might beat you to the finish or I might outlast everyone, surprising even myself in my longevity. No one really knew, but we were all still trying to survive. We survived because we wanted to live, and we wanted to live because we wanted to love, and we wanted to love because we wanted to be happy. Happiness was found buried in the living, in the journey, in the unknowing.

But in order to be happy, to be truly contentedly happy, we had to, like Ellie, hide behind the rose-colored glasses, because if we took them off even for a minute we'd see the world in shades of black and gray, stripped of all the colors that made life worth living. And I don't know about you, Ri Rose, but I wasn't done living yet. You and I still had more surviving to do.

I pulled out my computer and found the Ace of Hearts website. I clicked on Kari's email address and began typing…

*Dear Kari,*

*My name is Caroline Rose. Ten years ago, I rescued our dog, Riley, from Ace of Hearts. Riley is now eleven years old and most likely nearing his final years on this planet with us. Today, I'm home sick and lying here in bed with Riley beside me, and I just felt the need to reach out and thank you for all the incredible work you are doing. You are changing lives, and I'm so incredibly fortunate to be one example.*

*Riley has become my best friend. This dog is my therapy. He is the quiet constant in my life. Riley knows when I need his strength, and he has never once asked for anything in return.*

*In our ten years together, Ri and I have been through multiple rounds of cancer treatments, including two bone marrow transplants. This amazing dog has put his large head on my stomach for five pregnancies, and of the five has met two live babies. He has licked away my tears, danced with me in times of joy, lay with me when I needed companionship, guarded my children, and kept all of our hearts safe.*

*Because of my medical history, I was able to get a service dog vest for Riley, which has really been his ticket to freedom. Riley has flown back and forth to Texas with us more times than I could count, he has gone to Disneyland, countless hotels in Southern California, he played with Matthew McConaughey's dog on a Barbara Walters special as we were walking Runyon Canyon, and he has lived with me at our lake house in Texas when I needed a secluded place to recover from the potent chemo. Riley has run, swum, chased thousands of tennis balls, traveled, barked with joy, played so hard he couldn't take another step, and he has loved. This big goofy eleven-year-old that came to us broken has learned to trust and has learned that he will never, ever be hurt or abandoned ever again. But let me be clear, it was me that was rescued.*

*A few months back, through the recommendation of a friend, I treated myself to a session with a world-renowned healer. I had no idea what to expect and was a bit nervous to hear what he was going to tell me. I walked into his unassuming condo and sat down on his brown leather sectional. We started by taking a few deep breaths and then looked at each other for a few seconds. A smile slowly spread across his face. He lifted his head a bit higher and simply stated, "You have a dog. And not just any dog. You have your soulmate dog."*

*This healer believes that Riley came into my life to take on and carry much of the emotional energy that I have been too weak to bear. He said Riley's job has been to carry me when I've been too tired to walk on my own. And he said we only get one soulmate dog in our lifetimes, if we are lucky. What an honor that Riley is mine.*

*I cannot imagine a day without Ri. I can't fathom the thought of his leaving me, but I know, deep in my heart, that he won't leave me until he knows I'm ready. And right now, today, I'm not ready.*

*Kari, you've saved so many precious, defenseless animals. There must be a special place for you in Heaven. But maybe what is not talked about as often is the other side—the human side. I believe we all need love and support in different ways. These canine companions come to us and, without one word being spoken, naturally identify with our individual needs and plug into that area of our soul that needs recharging.*

*Thank you for changing my life. Thank you for making it possible for me to find Riley. You gave me my first child, and I will be forever grateful. I pray Riley will stay with me for years and years, but I know that someday I'll need to tell him that it's OK. He'll need to hear me say that I can handle it, that I can take on the energy he's been shouldering for such a long time, that I'm strong enough to hold it on my own. That will no doubt be one of the hardest days of my life, but it's a small thing to do for an animal that has served me so faithfully for so many years.*

*Please keep doing what you are doing, Kari. You truly are an angel.*

*All our love and thanks,
Caroline and Riley Rose*

# CHAPTER 21

# Christmas Cards

Dear Riley Rose,

Well, Ri, it was that time of year again. Like so many other families around the world, it was time for the five of us to spend an entire Sunday afternoon dressing up in color-coordinated outfits and striking the perfect authentically contrived pose with the big but not too bright smiles. We all dreaded this day—Christmas photo-taking day.

For me, holiday photos brought back not-so-fun childhood memories of putting on a smocked dress and some gold beads along with a huge matching bow on top of my head. I would have to stand next to Chad as he tormented me about my ridiculous-looking outfits, which he knew I'd been forced to wear. If I looked absurd, you should have seen him!

Our childhood annual holiday card tradition had lasted until we endured a painfully long session with Mom as our photographer, only to realize at the bitter end that she had forgotten to put film in the camera. Chad and I were scarred for life.

It was then up to me to create the image of our family that would be mailed out to 350 people a few weeks before Christmas Eve. California

Christmas cards were typically more causal than the cards we received growing up in Texas. These more relaxed images showed some families on vacation and others smiling at a sporting event. Some California families created a collage of their favorite pictures from the year, and some cards were even done with (gasp!) non-professionally taken photos. Shutterfly cards initially challenged my deep-seated southern values, as I was more accustomed to the embossed card stock. But over the years, as I studied the wide variety of holiday cards that were hung up in our kitchen throughout the Christmas season, I began to notice that the cards I liked to hang in front, the cards we would see the most, were the cards that were the least "fancy," the least "contrived," the most…honest.

I hadn't been thrilled with our card from the previous year. Our photographer had failed in his attempts to capture Ellie's and Tommy's attention and had offended both you and me by trying to use a squeaky toy to get your ears to perk up for the camera.

The pictures had turned out fine. Ellie had been wearing a cotton dress with no smocking and brown cowboy boots. Tommy had worn his Vineyard Vines wool blend zip-up sweater, and I'd just refreshed my new hair extensions. Tom looked handsome in his navy blazer and you, well, you were you, because you were incapable of being anything but.

I'd always supported the MD Anderson Children's Art Project by buying our cards from the children's holiday store and attaching our professionally taken photo on the front fold. I felt good about supporting this charity, but I think my choice of cards was more a way to say: I know I may look strong and healthy and even like my old self, but please, please don't let my looks fool you. Please never forget the hell I've been through. I needed people to remember why I couldn't stay out past 8 p.m. or why, without extensions, my ponytail was thinner than a rat's tail or why I needed to avoid crowded places. I begged everyone to recall the source of my low energy levels and chronic infections. I wanted our friends and family to understand that The Cancer was the invisible sixth family member in our annual Rose family Christmas card.

I'd recently tried a new doctor at a top Los Angeles hospital whom my sinus doctor highly recommended. Another very scary fungus had appeared again in my upper sinus, so a PICC line had been inserted into a vein in my upper arm so that I'd be able to infuse a strong antibiotic three times a day from home.

I was nervous to meet this new recommended doctor for the first time. She potentially held the key to figuring out why my sinuses were such a problem, so the pressure was on. I needed to make sure she understood the situation and that she had all the information so she could give me a path forward.

This new doctor began our appointment by looking over my medical history, my medications, and my notes from my most recent stay in the hospital. She examined my blood work and other test results carefully before looking up at me and saying, "I'm looking at your test results and reading the doctor's notes. I understand on paper what you went through, but then I look at you and can't for the life of me reconcile how you've been so sick when today you look so good, so healthy."

Okaaaay. Should I not have showered before this appointment? Would that have given off a more "sickly" vibe? My new doctor finished our appointment with an assertive request. "Why don't you see how you feel and come back in three months?" I left infuriated. But, more so, I left dejected.

After so many years of living with The Cancer, I'd grown used to my inner struggle and my outward appearance not coinciding. After being told I'd never have hair again after the crazy chemo involved in my second transplant, I was thankful that even some of my hair had grown back. But would living bald have been easier? Would it have been a constant reminder to those around me of what my body had gone through and that, even if I seemed happy and healthy, I was still not "normal"? Would it have given me the continued ability to play the cancer card even though I was in remission? Would my lack of hair have been a blessed gift, never letting anyone forget the past or that The Cancer was still very much a part of our lives?

Over time, my few thin strands of hair did grow back. The regrowth covered most of my scalp but still left noticeable bald patches. So I decided to try hair extensions. I was lured in by the hope that maybe looking like my pre-cancer self would in turn help me feel like my pre-cancer self. The extensions looked good, they really did, but then I put my head on the pillow to go to sleep that first night and felt a million small plastic tubes of artificial hair glued onto my precious and scarce real hair and felt an ick welling up inside. This new fake hair only added to the misconception I was putting out into the world that I was killing it. So which one was it? Was I damaged and struggling or healthy and kicking ass?

I sat down at my desk and opened my calendar. There was not much time left before Christmas. I opened my computer and looked at holiday cards on Pinterest. There were just so many options. Just kids or the whole family? Inside or outside? Dressy or casual? Tom felt that I needed to be in the photo. He wanted our friends to see how I was doing. How was I doing? I didn't even know.

And then there was the question of Brody...

Brody was never supposed to step foot into our house. I'd agreed to drive two hours to the high desert to pull him from the shelter that was keeping him, but when his foster mom fell through and Ace of Hearts didn't have a backup foster family, I became Brody's backup. Brody and I were both exhausted. This innocent Lab mixed with who knows what had been scheduled to be put down at 3 p.m. and I'd pulled into the parking lot at 2:50. Ace of Hearts had given me the identification numbers of four dogs they'd wanted me to pull for their rescue program. The shelter had known that I was coming for those four dogs but had already put down the first number on the list, a nine-month-old German Shepherd puppy. Brody had been next.

Brody jumped in the backseat of my car while the two small dogs I'd also been able to save sat together in the front. I'd never pulled dogs from shelters for a dog rescue organization, so I didn't realize I needed a better dog transport system. Kennels or dog beds would've been helpful. Up until that day, I'd only ever worked the adoption events at the Petco in West Hollywood with Ellie. But then they'd called me that morning and told me that if I wasn't able to pull those dogs, well, then...

The foster mom for the two small dogs was waiting for us when we got home around ten o'clock that same evening, but Brody's was nowhere to be found. Maybe there had never been a foster. Maybe the person had the wrong address. Maybe it was one of those meant-to-be moments. We'll never know.

So, Brody came into our house. Not knowing what to do with this dog whom I'd never met and knew nothing about, I decided to sit down with him in the family room. Tom was on a business trip, and you were upstairs asleep with Ellie and Tommy. Your older ears hadn't heard us come in.

I turned on the TV. Brody sat down on the floor and stared at me. I knew from my only other dog fostering experience when I lived in New York two decades prior not to get attached to the dog because it made the goodbye that much harder. Even though Chico had been a huge pain in the ass and didn't do stairs, which was a big problem with my four-story Upper West Side brownstone walk-up, my roommate and I had fallen hard for this "spirited" dog and cried ourselves to sleep when we had to say goodbye. Well, Lauren technically popped open a celebratory bottle of champagne and relished having the sofa clear of Chico hairs, but I like to think she was masking her grief in smiles and bubbles.

So that was my plan—not to get attached. I didn't want you to be upset about this unfamiliar dog invading your space. I hoped you wouldn't hear us, but then you sensed I was home and walked downstairs.

Annie, our neighbor's dog, had been coming into our house every day for the past two years. She tore through our downstairs as her young Golden Retriever tail wagged with a force that could have propelled a small boat. Every day was the same. Sue would call for her dog in a not-so-stern voice from the front yard. This neighbor knew the kids, and I loved Annie and welcomed her presence in our home anytime. We even started leaving a basket of balls for Annie on our front doorstep, trying to lure her in. Your well-worn body was no longer able to chase your beloved tennis balls, and as long as you had one by your side or in your mouth you seemed content to pass the rest of them on to the younger generation. But in all of our years of living across the street from Annie, you'd never acknowledged her. Not. Once.

But you acknowledged Brody.

You even LIKED Brody. When you walked into the family room and saw us sitting together in the TV chair, him sitting in the upright position with his eyes closed and a look of "I just came within minutes of dying but managed to escape" on his sleeping face, you walked up and sniffed his paw. Then, instead of going to your usual place on your brown dog bed, you sat down next to Brody and watched him. And waited with him. And waited with me.

Looking back, I now realize that you understood Brody in a way only you could. You saw yourself in that dog who'd lived in Hell and almost been killed before having the chance to know or experience goodness and love. While I was too busy thinking about the logistics of fostering this dog and what that would do to our home and our schedules, you were sensing his pure exhaustion and the deep, peaceful slumber he was feeling for the first time in his we-don't-know-how-long life. I think you also knew he'd wake up and never want that feeling of contentment to end.

The three of us slept together in the family room that night. You alternated between your bed and Brody's side. When he woke around 6 a.m., you led him to the backyard. I saw glimpses of young Riley as I watched the two of you play together under our orange tree. He was gentle with your aching bones, and you were patient with his over-eagerness.

At breakfast, you allowed your food bowls to be placed side by side and even yielded your bed to Brody at morning nap time. All of this was telling, but when our midday quiet time came—when you and I resumed our normal nap positions upstairs in bed, and you allowed Brody to lie next to you—it was at that moment that I knew you saw something in Brody. Something special. Something worthy. Something lasting. Something like you.

In contrast to your light-yellow fur and gigantic paws, Brody had red fur and small paws. His ears were small, and his tail curled up in the back. The markings of a white stripe had just started to peek through on his chest. Dr. Wantanabe thought this meant he had some Husky in him, but who knew? Brody was submissive and nervous. Other dogs seemed to pounce on him for no reason. He always tucked his paws under his body, which I later learned was a sign of him feeling he needed to protect his body, his limbs, probably his heart. Brody became deeply attached to you in the two weeks you knew each other. Little did I know that you were using those two weeks to teach him everything you thought he needed to know.

Including Brody in our Christmas card that year felt premature. True, he had become an official member of the Rose family after you made it clear you wanted to keep him around. But on the other hand, I didn't feel he had earned a spot in our family photo. Or maybe I just didn't want anything to take the focus off of you.

One thing I did know for sure was that I didn't want to use the same photographer we'd used in the past. It was nothing personal, but he tended to be more of a traditional, proper, elegant photographer, and I was feeling like I was ready to take out the extensions and find someone who could capture the possibly messy but real "thing" that made the five (six with The Cancer) of us "us."

I emailed some of my friends from Pacific Oaks, knowing that they'd be the people who could point me in the direction of a real-deal photographer. Most of our PO friends didn't send holiday cards, and I so envied them for that, but alas, I knew dropping the obligatory yearly "look at our cute family and of course we are always this put together and happy so get your act together because this is what a real family should look like" mailer was not an option, so I sent the emails and waited for the response.

Andrea emailed back within minutes. Her family always sent a holiday card, but they were that amazingly cool family that somehow managed to get the greatest family photo every summer, almost like a passerby took a photo of their family of four in the most authentically loving, joyful moment and texted it to them and bam! Perfect Christmas card. Andrea and her boys were all insanely beautiful, both inside and out, and really couldn't have given two shits about what most everyone else thought, and I admired the hell out of that. So in a meek effort to recreate some of their holiday card magic, I called her person (which, to be clear, she'd never had to use), and we scheduled the shoot for a week from that coming Sunday.

As D-day approached, I began thinking about our card for that year. I wanted to change it up, make it more "me." After twelve years in LA, I'd finally begun to figure out who that "me" really was. From an early age, I'd been aware of the importance of blending into my environment. It was a difficult social grace to master, but like most southerners I'd been given a lifetime of practice. If I went to lunch with my country club friends, I chose my outfit from the right side of my closet, the sundress and button-down shirt conservative side.

If I went to dinner and drinks with my Pacific Oaks friends, I chose from the left side of my closet, filled with ripped jeans and worn-in tanks. When I ordered food at the club, it was usually a salad with champagne. Dinner with my PO friends meant whatever the new vegan must-have menu item was at the time with Tequila. I was a bacon-eating vegan, an Ann-Taylor-wearing hipster, a confident lost soul.

And, Ri, the thing is, I really was both. To what side I leaned just depended on the moment I was in at that time. Through college and my time in New York and all the years in LA, I'd tried on a lot of different "Carolines." Some felt right, and some felt wrong. Over time, my life had become a collection of all the rights, even if they were oxymorons.

As I walked to my closet, I looked up at the two sides and paused. Which image would the Rose family project to the world that year? Ever since you'd come into our lives, Goofball, we'd sent a card each year. For me, it had always been a reminder to others that I was still there on the planet, fighting, with you and Tom always by my side.

Our very first card was a picture of me and Tom on the back of the boat at the lake, The Rock in the background, with you lying on the cushioned seat behind us. You looked so regal in the light of the setting sun. I had my brown and turquoise scarf wrapped tightly around my head to prevent the wind from blowing it off and into the lake water. Tom had his arm around my shoulder with a large grin on his face, holding onto his Miller Lite with his free hand. In that snapshot of our life, we were so happy, so hopeful, so good, so real.

And then the years progressed, and our family grew, as did our recipient list. With that growing number of cards came an increased pressure to project an even stronger image of, "Look at us! We are the perfect family!" It was almost as if, with each holiday card sent and received, we all absorbed by osmosis this unattainable image we felt we needed to show to the world even though we knew in our rational minds that the photo was one of hundreds taken that day and possibly the only good snap, the only good second, the only good moment out of so many messy and therefore unacceptable ones.

I looked down at your tired body sleeping on the floor. You were sleeping a lot more these days. I walked over and turned on our newly installed Sonos system, my favorite accessory in our new home. Van Morrison's Pandora station filled the house. The windows were open, and the crisp fall air poured in like a wave, a fresh California breeze. You opened your eyes and looked at me without raising your head. I asked if you wanted to go outside. You slowly stood up.

Our new home was a two-story house. Initially, the stairs were not a problem for you, but after your second surgery to fix your second torn cruciate ligament, and then especially after your time spent in Dr. Wantanabe's special Riley Rose ICU, the steps were not something you could climb without help. I'd become very used to picking up your back end as you used your front two legs to climb the stairs. My back gave out a few times, but I didn't mind.

As you and I slowly descended the stairs, I looked up at our family photos that lined the stairwell wall. I smiled as I passed the photo of you with the kids on the ski boat up at Big Bear. I saw the photo of you sitting on home plate, surrounded by Tommy's t-ball team. Then there was the picture of you in our front yard, the center of attention the previous Halloween. Maybe, for the first time, I realized that you were in every single family photo, every single family moment.

I opened the front door, and you followed. I sat down on our front porch step, and you sat in the grass. Our friends and neighbors always marveled at how you would sit in our fence-free front yard and never run off, never run away. On the rare occasion that you were not in the car with us, you liked to sit out front, patiently waiting for your family to return.

Passing dogs or taunting cats couldn't distract you from your watch. It was one of those certainties in life that I depended on so strongly.

I looked out across our front lawn. The grass was green, and the flowers were still blooming. Maybe this would be a good place for our pictures. We could put Tommy in a tree and have Ellie on Dad's shoulders. That was a pose we'd never tried and probably would never actually do in real life, but it might look natural enough. Or maybe we could all lie on the grass and laugh at some nonexistent funny occurrence as if that was what we would do on a daily basis.

I looked down and realized you were sleeping again. You hadn't eaten all your breakfast that morning, or dinner from the night before, but maybe you were not as hungry these days. As I looked at you, lying in our grass, I made a decision. Our card that year would be the card of Riley. Just as the wall of pictures had proven, you'd been the center of our family, the center of every holiday card, the center of every memory for as long as our family had been a family. So that year, that time, we were going to do an afternoon that fit with your image. We were going to do our Christmas card photos on the beach.

A few days later, it was Christmas Card Day. I braced myself for the familiar moans and groans of getting dressed and ready for our photo session. Shockingly, no one complained. I'd decided that the Rose family was going to wear…whatever we wanted. I told everyone that we were going to the beach, because that was where you always seemed to be the happiest. Ellie and I threw our hair in ponytails, and the boys pulled out their sunglasses. Our only goal was to get a family photo with Ri in the center. That was it. No pressure, no posing, no squeaky toys. Tom and the kids were thrilled.

The car ride over to the beach was a big dance party. The kids put on their playlist filled with all the usual favorite kid songs, "Paradise City," "Don't Stop Believin'," "Enter Sandman," and of course, "Stairway to Heaven." We pulled up to Santa Monica Beach in high spirits.

Instead of lip gloss and hairbrushes, I'd brought a bag filled with swimsuits and tennis balls. Our new photographer was waiting for us. She was wearing ripped jeans and a t-shirt. Her bag was small and light, just a camera and lenses. I liked her instantly.

After short introductions, the fun began. Ellie and Tommy ran through the large chilly waves. You took your time walking across the sand. I didn't even think to bring a leash, as you hadn't used one in months. Once you were closer to the water, I gave you your tennis ball. You took it from my hand with your mouth and sat down on the wet sand. You didn't toss it to me. You didn't want me to throw it for you. You just wanted to sit and hold your ball. So that's what we did.

Our photographer captured shots of Ellie and Tommy playing on the beach that afternoon. It didn't take us long to forget that she was even there. After the kids grew tired of running, they came over and sat with us. They were wet and their hair was filled with sand. Tom came over and sat down, too. We all wanted a minute with you as we watched the sun set over the California coastline. The photographer snapped a picture.

She captured a moment. She captured…us.

That moment became our Christmas card photo, and that Christmas card became my all-time favorite.

When I addressed the 350 foil-lined envelopes that year, I had no way of knowing that afternoon on the beach would be your last. I may have sensed it deep down, but I wasn't ready to acknowledge what I feared the most. I addressed those cards slowly, carefully, savoring every stroke of the color-coordinated pen.

Those moments on the beach that afternoon flowed in and out of our lives like the waves of the ocean we splashed in. Sometimes I wished we could all go back to that afternoon and feel that sun and that joy and that easiness we felt together. I wished I could cling on to those moments and never let go, but even I knew that would be a fruitless dream. Because even if we'd been able to hold on, choosing that would've meant not making room for new moments, new memories.

Attaching to a moment is like attaching to a label. Country club mom or hipster? Vegan or steak lover? Marathon runner or power walker? Cancer patient or survivor? We couldn't really attach to anything because we were all of it, all the time, a collection of our moments, a collection of our labels. Ri, you taught me over and over again to accept it, all of it. Accept where we were, in every second, every hour, every day. Accept how I was feeling, what I was or was not doing, what I looked like, what my family looked like, and accept that I had absolutely no clue what would happen next.

Sometimes it was difficult for me to find the line between fighting and acceptance. I'd been in battle mode for such a long time. It had begun to be the only mode I knew. Keep fighting, keep moving forward, keep healing, keep going. That was what I'd done, what we'd done. You healed your body, and then I healed mine. But were we done healing? Would that mean we were done fighting? Did acceptance look like giving up? It sometimes felt that way.

When I now look at the photo from the beach that afternoon that is framed above my desk and I look at our relaxed smiles on our sun-kissed faces, I think, that doesn't look like fighting. The joy in our eyes looks peaceful, and one thing I do know is that peace was never found in the depths of the fight.

No, my sweet Goofball, that afternoon you created on the beach was not an afternoon of battling. It hadn't been a struggle to get everyone to that photo session, and it hadn't been difficult to capture amazing pictures. No, Ri, that afternoon, you brought your family together, in your favorite place, with your favorite people.

You drew us around you in your own quiet way and the result was honest acceptance of the moment and renewed hope in the unknown. Nothing more, nothing less, just what was. After all, who ever needed to say cheese when all we ever had to do was love you?

CHAPTER 22

# The Nod

## Sunday, January 22, 2017

9:13 p.m.

"Mrs. Rose, my name is Dr. Schwartz."

"Call me Caroline."

"Okay, Caroline. I just examined Riley. I gave him medicine through his IV to help with his pain."

"What happened to him?" I asked in a shaky voice.

"Riley is bloated, which means his stomach is filled with fluid, and it's putting pressure on vital organs."

"How do we fix it?"

"Well, that's the hard part. There aren't really any treatments available for bloat."

"But...how do we fix it?" I asked again.

"Caroline, I hate to tell you this, but you need to make a decision right now. Riley doesn't have much time. We can try to go into emergency surgery and operate, or we can put him down. The risks of surgery are..."

"What are you waiting for? SAVE MY DOG!"

"I'll do what I can."

11:34 p.m.

You were in surgery. It had been an hour and a half. You were still on the table. Lauren left me in the upstairs break room to go check on you. My mind was spinning. I couldn't seem to slow it down enough to think. Or maybe I didn't want to think. Maybe I wanted to sit there with my friend and listen to her tell me that you were going to be okay. Because you were going to be okay, Ri Rose. You had to be.

11:37 p.m.

Lauren's husband, Mike, the owner of the animal hospital, arrived and assessed the situation. They told him you were still in surgery. Lauren came upstairs and gave me the code to Mike's office. I was granted access to see you, Ri, at any and all times for the duration of your stay. Lauren and Mike made sure that everyone in the hospital knew it. My friend came back upstairs to the break room and sat down next to me. When I thanked her, she covered her face with her hands and began to cry.

## Monday, January 23, 2017

12:08 a.m.

You were out of surgery. I knew you'd make it through! I ran downstairs to be by your side. Our eyes met through my pool of tears. You had tubes attached to your body. You were limp, listless, but your eyes—your eyes saw me, so I knew your heart felt me. That was good enough.

Just sleep, my sweet Goofball. I'll be right next to you when you wake up.

7:12 a.m.

Shift change. You had a new doctor, and I think I liked her. She wasn't warm, but I heard she was very good. I didn't think she liked me looking over her shoulder. Dr. Wantanabe called to check on you. I didn't know what to tell him. They took you back for another X-ray. I watched you all the way around the corner. I waited next to your now-empty spot until you got back.

6:26 p.m.

I knew you must have been so tired. You'd had a steady stream of visitors all day. Lauren came back early that morning. Anna-Christine brought me coffee and stayed for most of the day. Lauren picked up Ellie and Tommy from school and brought them to you. Ellie cried when she saw you. Tommy had been afraid to touch you. I told you Tom would be there soon. Just close your eyes, my sweet Goofball. Rest and know I am here by your side. I will never leave you.

## Tuesday, January 24, 2017

7:42 a.m.

Tom and Ellie came by to check on you before school. They'd noticed you'd been moved overnight. You were on a raised stretcher in the middle of the ICU. Ellie was worried you'd roll off and fall to the floor. I told her you were too weak to lift your head. A red crash cart lingered to the side of your stretcher. They'd asked me if I wanted them to resuscitate you if you went into cardiac arrest. I was surprised they even had to ask.

9:09 a.m.

You needed another X-ray. I waited for you upstairs in the break room. I was alone and cold, so very cold. I heard raised voices downstairs and alarms beeping. I assumed it was for some other critical patient. I never imagined the panic would be for you.

9:11 a.m.

Dr. Scotsman ran up the stairs. She told me I needed to come—NOW. Her eyes were wide and frantic. I flew down the staircase. I'd come out of my body, no longer attached to this Earth. I heard a sob and realized it was mine. I saw the red crash cart before I saw you. Then I saw you. I saw your eyes searching for mine. Then you saw me. And I knew. Ri, I just knew. I ran to you and folded my body over yours. My tears soaked your yellow fur. I pulled a stool over. My head was level with yours. I knew what I had to say, but I couldn't bring myself to say it. Instead, I asked you to please hang on. I asked you to fight. I begged you to stay.

11:39 a.m.

You were on life support. Dr. Scotsman pulled me aside and asked me to reconsider the crash cart. I was aware of what she was asking of me, but God damn it, Ri, I couldn't understand any of it. Anna-Christine and Lauren were with us. Your body was lifeless. But your eyes still saw me.

1:14 p.m.

I hadn't spoken a word in over an hour. I wasn't even sure anymore who was still there with us. I had my head on top of yours.

I need you, Ri. I can't do this without you. I'm not ready to say goodbye. Please, Ri, please don't leave me. Please fight for me.

2:11 p.m.

Tom was there. Anna-Christine had left to pick Ellie and Tommy up from school. The people around me were making decisions for me, for us. They were the right decisions, the necessary courses of action, but I still resented every single one of them.

2:32 p.m.

Ellie and Tommy were with you. Tommy gave you a quick hug before turning away. Ellie smiled when she saw you. Tom told her it was time for her to say goodbye. I watched as her face crumpled into raw grief.

2:51 p.m.

Dr. Scotsman was sitting on a stool near your body. She had a syringe hooked up to your IV. Her thumb was on the syringe. She was ready to push. Tom and Ellie were right there with you, with us. Anna-Christine and Lauren squeezed my shoulder. Everyone was looking to me to give the nod, the okay to push the syringe. I knew I needed to do it, but I couldn't bring myself to be the one to end your life. Just a few moments longer…

3:04 p.m.

I pushed my stool back and bent down lower so your ears and soul could hear my whisper. The words I needed to say were to be between you and me, the souls who saved each other, one last time. I said a prayer for strength. Sorrow ravaged my entire being. I told you that it was okay. I told you that you could go.

"I love you, Riley Rose. So much. I will never, ever stop loving you. I will miss you every second of every day of my life. It's been a good ride, Goofball—the best. You've changed my life, and I'll be forever grateful. The part of my heart that is yours will always be yours. Ri, thank you for everything. I know you're so tired. Thank you for fighting so hard. But it's okay now, my precious boy. You can go. I'm giving you the gift that you've always given to me—I'm going to give you the gift of peace. Yes, you can go now. Just please never forget how much I love you."

I raised my head and, through the blur that had become my world, against every instinct in my body, I forced myself into the ultimate expression of painful, brutal, selfless love. I lifted my chin, ever so slightly, and gave The Nod. Dr. Scotsman pushed her thumb on the syringe. Riley and Caroline, Caroline and Riley, Riley and Caroline, Caroline and Riley, Riley and Caroline, Caroline and _____

## CHAPTER 23

# Soulmate

You had left. And I knew you were never coming back. I didn't know if I could do life without you. I didn't know if I wanted to do life without you.

The first two weeks were a blur. I came home from the animal hospital and curled up on your dog bed. The smell of you had tricked my emotions into believing it had all been a horrible nightmare and that you were in some way still with me. The flowers and cards started arriving the following day. By the end of the week, our downstairs was filled with gorgeous bouquets and Hallmark cards sent from well-wishers.

Carrie and her husband, Jeremy, sent flowers from New York. The head of Ellie and Tommy's school sent an orchid with a note expressing his sincere sorrow. A child I'd only met once sent a drawing in orange crayon of her patting the top of your head in the back of my car before school so she could get all of the courage and luck she would need for the day. A mom friend sent you a picture of a black Lab she decided to rescue in your honor. Anna-Christine gave me a bracelet with a silver heart locket with your picture. None of these kind gestures seemed to help my grieving heart. Jill brought over a bottle of Tequila. That helped a little.

A week passed, and I began to resent the new routine that was beginning to develop, which didn't include you. We no longer needed to drive to school, so we began walking. There were no more early morning outings in the front yard for you to do your business. I kept turning around, expecting to see you as my shadow, but I never found you. The doorbell would ring, and I'd listen for your bark. I'd walk to the bottom of the stairs and wait so I could help you up, but you never came.

I began to wonder where you were. I believed you were in Heaven, but I still couldn't picture you anywhere other than at home, with us—your family. One friend sent me a poem titled "The Rainbow Bridge." It was beautifully written and referred to pets crossing over the bridge, which was supposedly made out of a colorful rainbow, from Earth to Heaven when they die. As I began reading the poetic words, I started to realize that those words were meant for dog owners who had lost their pets.

It told of dogs who had passed over to the other side and were running and playing all day long before stopping at the end of the day and looking around for their owners. It promised the two would be reunited when the human joined their canine in Heaven and offered the hope of eternal life spent together. This was all well and good, but it didn't apply to us.

Ri, you never were just a pet. You were rejected from doggie daycare due to your high separation anxiety and were only fully relaxed when I was by your side. You'd never be happily playing all day on the other side of a bridge if I were not right with you. The only image my brain could conjure up was a picture of you sitting next to God, just as you'd always sat next to me. I believed that God understood you and knew you weren't a dog who'd enjoy playing with all the other happy dogs in the nearby field. I'm sure He offered you a tennis ball, and you put it in your mouth before taking a seat by His side. And that was exactly where I know I'd find you.

My thoughts then drifted back to your physical body still remaining here on Earth. You were at the doggie morgue. You didn't belong there.

I worried about the way you were being treated. I hoped you weren't lonely, but I knew you were. Had they lifted you gently off the table? Were you in a comfortable bed? Were you scared without me? I found the paperwork sent over from the animal hospital and called the number for Pets in Heaven.

"Pets in Heaven. How can I help you?"

"Yes, this is Caroline Rose, Riley Rose's mom. I was just calling to check on Ri and see how he's doing."

There was a slight pause.

"Umm—yes, ma'am. Let me find his file. Okay, yes. We're just waiting on you to tell us what kind of urn you'd like to order for…let's see…your dog's name was…"

"Riley. His name is Riley."

"Okay. Riley. So, what kind of urn would you like for…Riley."

"I'd like the nicest urn you have to offer."

"Well, all of our urns are nice. The options are listed on the paperwork," the woman unhelpfully replied. I took a purposefully audible loud breath that reeked of agitation before glancing over the urn offerings.

"I'd like the pine box with the light finish, please."

"Not a problem. We can do that for you. Now what size box would you like to order?"

Seriously? Oh, come ON!

"Well, Ri is one hundred and forty pounds so…"

"Yes, Riley Rose certainly is a big dog."

Misunderstanding her meaning, my tone immediately did a 180 as I frantically yelled through the phone, "Wait—you have seen Ri?? How is he???"

"Oh, I'm sorry, I didn't mean to imply I've actually seen Riley because you know, Riley is… Well, yeah, I was just going off of the weight you gave me."

I sat heavily back in my chair.

The woman continued. "Based on his weight, I recommend the extra-large pine box."

"Sure. Fine. How soon can I get Ri back? He needs to come home," I half pleaded in a shaky voice.

"We'll call you within the week. And thanks for using Pets in…"

I hung up the phone.

Lauren had called me on a Wednesday, a little more than a week after my call to Pets in Heaven. I'd just picked up Tommy and his friend from baseball. They'd told me they were STARVING. They both REALLY wanted a toasted bagel from Starbucks. Absolutely nothing else in the entire world sounded good to them. So, I was driving them to Starbucks for a toasted bagel. Lauren called to tell me that she had you and was on her way to our house. Neither bagel-craving boy heard Lauren's call over my car's Bluetooth, as they were busy debating the fate of the Dodgers' upcoming season.

After hanging up with Lauren, I immediately pulled my car over, turned around, and told Tommy and his friend that Starbucks was totally out of bagels and that we'd have to toast some bagels at home. Before they could process the absurdity of my statement, I pulled a U-turn in the middle of a busy four-lane road. I had to be there when you came home.

I waited for you in the rocking chair on the front porch. I didn't rock. My feet were planted firmly on the ground. My head was turned, eyes staring up the street, searching for Lauren's car. I knew that at any moment I'd see the car that was bringing you back to me.

Lauren's car pulled up in front of our house. I'd planned on running to greet you, but my body didn't move. I saw the car door open. I saw a box, your box. Lauren began to carefully walk across our front lawn. She was aware of the importance of the box she was about to hand me. She understood the care and love with which it must be handled.

My friend stopped just short of the front porch. You were right in front of me. All I had to do was reach out and grab you. I wanted to, but I couldn't. I kept my tear-filled gaze pointed toward the squirrels running through the tree branches in our front yard. I wanted to feel relief, but all I felt was broken.

Ri, how could that box have been what was left of you? Part of me had been hoping that when Lauren stepped out of the car, her hands would be empty and you would exuberantly jump out behind her and run toward your home, toward your family, toward me. But you didn't jump out of Lauren's car, and her hands weren't empty. They were holding the one thing that I never wanted to accept.

My friend gently, cautiously placed you in my lap. I stared straight ahead. I felt the weight of you against the top of my legs. Your 140 pounds had been reduced to ten. I felt the box settle into my body. My hands gripped the sides. I tasted the salt from my tears that had traveled to my mouth. My feet relaxed and the chair began to slowly rock back and forth, back and forth, to the rhythm of my sobs.

Ever since The Cancer came to play, people had used the word hero in regard to The Cancer and all the treatment I'd endured, and it never had sat well with me. Whenever anyone referred to me as a hero, it had made me feel like a fraud. I knew I was no hero. Because I'd never been given a choice.

Heroes were soldiers who risked their lives to defend our freedom. They were mothers who gave their babies up for adoption so their child may have a chance at a better life. They were the passengers on Flight 93 whose brave actions saved the lives of countless others. I was beginning to grasp the understanding that heroes all had one thing in common—they all had a choice. They chose to put their lives on the line every day as they fought for our country. They made the impossibly difficult decision to sacrifice themselves for the good of others. They understood that sometimes the ultimate expression of love was choosing the thing that would cause them the greatest amount of pain.

In my situation, I'd never been faced with the question of to fight or not to fight. I showed up when I'd been told and endured the pain and discomfort of the treatment as a result. As humans, we fought for our lives. We were, in general, too scared of death. It was too hard for us to let go. So, we did what we had to do to live to see another day. So that was what I did. And then I did it again. And I kept doing it.

Some may argue that my moment with Nurse Jan was heroic. It could be argued that agreeing to do the chemo that morning when I was ready to give up, when I was begging to give up, was a choice I made so I could continue the fight. The reality was that Nurse Jan treated me with dignity and respect. She wanted me to agree to the chemo because she understood the importance of the patient feeling like they were playing an active role in their treatment and the positive effects that could have on the patient's ultimate outcome. But, Ri, I never really had a choice. That chemo was going to be hooked up to that IV pole and infused into my body one way or the other. All I did in that moment was make a choice.

The day you and I said goodbye was the day I had a choice—THE choice—the heroes' choice. I could've kept you on life support, kept praying for a miracle, kept you in pain for my benefit. But somehow God gave me the strength and love to do the one thing that I never, ever wanted to do. In my thirty-nine years of living, the only time I'd been a true hero was the moment I chose to end your life.

I wasn't sure how long I sat in that rocking chair, holding you on my lap. Lauren had left soon after giving you to me. She understood we needed that time. I remember the air growing colder as the sky grew darker. I didn't want to stand up, because I didn't know where to go. So, we sat there, you in your pine box and me in my rocking chair. After a long while, I heard Ellie and Tommy calling to me, asking for help with their homework.

The young voices of my two children snapped me back into the present moment. I stopped rocking. I now had a place to go, people to go toward. I stood up. I turned toward the front door. But before I could open that door and take you back inside to the warmth of your home, I knew there was one more thing I had to do. I looked down at your box. I looked down at you. I held you up closer to my face and, through the fading sunlight, was just able to make out the inscription on the shiny gold plate nailed into the side of your pine box. It read:

## CHAPTER 24

# Fucking Awesome

Dear Ri,

I was back in Chicago. That's right—but this time I wasn't on a college small group field trip led by our professor. I still had regret for going out to dinner after Herb Kelleher's inspiring speech to the room full of hundreds of students at the Navy Pier. But Jon had insisted we MUST try this steak place a few blocks away, and since he was the foodie of the group I'd listened and followed. So had Carrie. And so had Allison. And, well, the rest of the night was a blur.

None of us had shown up for the second day of the entrepreneurship conference the following morning. We'd left Professor Krause sitting at our class table with half of the seats empty. The look on his face the following Monday in class conveyed his deep sense of disappointment, and if there was ever a Vanderbilt professor we hadn't wanted to disappoint, it was Professor Krause.

But, Ri Rose, it looked like the universe had given me a shot at redemption. Three weeks prior, I had received a call from the speakers bureau at City of Hope. One of the powers that be had heard me speak at a prior event and requested me for the keynote at the annual Spirit of

Life event. That year, it was being held at Navy Pier with an estimated attendance of 800.

Goofball, do you remember the first fundraiser we did for City of Hope? I was in a Monday morning class at SoulCycle with my favorite instructor, Heather, and was struck by a bolt of inspiration (which I now like to call God's voice, loud and oh-so-clear). What if I tried to do a charity ride for friends and family and donated the money raised to research at City of Hope? This may sound fairly commonplace to you now, but this was before the days of benefit rides every other week. I like to think I was one of the first innovative charity rides forward thinkers. Well, I guess God's voice was, but anyways…

On that particular Monday morning, I got off my bike after the cooldown and gave Heather a sweaty hug. I was always awestruck in her presence. She exuded badass authenticity. Heather was not the typical size two, but, man, her body was ROCKIN'. She had the perfect rebel tattoos and such great taste in music. She didn't talk too much during class, but when she spoke, we listened. Every now and then, Heather would inspire the class with nuggets of her personal story. She used to be hardcore addicted to some hard drugs and then found SoulCycle and Lululemon, and holy freaking moly—look at her now. And, Ri, I have such mad respect for someone who'd been in the deep, dark trenches and has clawed their way out. You could almost still see the mud under her fingernails, and it made me love her even more.

After we swapped sweat, I asked Heather about the possibility of a charity ride. She said it had been done and offered to be the instructor, free of charge. Heather knew pieces of my story. I'd had to let her know on the days I'd shown up to her class weaker than normal because I'd been fresh out of a week-long hospital stay. I didn't want her to think I was being a slacker. I cared deeply about what she thought of me and was desperate to keep up with the pace of her class. I never wanted to be that front-row rider who couldn't keep the beat. Can you imagine?

On my weaker days, I listened to my body and bumped back to the second row. On these days, I preferred a row of protection in front of me to hide my shortcomings. I felt a bit more invisible there and found I even enjoyed those rides the most. I was able to close my eyes and find my Zen. In the second-row corner, I gave myself permission to be wherever I was physically that day, for better or worse. And it was in that corner where Heather always found me after she lit the candles toward the end of class and put her hand on mine.

After discussing the charity ride a bit longer, Heather referred me to the front desk for further guidance, and the front desk referred me to Zoe. Apparently, Zoe was the person to make this thing happen, and Zoe did. Within an hour, I had approval, a date, and a time. Now all I needed to do was figure out how the hell to get money funneled from my friends and family to the researchers at City of Hope. In acknowledging my stroke of divine brilliance, I hadn't actually thought through the details.

I asked God for guidance, but He sat back and let me figure this one out for myself. You were waiting for me in the back of my car when I walked out of the studio, and you were with me as I drove around and around the three-mile Rose Bowl loop as I waited for the answer to come to me in the form of eighties rock. I never did find any answers that day. My big break came to me the following day over cocktails.

I was sitting at the bar by the pool at the local country club. It was cotillion time for Ellie and her friends, which meant social time for the moms. You were just on the other side of the white brick wall covered in perfectly trimmed ivy that hid the parking lot from the club patio.

Many of Ellie's friends had paused to rub your head for good luck before their dancing class out of habit. I knew you were blissfully happy listening to the soft sounds of the dancing music and muted children's voices drifting out from the ballroom while enjoying the cool fall Pasadena temperatures. Technically, dogs weren't allowed on club property, but I felt those rules never applied to us. So in the car you waited and in the bar I sat.

And then Paula sat down next to me, and we started talking.

Paula's son and Ellie were the same age and had known each other since our first music class. After sizing each other up from across the circle for the first few weeks, we'd decided we were ready to try out a new mommy friendship, and that led to a few years of fun times together. Since we'd chosen different schools, we'd lost touch over the years but still had fond memories of our times together and considered each other friends. We began to catch each other up on our lives. Paula mentioned that she'd just started a job at City of Hope, working in the research department. BINGO.

By the time the last dance ended, I held the names and numbers of the people I needed to contact to make the charity ride a reality. I called the following morning, and by the afternoon I had a website set up by the charitable giving department ready to accept donations. Now, all I needed were the donors. The donors. Ugh! My friends had already given so much. Was I really about to ask them for more?

In the many years since my initial diagnosis, every single relationship in my life changed. Some grew stronger, and some faded away. Some people showed up in huge ways, and some didn't show at all. Some of the people I'd thought would for sure, without a doubt, be the first in line to offer support were the people who disappeared without a word of warning. A part of me kept wishing they would come back, hoping they would reappear, wanting them to reach out, and then I stopped waiting. The part of me that assumed there were certain things and certain people in life that, no matter what, you could count on, stopped believing. And that part of me grew angry and dark. I'd felt abandoned and betrayed. But more than that I'd felt sad.

There were, of course, the friends and family who supported and carried me. Those were my people. There were unexpected friends who arrived in silent ways that spoke volumes, and there were close friends who wanted to do something, anything, but couldn't. It was too much for them. And I understood.

I was that story, that urban legend that freaked people the fuck out. I was that young health nut who was, out of the blue, diagnosed with a stage IV incurable cancer, even though she'd never experienced one symptom. It hit too close to home. If it could happen to me, it could happen to any one of us. My story brought mortality into the invincible mindsets of our late-twenties peer group. And some just couldn't handle it. And I think, had the roles been reversed, I might have even been one of those friends.

As the years with The Cancer passed and my support group's resolve began to weaken, my expectations had grown stronger. I understood that they were scared, but I'd needed them not to be. I couldn't have their fear reflected back to me. I'd desperately craved a safe space where I could be honest about my pain, my fears, my despair, but instead I always found myself reassuring others. The Cancer set up an impossible situation where no human had been capable of offering the perfect love and support I'd so desperately needed. But you always could.

The Cancer had created a decade-and-a-half-long battlefield where every single day I was forced to fight to stay alive. It had brought out the best AND worst in all of us. People had hurt me, but I'd also hurt people. *My* People. Together, My People and I had felt deeper sorrow, which had left deeper scars. We were all wounded. The Cancer didn't just pick a fight with me. By default, it had picked a fight with my family, with my friends, and with those who loved me most in this life. And we all just did our goddamn best to get through to the other side.

So, there we were, on the other side. None of us looked the same. We are all a little slower to trust and a lot slower to love. Once you'd withstood a punch from The Cancer, you instinctively wobbled at the thought of a subsequent blow. And yet, here I was, about to ask them for more.

I sighed as I stretched my arms in the air and looked up to the ceiling above our kitchen table. Ri, I had no clue how to write that email. Wasn't it my turn to give something to them? I typed the email that would ask My People to help one more time. Before I could stop to think or second-guess my decision, I pressed send. And then I waited.

It was like when you threw a party and worried that no one would show up, or when you walked into your first music class with your new screaming baby who had a severe case of acid reflux and were wearing the totally wrong thing, or like the first time you left the house without a scarf to cover your bald head. I felt exposed and vulnerable and terrified.

I looked down at you lying on your well-worn bed. You looked up at me with your calm eyes then put your head back down to resume your nap. And then I heard the ping of a new email. And then another. Then another.

I opened my inbox. I read the subject lines of the top three messages. DONATION RECEIVED. DONATION RECEIVED. DONATION RECEIVED. Had this been a test run from the automated website? I clicked on the first link.

"Anna-Christine R has sent you a donation." "Carrie G has sent you a donation." "Lauren K has sent you a donation." "Landon L has sent you a donation." "Andrea G has sent you a donation." And the pings kept coming.

Our charity ride happened three weeks after I sent out the email. Every single bike in the SoulCycle studio was full. We even had a waitlist. You sat in the lobby with Ellie and Tommy while all our non-sporty friends drank wine and the kids munched on goodies donated by our favorite local bakery. Dr. Forman from City of Hope stayed and chatted with our friends. We raised $22,000 that night. $22,000 of love and support from the people who'd already given so much but who still wanted to give more. $22,000 of hope. $22,000 of love.

After the ride, I talked to Instructor Heather and a friend from Vanderbilt who lived in Pacific Palisades. I hadn't seen this friend since college and had been both shocked and incredibly touched that she'd come with her husband. I mentioned to my friend how nervous I'd been to ask people for more after they'd already given so much to me and to Tom and the kids over the years, and my old friend looked me in the eyes and said, "Caroline, you don't understand. For so many years, we've followed your story. We've sat back and felt powerless as we watched you battle this disease. We wanted to help but didn't know how. This is the first time we've felt able to do something in some small way, and it was an honor to do it."

I was unable to find the words to respond. I looked up at Instructor Heather. I needed to pull from her warrior strength. She squeezed my arm as she said, "Honey, I've done a shitload of rides, and that one rocked my world. The love in that room was fucking awesome."

And you know what, Ri, it really was. It really, really was.

So awesome, in fact, that the marketing department and speakers bureau caught wind of our fundraiser and contacted me about doing some ad campaigns and speaking engagements for City of Hope. I'd said yes, and one thing led to another, which led to the night in Chicago.

So there I was again. Back in a room filled with individuals who'd been touched by cancer in one way or another. Except that time, I didn't know a single person, and no one was sitting on a spin bike in front of me. I was in an unfamiliar city, and instead of wearing a ripped muscle tank and clip-in spinning shoes, I was wearing high-waisted black pants and platform heels. I was not in the second row. I was not tucked into a dark corner. I was the one and only person standing under the bright lights in the center of the large wooden stage, the same stage where Herb Kelleher stood all those years ago. On that particular night, I didn't want to blend in. That night, I felt worthy. That night, I was confident. That night, I was ready.

After a brief introduction, I walked up to the podium. I didn't need my notes. I'd given that speech numerous times and to many different audiences. I started small, with groups of thirty at small fundraisers, and maxed out at an event for three thousand music industry cancer research supporters. The larger the crowd, the lower my nerves. The larger the crowd, the more potential to affect a life. The larger the crowd, the larger the hope.

I dived right into my battle with The Cancer. I tried to make it succinct and to the point. I gave a brief description of my life before The Cancer, just to set the stage. I didn't do this for dramatic effect. I told the story exactly as it happened. It just so happened that The Cancer had a knack for the sensational, so the dramatic effect was a natural byproduct.

I tried to give short recounts of my first eight rounds of chemo, my first recurrence, and first bone marrow transplant. My story really began when Ellie and Tommy had been born and The Cancer had been rediscovered.

I didn't tell the audience about you, Ri. Our story was something separate. Even though you rode the ride with me, you were not the element that was always seen or talked about. No, my sweet Goofball, you were the silent weapon, the secret to my success. Your love bolstered me, and your loyalty sustained me. You were not just a part of my story. You were my beginning, my middle, until you reached your end. And I didn't feel that, on that podium, I could give our story the justice it deserved.

The end of my speech changed every time. I knew the events of my story and understood the relatable threads that were important in sharing the message of hope, but I never knew quite how to deliver the finale. It used to include a touching story involving the kids and my doctor and their pacifiers. But then you passed away, and that ending seemed too…lighthearted.

On that particular evening, I found myself telling the audience about love and trust. I told them that sometimes I'd wished for a different path in life, one that did not include The Cancer. But, somewhere along the way, I'd realized that The Cancer was actually the reason I had the things I cared about most in the world. Had it not been for my diagnosis, I may have never gotten married, or had kids, or…found you. I may have been too stuck in my rigid, type-A, goal-achieving ways to ever make room for the love of another.

"Maybe, sometimes, the lessons that are the hardest for us to learn are the lessons we need to learn most. For so many years, I've looked at my disease as the enemy that was sent to destroy. But what if it was sent to save?"

I heard a muffled sob from the front row. I tried to find the face behind the sound, but the lights blinded my vision. I looked out across the sea of blurred faces. I looked across the entire room before I offered up my final remarks.

"I think it's time I lower my defenses and call a truce. Maybe instead of treating The Cancer like a deadly intruder, I instead accept it into my life as my invited guest. Maybe, if The Cancer and I stop throwing punches, we could come to understand each other, the essence of one another, and discover why we needed each other.

"I think it may be time for me to claim The Cancer as mine—My Cancer. I'm not quite ready to pull up a chair for it at our dinner table, but I do promise to at least agree to hear it out and listen to what My Cancer has come to teach. You know, when you really think about it, My Cancer is pretty damn clever. Maybe the two of us working together on the same team could produce big, beautiful results. I guess only time will tell.

"So to all those who doubted that I'd make it…" I paused as I allowed a sly, wide smile to spread across my face.

"And to all my loved ones who have gone to Heaven before me, please be patient while you wait for me to finish living. I think it might take me a little longer than I'd thought."

Standing ovation.

Their applause was not for me, Ri Rose. This one was dedicated to you. That night in Chicago, you were that relatable thread of acceptance and hope. You touched 800 hearts and inspired 800 lives because you, my sweet boy, were and always will be fucking awesome.

CHAPTER 25

# A Boy, a Ball, and a Boat

**Dear Ri,**

I was thinking about booking an appointment with a medium. I'd heard about one who was supposed to be pretty good. Apparently, one hour with this medium was more effective than years of therapy combined. I was doubtful, but what if she could talk to you? After my one and only other experience with a clairvoyant type, you can't blame me for being doubtful.

Toward the end of our six-month stay in Houston for my first bone marrow transplant, Aunt Karol surprised me with a psychic. He was waiting for me in her living room when I got home from a full day spent in the MD Anderson outpatient infusion clinic. I could tell that you were wary of this strange man. You sat patiently at my side as he took my hand in his and studied the converging spiderweb-like wrinkle lines that crisscrossed my palm. He was quiet for a long while before he looked up at me with worry lines running the length of his forehead. I felt your gaze intensify. You already didn't like what you sensed he was about to say.

This strange man took a deep breath before saying, "I'm sorry to tell you this, but you will not live past the age of forty."

Was he joking? I'd been twenty-nine at the time and had just been trying to live to see another day. Did he really think I cared about knowing anything further out than my next PET scan? Forty had seemed like a lifetime away and at the time one I would've gladly traded my soul to guarantee.

My lack of response seemed to surprise the psychic. I hadn't said a word. I hadn't flinched my hand away or diverted my gaze. I was still waiting for a piece of information that could help me in that moment, in that particular struggle. The psychic man looked back down at my hand and tried again.

"Ahh, now I see. Yes, yes, yes. Now I see clearly."

I scooted a bit forward on the edge of my seat. Your ears perked up.

"You are going to buy a boat."

Still no reaction. He kept going.

"Yes, you are going to buy a boat one day, and THAT'S when you will know you have been successful."

What the living hell was he talking about?

My snicker was misinterpreted as excitement. He kept going.

"A YELLOW boat. With a white stripe. Yes, yes, yes. Yellow boat with white stripe."

"Interesting," I managed to say. You stood up.

The psychic turned his head to look at you. Your height paired with your "get the hell out of here" stare were the only clues he needed. He stood up, thanked me for my time, and walked out of the room.

As soon as his energy had cleared, you and I walked over to the L-shaped sofa and resumed our post-treatment-day positions—me in the corner and you off to my left side. I turned on *Friends* reruns, and we never thought about the psychic man again.

It had been eleven and a half years since that reading and eight years since my second bone marrow transplant. Eight years without My Cancer showing up on a scan. Eight years without chemo. Eight years without the active cancer patient status. But you and I know that My Cancer never left. It just masked itself in sinus infections and chicken pox and salmonella and countless other maladies.

I was sitting in Dr. Andersson's exam room. I was back at MD Anderson for my annual July appointments. Tom was sitting in the chair next to me. Tommy was in my lap. We had dropped Ellie at sleepaway camp two days prior, so Tommy was enjoying all the attention that came with the temporary only-child status. Tommy was tossing his football back and forth to Tom. I heard voices outside in the hallway—other patients leaving their appointments, other doctors giving instructions to their nurses. I knew Dr. Andersson was in his work room. He never came into an appointment without personally reviewing all my test results. We'd come too far. He wasn't going to risk taking another doctor's opinion on the recorded test results. He was always the last line of defense.

I shifted my weight in my chair. My hips were still sore from my bone marrow biopsy the previous day. My two large bandages were soaked through with blood. The pain shot up my hip bone as I shifted to the other butt cheek. Tom noticed my facial muscles tighten as I changed position. He understood. I gave him a silent, reassuring smile. The physical pain was tolerable. It was the unknowing that was torture.

In that chair, in that exam room, in that clinic, I was a cancer patient. Each time I walked through the sliding glass doors and into the MD Anderson aquarium lobby, My Cancer was given permission to come out of hiding to play with all the other patients' cancers. It no longer had to mask itself under other physical ailments. It was like a playground for all the cancers that had become a part of us. And it felt oddly liberating to be able to not only acknowledge our other halves but to let them out in public with no judgment. It was the most honest place in the world. It was the only place where our diseases were discussed, understood, accepted.

Eight years in remission had been filled with a total of seven sinus surgeries and countless hospitalizations. I'd spent the past eight years trying to convince those around me I was fine, good, all better, even though I was anything but. My People were worried and tired. They deserved a break from the fight. After my second bone marrow transplant, I turned around to assess the damage on the battlefield. I'd made it to the other side, but it wasn't without casualties. Many relationships from my pre-cancer life had become fallen soldiers. I understood that life would never again be the same, but not in the revolutionary kind of way.

I was able to get through the war because I'd had you acting as my general. But now you'd fallen too. And now I was back in that room, back in the unknown. I heard the footsteps I recognized all too well. The door to the room opened.

"Your scans look clear. This is very good news."

I exhaled. After more than a decade together, Dr. Andersson knew to skip the pleasantries and get straight to the point.

"Thank you, Lord. Phew. Ugh—so relieved. Hi, Dr. Andersson. It's so good to see you again," I sincerely replied.

"Yes, good to see you too. Always." And I knew he meant it.

"Dr. Andersson, I know you don't remember…"

"Tommy," Dr. Andersson finished my sentence for me. "This must be Tommy." He remembered.

"Tommy Bug, I want you to meet Dr. Andersson. This is the doctor that made Mommy all better."

Tommy tucked his football under his arm and stepped forward to shake Dr. Andersson's hand.

"Tommy, the last time I saw you, you were just a tiny baby. It's amazing how fast time..." I heard a crack in Dr. Andersson's voice. He wasn't able to finish his sentence. I looked up at my doctor and watched as he turned his head away from us. He needed a minute.

"Hey, dude, can you tell Dr. Andersson about your flag football team?" Tom offered as an emotional neutralizer.

"Oh, yeah, I'm on this football team. And we're the Steelers. And my best friend, William, is on the team also. We are REALLY good. Probably the best team. We'll win the Super Bowl for sure."

Dr. Andersson recovered his composure. "That sounds good, very good indeed. You must have a very strong arm."

"Oh, I do. Probably the strongest on my whole team," Tommy replied. We all laughed at his lack of modesty.

I decided to step in and take control of the conversation. "Okay, Bug. Sit in this chair for me while your dad and I talk to Dr. Andersson."

Dr. Andersson handed me the printed test results. I knew I didn't need to read the numbers. I could tell by the smile in my doctor's eye that they were good. The details were, at this point, irrelevant.

"So, eight years. This is good. This is very good. Eight years was the goal," said Dr. Andersson.

"It was?" I asked. This was news to me.

"Yes, eight years. The clinical trial results are showing that the patients who make it to eight years without their lymphoma coming back are the patients who have the smallest chance of their lymphoma coming back."

"Well, that's great news," Tom exclaimed.

Tommy, already bored with the adult talk, began tossing his football up in the air and catching it in his hands.

"Yes, yes. This is good. This is very good news indeed. Now I can tell you that we feel very good about the decision we made eight years ago not to radiate you."

Huh? Radiate me? I was lost.

"Was that an option?" Tom asked.

"Yes, yes. We debated. All the doctors in the transplant department discussed your case numerous times at great length. We were divided. Some wanted to do full-body radiation after your transplant, and the other half voted for no radiation. This was a very difficult decision for me."

"So you made the final decision?" I asked.

"Yes, yes. I did. I lost many a night's sleep over this decision. The trouble was…if we radiated you, we knew the initial success rates were much higher. However, you were so young, and you had young children." He paused as his eyes shifted down to watch Tommy tossing his football.

"The problem with this particular type of radiation is that when it is combined with your transplant chemo, we find a very high rate of secondary cancers developing between five and seven years post-transplant. It was incredibly difficult deciding which risk to take—your immediate success or long-term survival."

Neither Tom nor I had ever heard this debate mentioned. Dr. Andersson knew this was a decision so monumental that he had to shoulder it and assume the corresponding consequences.

"So now that I'm eight years out from my transplant, does this give you comfort regarding your decision?" I asked, still trying to comprehend what Dr. Andersson was telling me.

"Yes, yes. It does. It is good. Very good. I can say now that I do not think your lymphoma will return."

"REALLY?" Tom and I both exclaimed at the same time.

Dr. Andersson continued, "Yes, yes, but we do need to start watching you very closely for secondary cancers. We are seeing them develop in patients eight years out in different ways."

"But I thought you said that was only if I had done radiation?" I asked.

"Patients that received radiation in this protocol have over a seventy-five percent chance of a secondary cancer occurring within the first seven years. Patients, like yourself, who did not receive radiation and achieved remission with the transplant have a lower recurrence rate in the first seven years, but we start to see the recurrence spike around year eight."

"Well, shit," I muttered.

"Mommy said a bad word!" Tommy blurted out.

We collectively ignored him.

"So, are you saying that we need to worry?" Tom asked.

"I think we always need to worry. I also think making it eight years is a huge relief, as it means your lymphoma has an extremely low chance of returning. And this is very, very good news. Our worry now becomes a secondary cancer, and that is what we need to watch out for and catch early."

"But, why?"

"Caroline, you have had one hundred and eighty eight scans and X-rays. And that is not counting the other forms of radiation you have been exposed to in your fourteen years of being a patient with us."

"Seriously? One hundred and eighty eight scans?" Tom asked incredulously.

"Okay, well, what types of cancers are you NOW worried about?" I asked with a bit of an edge to my voice.

"Colon, optical, oral, breast, pulmonary, ovarian—"

"Okay, I get it," I said quickly, not wanting to hear the rest of the list.

"So what do we do about this?" Tom asked.

"I'm going to monitor you closely. I will order some new tests each year. We will get samples of tissues from different areas. I want to look at your cells under the microscope. I know your cancer's personality, and I want to see if it starts to act up again."

My Cancer's personality. Dr. Andersson knew My Cancer as intimately as I did. I was suddenly out of questions, but Tom wasn't satisfied.

"So we just wait and see?"

"We wait. And we watch. And we stay in close communication," Dr. Andersson offered.

I could tell that was not a good enough answer for Tom. It wasn't good enough for Dr. Andersson either, but it was all we were going to get. It was all we had ever gotten since the day My Cancer was discovered in the funky blood work collected at Dad's office before Kilimanjaro. Wait and see. Wait and watch. Wait and try to live during the waiting.

"Okay, hop up on the table and let me have a look."

I removed Tommy from my lap as I stood to walk toward the exam table. I knew Dr. Andersson would first wash his hands and put on latex gloves. I knew I'd begin the exam in the upright position. I knew he'd start with my neck and move to my underarms. I knew he'd divert his eyes to the right side as he concentrated on his fingers and what they did or didn't feel. I knew to lie down before he had to tell me. His exam continued to my stomach before it ended with an examination of my skin. Light chit-chat usually accompanied this physical exam. It always helped to lighten the mood, even though there'd never been anything unexpected found on an exam like this. I'd always found My Cancer before my doctors had.

I returned to my chair, and Dr. Andersson returned to sitting halfway on the small work desk on the right side of the exam room. He offered his closing medical remarks.

"I'd like to see you back in one year. I will order a mammogram and colonoscopy to be done as soon as possible. I may order other tests as well. I will call you to let you know."

"Sounds like a plan. Thank you, Dr. Andersson," I said with heartfelt emotion.

"Yes, yes. You are very welcome. Now, one last question. How is Riley?"

"Oh, Riley died," Tommy stated matter-of-factly.

"Oh, no, no. I am very sorry to hear that. That is very sad, very sad. He was such a handsome dog. I have all your Christmas cards lined up in my office. I will miss seeing him in the pictures."

I was unable to offer a response, so Tom stepped in.

"Yes, it was a very difficult time. He passed this past January. We miss him every day."

I nodded in agreement.

Dr. Andersson thankfully changed the subject. "Well, I think there is only one thing left to do. I know it is getting late, but I think Tommy and I need to play some football."

"Really?" Tommy asked as he jumped out of my lap.

"Yes, yes. Come on, young man. I will show you MY very good arm."

Tommy followed Dr. Andersson out of the exam room and through the double doors that separated the bone marrow transplant clinic from the main hallway. The summer sun had already set. The evening light was softly streaming in behind the heavily tinted windows. The lights of the South Texas Medical Center twinkled in the distance.

The hallway was empty. The clinic was quiet. Everyone had gone home for the weekend.

"Now, Tommy. You stand here. I will back up and throw the ball to you, and let's see if you can catch."

"Okay!" Tommy exclaimed in response.

Dr. Andersson walked backward down the long hallway. His white lab coat flapped a bit as his pace quickened. He raised his arm, drew the football back behind his head, and extended his arm forward as he released the ball into a perfect spiral.

"Wow, good throw!" Tommy said as he caught the ball. My son was finally impressed with my doctor.

"Yes, yes. Now, let's see you throw it to me."

Tommy threw the ball down the hallway in a semi-spiral. Dr. Andersson caught it.

Tom and I stood to the side and watched Tommy and Dr. Andersson play football for half an hour. As I processed the conversation we'd just had in the exam room, I began to think about the future. I began to remember the psychic's prediction.

Would I really die by age forty? Would a secondary cancer take me away from my precious son and daughter? Would Dr. Andersson be at my funeral and feel like a failure because of his medical decisions? Would Tom be putting roses on my grave?

Ri, as we stood in the hallway at MD Anderson, watching the football being thrown back and forth, I had no idea what would happen with my health in the future. I felt back on edge as I tried to imagine what new form My Cancer would take and when it would decide to reappear. I wished you were there to help me bear the weight of that crushing reality.

As I watched my son and doctor laughing together in the quiet peacefulness of my honest place, I reminded myself to breathe. As I filled my lungs with the sterile cancer clinic oxygen, I began to feel calmer, and with My Cancer off playing with the other cancers, my body felt lighter.

Tom squeezed my hand. I felt a jolt of energy run the length of my arm. Tommy was spiking the ball after he made a "touchdown." Dr. Andersson did a little touchdown dance. I took another breath, trying to suck in every ounce of goodness I was feeling.

Ri, that moment was a snapshot of everyone feeling peaceful, contented, happy. That snapshot became the internal vision board I clung to, because I knew in the end that if I could cling to those moments, the moments of joy and peace and contentment, I knew deep down in my damaged soul that those moments just might be enough.

That, and a big yellow boat with a white stripe of love down the middle.

## CHAPTER 26

# The Waiting Game

Dear Ri,

As hard as Tom and I tried, we couldn't get what Dr. Andersson said out of our heads. We kept thinking about recurrence spikes and secondary cancers and living in waiting. By definition, waiting meant staying in one place without doing very much until something that you are expecting happens. It just turned out that the something we were waiting on was My Cancer.

Tom and I had met when we were so young and so innocent. We'd met when neither of us had a care in the world and carried no responsibilities on our shoulders. But there we were, all those years later, having discussions about what would happen when the waiting was over.

It was impossible to plan for the unknown, but since we were parents we had to be as responsible as we possibly could. It was true, Dr. Andersson did know My Cancer and its personality better than anyone. He had been the one to study it, to treat it, and to cure it.

During my time in Los Angeles, City of Hope had done an incredible job of following me and helping me and supporting me, but

Dr. Andersson lived in Houston, and Houston was a very long way from LA.

With too many unknowns to factor into any sort of an equation, Tom and I focused on the facts. If and when my cancer came back, we knew we would need to move our family to (or close to) Houston. We knew the emotional toll another cancer diagnosis would have on Ellie and Tommy and didn't want to have to uproot them from their current school and friend group and life just so we could all temporarily move to Houston together as a family. And who knew how long we would need to stay close to Dr. Andersson.

And my family—they were always my biggest support, but it was difficult to offer the support they wanted to give when we were 1,000 miles away. No, Tom and I knew what we had to do. We needed to move back to my home state of Texas.

Tom had been with his company for over a decade and had kicked some serious ass. When he approached his boss and asked about the possibility of a move to Texas, they told him they would accommodate. Even though the thought of moving home felt like a deep breath and a warm hug, I felt tremendous guilt and sadness over leaving Los Angeles.

Ellie and Tommy were devastated when we told them. Life in Los Angeles was all they'd ever known. They kept asking why, why do we have to move? I was never sure what to tell them because I didn't want them to know the truth. If they knew we were moving because of My Cancer, I worried they would resent me by default. Thankfully, Ellie and Tommy loved my parents, and they REALLY loved their Uncle Chad, so the prospect of spending more time with them definitely softened the moving blow.

And then there was Gus. Augustus McCrae Rose was the newest addition to the Rose family, and man, oh, man was he making his presence known. After several more foster dogs had come and gone through our house, Tom kindly requested we hit pause on the dog rescue hobby for a while. I understood. The thousands of dollars of damage that Hanson had caused to the pool house and the tranquilizers we'd had to use on the 160-pound Great Dane, Bud, to get him *down* the stairs were traumatizing for all of us. After you left, Brody had been a trooper with the revolving door of foster dogs, but he had not bonded with any of them. Until...he met Gus.

Augustus McCrae Rose came from a breeder. Yes, a breeder. I know, I know. I said I'd never do it. But I did it. And for Gus I'd probably do it again.

It had all begun with a Google search. Although this time instead of typing in, "rescue dogs Los Angeles," I typed in, "best dog breeder Southern California." Instead of empty eyes staring blankly into the cameras, I was flooded with photos of fluffy yellow puppies with fuzzy colorful blankets tucked around them. The website advertised bloodlines and pedigrees. The puppies' parents' photographs were included. It seemed like we could know all we'd ever wanted to know about these innocent little angels. These puppies seemed safe. They seemed uncomplicated. They seemed foreign.

True to style, I impulsively picked up the phone and called a breeder about an hour away. She was just finishing up with a litter but had one puppy left, a boy. An hour and a half later, I was holding Gus in my lap, heading toward his new forever home.

Brody was not surprised to meet Gus. Tom and the kids were shocked to meet Gus. I took Gus to Tommy's baseball lesson that afternoon. He looked so tiny napping in the netting of the batting cages. We could hold him with one hand.

And then Gus grew. And grew. And grew. The size of Gus's paws should have given us a clue as to how tall he would be, but we were still surprised at his large size. Brody tried to teach Gus all the wisdom that you'd passed along before you'd left, but Gus had a mind of his own. He was determined to do life his way. Gus wanted to pave his own path.

Ellie and Tommy adored Gus. They had worried that Brody had needed a friend, and Gus filled that role perfectly. They loved showing Gus new things and taking him on new experiences. They were overjoyed when Gus learned to sit, and they felt enormous pride when Gus *finally* learned to potty outside.

At the thought of a move halfway across the country, knowing they would be able to show Gus and Brody a whole new world gave them a reason to find some possible good in this upsetting news. That was the thing, Ri. As difficult as some things could be, having an animal by your side always seemed to make it a little more bearable.

The move happened fast. As in one week fast. Since it was halfway through August when we made the decision, we needed to act quickly so as not to miss getting Ellie and Tommy into their new school in Texas before the school year started.

We trusted our Los Angeles-based realtor to sell our home while we began to build our new life in San Antonio. Ellie and Tommy started their fourth and second-grade school years on schedule. They made friends quickly and seemed to love their teachers.

With Tom settled into his new routine of working from home when not traveling, I began to settle in myself. Old friends introduced me to new friends, and new friends showed me the mom ropes in my old high school stomping ground. Everything looked different when viewed through the eyes of a mother.

As wonderful as it was to be back in Texas, I had one problem that I couldn't seem to solve. Cats. Lots and lots of cats. I've never owned a cat but have nothing personally against them. Mom always said she was allergic, but I'm not so sure. I think sometimes we don't like what we don't know.

I've met a few cats that are sweet and cute and fluffy, but these are not the cats I am talking about. I am talking about feral cats. I am talking about ALL of the feral cats. Lots and lots of feral cats. Because they seemed to be everywhere. I heard they were in our neighborhood to keep the mice at bay, but I think I would have preferred to take my chances with the mice. You see, Ri, it wasn't so much the cats that were the problem. It was that Gus liked to chase the cats. And, by chase, I mean full-speed-ahead sprint and let me try to catch and eat the cat. And since he had grown to weigh a solid 104 pounds, I was powerless to try to stop him.

The daily walks with Brody and Gus were a disaster. Every block seemed to have a cat or multiple cats, which meant that while every block was cat-filled-Disneyland for Gus, I was constantly watching my dog run through my neighbor's yard while chasing their cat up a tree.

I got a referral for "the best dog trainer in town," so I had high hopes he would be able to help. I thought he was making progress until he said goodbye and asked me kindly to please not use his name when referring to Gus's training or lack thereof. Guess he didn't want to be associated with my unruly but oh-so-sweet Lab.

After a few months of cat chasing, I was truly despondent. And that was when a new mom friend told me about the Disneyland for cat-crazed dog owners. It was described as a truly magical place that would soon solve all of our cat-chasing problems… Doggie. Fucking. Daycare. Boom!

Feeling good about this new plan of doggie daycare attack, I called and made the first available temperament test appointment. Tom had seen the value in having our two large dogs exercised by professionals in a gated yard with no cats so had readily agreed to a five-days-a-week package. As enticing as it was to leave Brody and Gus at daycare for the full day sometimes, we agreed that half-day was sufficient to give them the exercise they needed.

Three days later, Brody and Gus (miraculously) passed the doggie daycare temperament test. I met the owner, Kind Kara, and she went over all the policies and rules. The entire time Kind Kara was talking, I did my smile and nod because all I could think about was how much this was going to change my life. Kara was my real-life version of Mickey Mouse, ready and waiting to cast all my problems aside by leaving my crazed dogs at the happiest place on Earth.

And cast my problems aside it did.

A few months into Doggie Daycare Heaven, I was at lunch with an old friend. We laughed and talked, which resulted in me completely losing track of time. The half-day rate at doggie daycare had a strict five-hour policy with little grace period for late moms, and I didn't want to get charged the full-day rate for both dogs. After throwing some cash on the table and giving my friend a hasty goodbye hug, I pulled my car up into the circle drive and raced through the white wooden door.

"Hi, Kara! I'm here for Brody and Gus!"

"Great. Let me get your boys for you," Kind Kara replied as she turned toward the wall of leashes.

"How'd they do today?" I asked with dread.

"Brody did great. He's such a love. He seems to be warming up to us and even approached Mike at one point. He's still not really playing with other dogs, but I think the more you bring him, the more he'll find his comfort zone," Kind Kara replied.

"Aww, Brody is such a good boy. I'm so proud of him for going up to Mike!" I exclaimed.

"I've never asked you, but why is Brody so scared of strange men?" Kind Kara wondered.

"We're not totally sure. When I pulled him from the shelter, he was in pretty bad shape. We don't know what happened to him, but we know it was bad, and we know he was abused by a man."

"That's awful. Just awful. Well, thankfully he's living the life of Riley now. Hopefully, he'll learn to trust again," Kind Kara continued, "but I've found that the trauma that happens to dogs before nine months tends to stick."

I was taken aback. For a moment, I assumed Kind Kara was referring to you, Ri, but then I quickly realized she'd never had the honor of meeting you so couldn't have used that expression in reference to your life. I remember Dad used to use that phrase when you were enjoying a particularly wonderful or luxurious doggie moment. Dad would say, "That dog really is living the 'life of Riley.'" At first, I thought it to be such a blatantly obvious statement—I mean, your name *is* Riley—but Dad was not one to state the obvious. So, one day, I just asked.

"Dad, what are you talking about? What is the life of Riley?"

"It was a television show when I was growing up. We used to watch it after Sunday supper. That's when Nonnie would make her chicken. Ahh, that chicken. Have you ever tried Nonnie's chicken? And the biscuits! Nonnie used to use this butter and honey…"

Unsatisfied with Dad's trip-down-memory-lane answer, I turned to my trusty and never-reminiscent source: Google.

The *Urban Dictionary* definition: "To have a happy life without hard work, problems, or worries." Another definition listed: "An ideal life of carefree prosperity and luxurious contentment."

After pausing to reflect on Kara's words, I realized Kind Kara hadn't mentioned Gus. I sighed as I asked the next question, already half knowing the answer.

"So how'd Gus do today?"

"Well, Gus did okay." This was kind Kind Kara code for "he was a little shit."

"Really?"

"Gus was really humping the other dogs, and he didn't listen when we tried to correct him. He spent about an hour demand barking at a Golden Retriever, Shelby, so we had to put him in time-out for a while. But overall he's doing great!"

Umm, was he though?

"Kara, I don't know what to do with Gus. I've never had a breeder dog before. Gus has never had a bad day, so nothing scares him. I have no emotional baggage to manipulate. Brody is desperate to please because he knows how great he has it now, but Gus…"

I pondered again what to do with this young and energetic and hard-headed yellow Lab.

I saw Brody's brown head peep through the glass window. He must've heard my voice. He jumped up onto his hind legs and started crying. Kind Kara opened the door as I braced myself for the "Brody Hug." Sure enough, Brody ran up to me before pausing and standing up on his hind legs while placing both front paws on either of my shoulders. In the process, he covered my face in gentle kisses.

I heard Augustus McCrae Rose before I saw him. His bark was unmistakable. He left the play yard barking at the other dogs, probably telling them to fuck off. Kara opened the door as Gus bounded across the room, large ears flapping in the wind. Gus barreled into Brody and knocked him out of the way. He then nearly knocked me over as he slathered my face in wet, sloppy kisses before checking the nearby trash can for scraps.

"Okay, then. See y'all tomorrow!" Kind Kara exclaimed with palpable relief.

"Thanks, Kara. See ya tomorrow." And with that, we were off.

The other night, I awoke in the middle of the night to hear Gus making a horrible, horrible noise. It didn't sound like a cough or a gag. It sounded deep and scary. I immediately jumped out of bed and grabbed my phone to call Lauren or Dr. Wantanabe before remembering that they were no longer able to help because we no longer lived in Pasadena. My animal support system was no more.

I desperately needed my close friend Lauren, who could guide me through any animal health crisis no matter what time of day, but she was a thousand miles away. I had no one to call. I could only wait and watch as Gus looked up at me with his terrified and pleading eyes. In that moment, I felt like a total and utter failure. Because, in that moment, all I could do was wait.

So, we waited. Gus crawled into his usual place, lying all 104 pounds lengthwise along the top my body. Brody watched and waited from his dog bed. At some point, we all fell asleep. And then the sun came up, and we knew that Gus was going to be okay.

Ri, hearing Gus making those horrible noises took me right back to the night—to *that* night. Fifteen days after I'd pulled Brody from the shelter, we'd decided to order Chinese food for dinner. This was not your favorite meal, but as long as it wasn't sushi you were game. Brody waited on your dog bed as you took your seat at Dad's side during dinner. He flipped you some orange chicken, and Tommy snuck you his beef and broccoli. We cleared the plates from the table and the kids headed upstairs to take a shower. You and I followed.

And that was when it happened. I first heard you gag and pant in our bedroom. Then you went downstairs, and it worsened. Five minutes later, Tom lifted you into my car and we were speeding toward the animal hospital. Eight minutes later, we spotted Lauren waiting outside the emergency entrance. Forty-three hours later, you were gone.

On the car ride home without you, I asked Tom to get Brody out of our house. I didn't want to look at him. I'd lost you, and it was everyone's fault. I needed time and space to grieve, and having another dog in your space was the ultimate betrayal. We walked in the back door with just your collar in my hand. Brody was there in the kitchen. He didn't approach me as I walked in and collapsed onto the floor. Brody knew you were gone, so he sat down and watched. And he waited.

And he kept waiting. The days passed, and he stuck around. Brody patiently gave me my space as I stayed in bed and avoided eye contact with him. He played along as other potential forever families came to meet him, and he posed for the photos I took of him for the Ace of Hearts website. Brody did what he was supposed to do. And he waited.

One day, weeks later, I woke up and looked at Brody. I mean, I really looked at him. A potential forever family had fallen in love with him and had said they wanted to adopt him. I was in the process of scheduling a home check when I, maybe for the first time, looked into the deep, dark eyes of this unknown dog. And when I looked, I recognized parts of you.

I cancelled the home check and told the family he was already taken. I filled out the adoption paperwork and told Tom that, unlike Chico, this foster was not leaving. Tom wasn't thrilled, but then I explained that Brody had been picked by you. He was the only dog who'd had that time with you, and that was enough for me. I told Tom that I was starting to believe that once Brody came into our lives you felt comfortable leaving me because you trusted this damaged dog to take care of my broken heart. And, Ri, that was just what he had done.

Brody has always known his role in our family. You handed it down to him and he has fulfilled it to the best of his abilities. He is weird and overprotective at times, but his unwavering devotion is the surest thing I have in my life. His intense attachment scared me because I knew I wasn't ready for a strong bond with another dog. So in an effort to dilute Brody's love, we got Gus.

I think my plan worked. Brody and Gus share a bond that only they can understand. Brody has raised Gus and taught him his street-dog ways. Gus looks up to Brody and gives him the confidence he needs to interact in the world outside our home. I don't worry when I leave them at home for hours at a time because I know they have each other. Their dependence on one another makes them less human in my eyes and lessens the guilt of my treating them more like dogs. Because they are not you.

Hearing Gus make that terrified noise took me back to our last moments together and the guilt I felt about not letting you go sooner. And then I thought about Kind Kara's comment when I picked up Brody from doggie daycare. As I looked at Gus's face two inches from mine and felt his breath rhythmically brushing against my chin, I smiled. Augustus McCrae Rose was definitely fitting the "life of Riley" definition. Not a care in the world and never a bad day. I turned my head to look at Brody. His eyes were open. He was still waiting.

Ri, that was when I understood the common thread between you and Brody and me. The three of us exist in a constant state of waiting. We are waiting to heal, waiting to be saved, waiting to finally be free of paralyzing fear. You and Brody waited to see if you would be returned to a shelter or even returned to death. I waited to see if My Cancer would take my life or if it would spare me another day. We feel there may not be any more time, so we have to make this moment count, and that can rob us of the peace of the moment. I guess that was what trauma did to a soul.

I looked back at Gus as he stared me down, his not-so-subtle sign that he was ready for breakfast. I envied the sheltered innocence that Gus will always live within. He'll never know the feeling of not knowing if he is living or dying. He'll never live in a constant state of waiting to find out that answer. And you are finally done waiting, my sweet Riley Rose. The slight nod of my head sent you into your long-awaited peace. But I'm still here, alive while also dying. And maybe that's just what life is—living and dying. Being present while also letting go. Allowing ourselves to love while not holding on too tightly to the fear of losing it.

I closed my eyes and once again pictured you in Heaven. I smiled thinking of you with a tennis ball in your mouth while you patiently and peacefully kept waiting for me. Thank you for picking Brody to protect my heart in your absence. You knew our wounded spirits would recognize one another once you were gone. And they have. And they will continue to do so as long as we live and wait in this life together. And even though Brody may sleep on your monogrammed Riley Rose dog bed at night, he will never, ever live the life of my Riley.

## CHAPTER 27

# The Dash

Dear Riley Rose,

I leave the house before anyone else is awake. I need to do this by myself. I drive my rental car to the base of the trail and park just as the sun begins to show its glow above the Colorado peak.

I've done this hike many times before, but now everything seemed unfamiliar. It has been two decades since my hiking boots had made a track on this trail. So much had happened. So much had changed.

I pull my backpack out of the backseat. The double water bottles and sack lunch create more weight than I'm used to carrying. My pre-cancer body only needed one water bottle and a protein bar, as I'd easily make it back down the mountain and into town by lunch. I know this hike will be longer and slower with the weight of My Cancer.

I walk across the small parking lot to the dirt path. The morning light illuminates the trail map. Six and a half miles round trip. I resist the urge to set a time goal for myself. Old habits die hard.

I draw in a deep breath and take my first step onto the trail. Within minutes, my legs begin to burn. It is a welcome feeling after the countless days I've spent in bed, recovering from a sinus infection.

As the incline of the path increases, so does my struggle to find oxygen in the thinning air. Cousin Kelly and I used to jog this trail in a race to the top—the altitude had never bothered me. But it was different now... On this morning, my only focus is to accomplish the goal I'd set for myself eight years prior. On this morning, I only needed to reach the top.

I come up to the river with the log bridge. I remember this scene vaguely from years prior, an image in the background as I'd charged on toward my destination. It hadn't occurred to me to pause and take in the natural beauty of this spot—beating my previous round-trip hiking time had been way more important. But this day is different. This day, I sit down on the side of the river. This day, I take time to soak in the energy radiating from the rushing mountain water. This day, I allow myself to just be.

In this moment, I find myself thinking back to the first day we met and the despair I felt when I tried to take you for a walk around the block. I recall being nervous the first time at the beach when I unclipped your leash from your cowhide collar, and the relief I felt when you never strayed far from my side. I remember hiking with you in Runyon Canyon as your legs grew stronger and relishing the sight of your strength.

I hear voices, and the images fade. I feel the familiar pang of panic now when faced with a potential social situation. Will these hikers want to stop to chit-chat? Will my post-cancer brain be quick enough to come up with the right words to say? Will I be able to carry on a conversation, or will the brain fog overwhelm my once Theta-Social-Chair-worthy personality? My Cancer has morphed into a dark cloud that infiltrates my mind in the most inopportune moments, causing previously normal social interactions to be high-stress and awkward situations. Lately, I much prefer the quiet of solitude. I much prefer being in peaceful connection with you.

I lower my head as the hikers acknowledge my presence with a hello and keep walking. Relief floods my body. I remind myself to breathe. After waiting a few minutes to reclaim my solitude on the trail, I stand and start to climb once again.

I come upon another familiar landmark—a large log fallen across the trail. This barrier has been here for as long as I've been hiking this path. I remember a time, decades prior, when we were on a designated "cousin" hike, and we carved our names in the aging bark. I bend down to see if I can find our markings but only see smooth brown wood where the bark used to be.

I think about Cousin Paul and the words he said to me all those years ago at the ranch after he heard about my diagnosis. "Well, Caroline, fuck this."

I smile at the memory and marvel at how much has changed since those never truer words were uttered. Cancer had shattered our family dynamic as we'd known it and threw the pieces up into the wind. Now we live the new and beautiful puzzle that formed as the result of the pieces falling down, only into a new and sometimes strange arrangement.

Life with My Cancer after the treatment ended is, in some ways, more difficult than the time spent in the active fighting stage. I experience deep, paralyzing fear that has yet to let up. The innocent trust I had that life would take care of me is gone. I've danced with death and still feel its presence looming. But, Ri, the thing is, even though I've lost my trust in life, I trust fully and completely that God and the universe are a whole, taking perfect care of me.

The heavily tree-lined trail eventually gives way to a large grassy field. I look to my right and see a bluebird. I feel your presence. I know you are with me. I know you've always been with me.

The switchbacks are harder than I remember. My lungs heave, and my muscles shake. My legs feel like noodles. My foot catches on a rock, and I lose my balance. My hands help to brace my fall, but the pain tells me I'm still injured. I look at my knee and see the blood starting to seep through my broken skin. I watch as my blood, which has been altered into my brother's blood, falls onto the rocky trail. I think about turning around. I think about pulling the cancer card and justifying my surrender with the excuse of falling and My Cancer weakening my body to the point of failure. I recall Nurse Jan and can almost feel her squeezing my hand. I stand up. And I put one foot in front of the other. Breathe in, breathe out...

The trail flattens out. I feel the sun shining down on my sweaty face. I hear the faint sound of the creek in the distance. A little farther...

And then I arrive.

Cathedral Lake looks similar to my memory from childhood. Or maybe it's something different. Maybe it's what I'm remembering from the framed photograph that hung on the wall in the hospital and became my goal during my second bone marrow transplant eight years prior.

Three times a day for sixty-five days, I walked the halls of the MD Anderson bone marrow transplant hospital floor. And three times a day I tried to summon the strength to take one more lap around the nurses' station. As I began each lap, a decorative framed photo of a lake surrounded by snow-topped mountains and yellow wildflowers awaited me. And, initially, it taunted me.

For the first three weeks, I looked at this photo while trying to put one foot in front of the other and felt sadness. For the first three weeks, that framed photograph of this gorgeous mountain lake represented all the things in my life that I loved so deeply but would probably never be able to see again. Things were dire, and my making it out of that hospital alive was uncertain. For me, this decorative photo was my real-life reminder of everything I was about to lose. And for a while I never wanted to look at this taunting remembrance.

And then Nurse Jan held my hand, and I made it through the final chemo. My spirit slowly began to heal, and my blood work numbers started to rise. After that, instead of trying to ignore this taunting image, I began to pause in front of it and began to think, began to dream. What would it feel like to stand on that mountain? What if I could run through the field of yellow wildflowers toward the healing lake water? What if... What if...

And then I got a little stronger, and my walks through the hallways with my IV pole became a little faster. I began to turn the "what if" into a "when will," and reaching my own version of that mountain lake, Cathedral Lake, became my goal. I began to pass that photo and say to myself, "I WILL get there again. I WILL get back to the top of that mountain." It was the promise I'd made to myself. I guess I'd just always pictured you would be by my side when I reached the top.

I walk up to the lake. I want to feel the water. I'd imagined so many times what this water would feel like. I'd pictured it cold and startling to the touch. I'd dreamed of the healing powers this water must contain. I look down into the glass-like surface and see my reflection, and in that moment, Ri, I see your face next to mine. Caroline and Riley, Riley and Caroline. And then a burst of wind waltzes across the surface of the water and the ripples erase our perfect image.

Ri, this life is so much different than I pictured it to be. You've been gone for two years. It's been two years since I've heard your bark or felt your paw on my leg. Two years since you waited for me by the back door or rode around town in the back of my car. I find myself looking for you less and less. I've memorialized you around the house. Your pine box rests on the table beside our bed, and your pictures adorn our walls.

And then I think about the engraving on the gold plaque centered on your pine box:

And I think about the dash.

Ri, here's what I've come to understand about your life. It isn't about the year you were born or the year you died. It's about everything in between. It's about the dash. It's about every single day you existed on this Earth and every single moment you lived and every single breath you drew.

I think about my own life and envision again the funeral I've so perfectly planned out in my head. I think about my tombstone and wonder what it will say. I wonder what the year of my death will be, what number will come after my dash. And then I stop wondering. Because it doesn't really matter. What matters is the moment.

It is about the beat of a heart or the allowance of a feeling. It's the shed of a tear or the burst of fear. It's about the feeling of laughter or the hug from my kids. What matters are the treasured seconds of perfect peace I'm blessed to feel at certain times in my life. And, Ri, all that happens within the dash.

I pick up a flat rock and skip it across the lake's surface. The small rock bounces twice before sinking. I consider it floating to the bottom of the cold waters and wonder if it will ever see daylight again. I desperately regret my decision to throw that rock. I don't want that rock to be confined to the darkness of the lake for the rest of time—I want that rock to fight, to rise, to find its way back to the light. Like I've been doing for years.

Ri, I've been fighting for so long. I've fought for my life. I've fought for your life. I've fought for our life together. I fought for Ellie and for her twin that we lost. I fought for my other lost children and then again for Tommy and for his life. I've fought for my marriage when the stress threatened to break us. I've fought for friendships when we were broken and fought for forgiveness when it was the only way forward. And I've fought for the strength to live each and every day in the face of the fear that it could be my last.

I've tried to embrace the "live like you are dying" philosophy, but that doesn't always fit in with retirement savings and delayed gratification.

And some days, I just want to stay in bed and binge-watch Netflix and Bravo. But where does that fit in with the YOLO lifestyle? If I live a day quietly, did I fail to live out loud? Does spending time numbing out make this life I fought so hard to save less worthy?

I find a grassy spot in the sun and sit down. I look up into the crystal-clear Colorado sky and say a prayer. I thank God for my strong body. I thank God for my family. And I thank God for every single day I had with you.

As I inhale in the fresh, crisp air, I feel a sense of calm wash over me. I close my eyes and sink into the moment. And in this moment I know I'm going to be okay. I understand life will have its challenges, because—let's face it—life can be fucking hard. But the solid, unbreakable knowledge that no matter what may be thrown at me I'll be okay is bigger and more powerful than any potential life hardship.

I made the choice to live a long time ago. And I keep making it every single day. And on this grass, sitting by this peaceful lake, I promise to never stop choosing life.

Ri, I know that this, today, by this lake, is my love letter to myself. Reaching the top of this mountain is my honoring the goal I'd set for myself and the reaffirmation to my soul that my life will go on for as long as my body will allow. This day, sitting by Cathedral Lake, I feel so close to Heaven, close to God, so close to you.

I miss you, Riley Rose. I miss you every single day. I'll never stop missing you, but I also know you left me stronger than when you found me. You took care of me when I was not strong enough to take care of myself, and you stepped back when you knew I needed to find my footing. You loved Tom and our children, and you welcomed the many you deemed worthy. You gave children courage just by a rub of your head. You marked so many hearts, more than I'll probably ever know.

And now, Ri, it's my time to make a promise to you. Ri Rose, I promise to carry on your legacy by doing my best to emulate your love and kindness to those around me. I promise to tell my story so that I may be able to offer hope to someone in need. And, Ri, I promise to live this gift of life that I've been given to the absolute fullest.

Clarity and Courage. Two words, one prayer.

Caroline and Riley. Two hearts, one journey.

Palms open.

Heart full.

Inner truth heard.

A few months back, I came across a quote from an unknown source: "Life may not be the party we hoped for…but while we're here, we may as well dance."

Riley Rose, I promise to always, always keep dancing.

Preferably to eighties rock. But who am I to choose the tune? I'll leave that up to you.

I love you, my sweet Goofball.

Forever and always,<br>
Me

## ACKNOWLEDGEMENTS

First and foremost, I want to thank my brother, Chad. Not only did you save my life twice over and make Ellie and Tommy's lives possible, but you also spent your life loving and protecting me as no one else ever could. You are the reason this book exists and the source of my courage for publishing. Not a day goes by when I don't think of you and miss you with my entire heart and soul.

Paige, this book would never have come to fruition without your encouragement, guidance, time, love, and support. We met two decades ago in the dog park, and even through distance and time, my love and admiration for you have only grown stronger. To all the dog park posse, humans and dogs alike, meeting you was no coincidence. You left marks on my heart that I'm proud to carry.

To my family—Tom, Ellie, Tommy, Mom, and Dad—you are my reason for living, fighting, and smiling. Your love has sustained me, and your support has saved me. I will be forever grateful for all that you have done for me and all that you continue to do day in and day out.

To Kelly, Lila, Paul, Katie, Wynn, Ada, Aunt Karol, and Uncle Paul-they say you can't choose your family, but if I could, I'd still choose y'all. Thank you for all the support, love, and laughter y'all have given Ellie, Tommy, Tom, and me over the years. Y'all made our time in Houston not only bearable but meaningful and, dare I say, enjoyable. I will be forever grateful for your opening your homes and lives to us time and time again.

To Francis—my angel sent from up above. You were not just our nanny; you are forever our family.

To my friends who have contributed to reading, editing, encouraging, or inspiring this book, I hope to repay the favor one day. I would hate to think what this life would look like without you.

To Linda and my Carmel writing squad, I met you with only a dream of a book and left knowing the dream would and could become a reality. If only we could all be so lucky as to have friends, mentors, and coaches like y'all.

To all the doctors and nurses who have saved, healed, and stood by me-doctors and nurses like you don't come along often, so I feel insanely blessed to have crossed paths with you. Thank you for your dedication to your profession and to your patients.

A special note to Dr. Andersson- you saved my life twice over, but more than that, you became my source of comfort and confidence against the disease that wanted to end my life. Because of you, I am both alive and thriving. Because of you, my children have their mom. Because of you, I lived to tell the tale.

To anyone who has signed up to be a bone marrow donor- you are a true hero.

To Kari of Ace of Hearts Dog Rescue and to anyone connected to rescuing and/or saving a rescue dog's life in any way, this world is a kinder, happier, and more comforting place because of each of you. You bring out the best in humanity, and I'm honored to be walking beside you.

Lastly, I thank the dogs that have blessed my life. Snoopy, Toffie, Rudder, Sam, Abby, Riley, Brody, Gus, and Axl. Thank you for your dependable love and constant faithfulness. And, for the record, we didn't save you. Y'all saved us.